About the Author

Rupert Isaacson was born in London in 1967 to Southern African parents. He currently lives in Austin, Texas. His books include *The Healing Land*, which chronicles his time spent living with the San Bushmen of the Kalahari Desert and his adventure helping them to win back their lost hunting grounds; *The Wild Host: The History and Meaning of the Hunt*; and *The Horse Boy*, which tells the story of his quest on horseback across Mongolia to find healing for his autistic son, Rowan, which was translated into thirty languages.

Rupert Isaacson is also an independent film-maker, whose feature documentary of *The Horse Boy* was screened on television worldwide and in cinemas all over America. His journalistic work has appeared in national newspapers and magazines in the UK and USA. Still a human rights activist for the Kalahari Bushmen, Isaacson also founded and runs the Horse Boy Foundation, which specializes in helping children find communication and learning both by using horses (Horse Boy Method) and by using play equipment and the environment (Horse Boy Learning).

To find out more, visit
www.horseboyworld.com
www.horseboyfoundation.org
and 'like' us at
www.facebook.com/horseboyworld

The Long Ride Home

*The Extraordinary Journey of Healing
that Changed a Child's Life*

RUPERT ISAACSON

HORSE BOY PRESS

P.O. Box 1362 - Elgin, TX 78621 - USA
www.HorseBoyWorld.com

First Published 2016

ISBN-13: 978-0-9966276-0-3
LCCN: 2015912266

Distributed by Itasca Books

Printed in the United States of America

To Besa, Healer of the Bakoko Bushmen, Groot Laagte, Botswana, rest in peace (which isn't likely as now that you're an ancestor yourself, we'll be badgering you for all kinds of help)

Contents

List of Illustrations

Illustration acknowledgements

I am grateful to the following people for their help and for providing the following photographs: Rufus Lovett, 1; Iliane Lorenz, 2,19, 20, 33, 35, 37; Megan Biesele, 5; Tayabe Nicholson, 6, 7, 8, 9, 10, 11, 12, 13; Polly Loxton, 14; Margot Gordon, 15, 16, 17; Dewaine Drew, 18; Nico Lorenz, 21; Amy Hammond, 23; Olivia Rutherford, 24, 25, 26, 27, 28, 29, 30; Martha Lamarche, 31; Gemma Barerra, 32; Alexandra Diaconu, 34. Photographs 4, 22 and 36 are the author's.

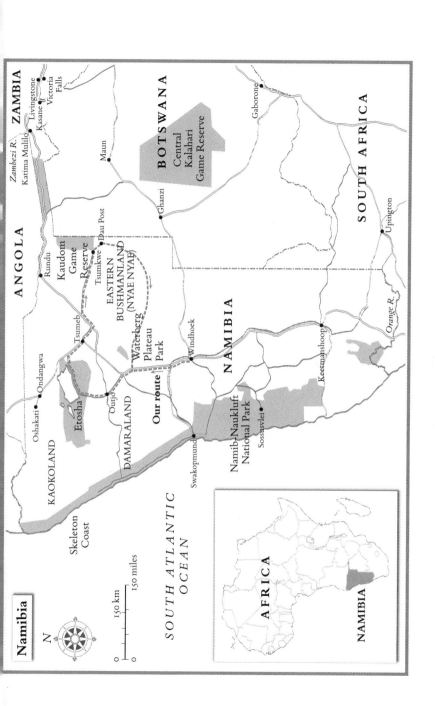

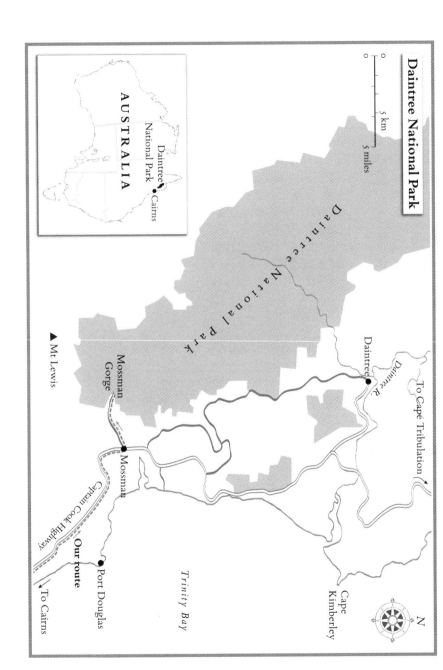

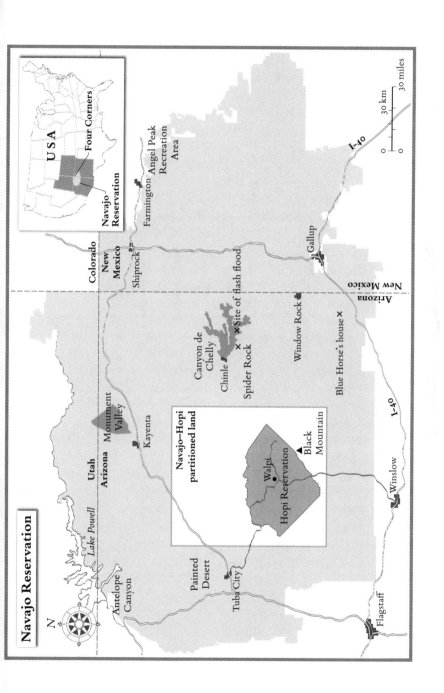

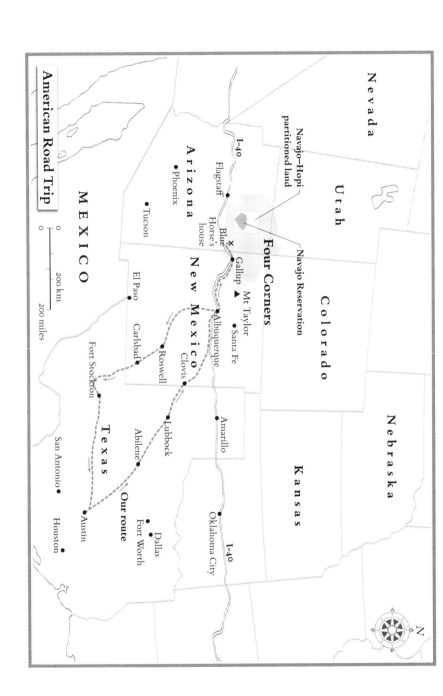

American Road Trip

Prologue

A Shaman Once Told Me

It was time to go. The tents were packed away, the horses saddled for riding or laden with gear. There remained only one last thing to do: say our goodbyes to the old shaman, Ghoste, before we rode back down the mountain, back through the forest below, back out to the vast plains of the steppe and ultimately, at the end of our great trek through the wild north of Mongolia, back home. Had the rituals worked? For three days Ghoste had worked on my autistic son Rowan, dancing with the spirits, telling us what they told him, our hopes – those of my wife Kristin and myself – rising and falling with every passing hour. Had it worked? Had this long, killing journey been worth it, or had it all been for nothing? Would my son be healed?

Old Ghoste, the shaman of the reindeer people, held Rowan in his arms. The mountain breeze – cool, moist – ruffled his grizzled mop of hair and my son's rich brown locks as I looked on, wondering, not wishing to be in the way, yet wanting so badly for the healing to be complete. The horses, saddled, ready, cropped the green upland grasses while – further up the mountainside – the great reindeer herd grazed in close-knit ranks, their antlers knocking together as they moved, the click and clack of them echoing down the slope to where we were sitting. All of our party – including Tulga, our Mongolian outfitter and translator, and Tomoo, his solemn-eyed, six-year-old son – watched as Rowan, happily munching a chocolate biscuit, the chocolate smearing all round his mouth, submitted to the final, very gentle ministrations of the shaman. As Rowan sat in his lap, Ghoste moved his fingers in delicate, grabbing flutters up and down my son's spine, shaking and twitching his head, eyes half closed, as he slipped in and out of trance. He seemed to be pulling something out of Rowan, some kind of invisible matter that one could sense if not see. Or was this just wishful thinking? We had come an awfully long way for it to be all for nothing, after all.

The shaman's fingers fluttered down Rowan's back once more, as my son – still oblivious – reached forward from the old man's lap to grab another biscuit; they danced back up to the top of Rowan's spine and gave a final sharp pull, then Ghoste let his hand drop back to his side. He looked at us, his brown eyes rheumy in the grey, wet morning, and grinned a gap-toothed smile.

'That's it,' he said, and let my son go. Rowan got up, trotted over to me and dived into my arms where I sat cross-legged on the turf. I fell backwards, hugging him to me, then just as suddenly he was gone, shouting, 'Wrestle!' and diving on to Tomoo, who, delighted, immediately began to try and roll out from under Rowan as my son attempted to pin him down. Around us the guides were busy, tightening the horses' girths, getting ready to mount up. As I went to fetch my horse, the brown-and-white gelding that Rowan had christened 'Blue', the shaman stopped me. 'Wait,' he said. 'I have something to tell you.'

Tulga and I squatted down in the grass, while Rowan and Tomoo chased each other around the remains of the campsite, diving and wrestling like ordinary boys anywhere. My son seeming ordinary – almost. It was still something I could hardly imagine.

'Listen,' said Ghoste. 'This is what the spirits have told me. Rowan will become gradually less autistic until his ninth year. Then, if you follow their instructions, his autism will get less and less, and gradually disappear. But the stuff that's been driving you crazy, the incontinence, the tantrums, these things will end now. From today.'

I tried to take this in, found I couldn't. So I just kept listening.

'But to make this happen, every year for the next three years you must make another healing journey to see a good shaman. It doesn't have to be me, or in Mongolia even, but a good shaman,

somewhere. You told me you know healers in Africa, the Bushmen. I have heard of them; they are powerful healers, more
powerful than we reindeer people, perhaps. But one good healing
journey a year for the next three years to make the healing complete, to make the autism no longer . . . no longer a problem, you
must do that.'

I nodded, not knowing what to think, whether to wince or to
whoop for joy. Three more journeys. Like this one? Well, it
would be another adventure, an amazing adventure such as few
people ever get to do. But also so much stress, effort and anxiety,
not to mention expense. Then from that place somewhere
between the solar plexus and the gut a little voice said: *He's right
– you have to do this.*

The same gut feeling that had told me to bring Rowan to
Mongolia in the first place, half a world away from our home in
Texas.

1. The Horse Boy

Our journey to Mongolia had happened like this. In 2004 my son Rowan was diagnosed with autism. Completely stunned and unsure where to turn for help, we floundered around like most parents of newly diagnosed special-needs kids in the shock of the diagnosis. It had been presented to us as a catastrophe: '*I regret to inform you, Mr Isaacson, that your son has a diagnosis of autism; there's no cure, the therapies are going to cost you about a hundred thousand a year that you haven't got – oh, and by the way, you are going to have to limit your life to a rigid schedule of daily activities written on a piece of paper on your fridge because your child will never be able to deal with change, and if you don't do these things you'll completely lose your child, who's actually kind of lost anyway. So goodbye and good luck.*'

No wonder parents of autistic children despair initially, until that other part of them asks: hold on, is this the complete picture? Can it really all be *that* bad?

Well, yes, it can. Tantrums like tsunamis, like storm fronts moving in from nowhere, erupting even in sleep. No language. My son floating away from me, absent, not there. So tantalizingly affectionate one moment and so lost the next. Enough to break any parent's heart. But I did notice one thing: despite my son's endless tantrums, his obsessive behaviour, he became better outdoors. He tantrummed less, seemed happier, more 'present'. So we spent hours and hours exploring the little trails in the woods behind our house in the Texas countryside, thirty minutes from the city of Austin. I wasn't working – my wife Kristin was teaching at the university, where she was a junior professor of psychology. My journalism, which routinely took me to Africa and other parts of the world to report on the environment and human rights, had dried up since Rowan's diagnosis. Autism is a full-time thing: usually one half of the couple gives up their career, at least in the early years. Single parents have an unimaginably hard time of it.

And into the bargain I had given up my principal passion in life – horses. Because I assumed that my wild, uncontrollable, two-and-a-half-year-old, non-verbal, raging bundle of utter enigmaticness would not be safe around horses.

So, into the woods we went. Much as I love nature, being outside in Texas from April until October can be pretty uncomfortable: hellishly hot and humid and with everything nature can throw at you, from mosquitoes, fire ants, bull nettle, poison ivy, poison oak and poison sumac to chiggers (if you've ever had them, you'll shudder and start itching just reading the word), brown recluse and black widow spiders and four species of venomous snake. There's a reason why people in the American South spend much of the year inside with the air conditioning on. But Rowan needed to move, move, move, so out along the sweaty trails we'd go, for hours at a time, under the elms and hackberries, me tagging behind in lonely silence as he dashed ahead, chirruping to himself in his private language, from which I was firmly excluded. Swatting at the flies and mosquitoes as I lumbered along, I wondered if this was it, this was what life would be like from now on, following in the wake of a child who didn't communicate, didn't really engage with us, who seemed to be floating away from us no matter what we tried.

Our marriage was suffering too. Badly. Kristin's parents – long since divorced – were about as far away as it was possible to be: her mother in Seattle, her father in Copenhagen. My parents lived in London, though both were southern African by birth. They had brought me up in England, but had always retained a strong link with Africa – hence my journalism and human-rights activity down there – for ours had been a political family, some of our cousins in jail for fighting against apartheid, others actively helping the regime. With offshoots in Zimbabwe, Botswana and Namibia, we were colonials through and through. But all that meant for me and Kristin, far away in Texas, was that we had no babysitters. And none of our friends could cope with Rowan's emotional and –

though we did not know it then – neurological firestorms, let alone the incontinence. Having no one else to turn to, no safety valve of any kind, Kristin and I had begun to eat at each other. And as all couples know, that can only go on for so long.

So there I was, traipsing behind Rowan, passing under the big post oak, through the evergreen yaupon holly, as we headed for the mustang grapevine he liked to swing from, when instead of heading to the right along the trail as he usually he did, he suddenly switched direction and charged to the left. Barging through the undergrowth, faster than I could follow because of all the thick bushes, he'd got through my neighbour Stafford's fence and into his horse pasture before I could catch him.

As sod's law would have it, all five of Stafford's horses were grazing right there by the fence. In a flash, Rowan was in among them, throwing himself on his back, impossibly vulnerable and exposed, among the horses' hooves, giggling and gurgling up at them, as they looked down at him, snorting their surprise.

My God, I thought, *he's going to be killed!* The very situation I'd tried to avoid by giving up horse riding in the first place. So there I was, creeping up to the fence, ready to grab Rowan by the collar or shirt tail and drag him to safety before the horses trampled him.

Except they didn't trample him; instead something extraordinary happened. Gently – very gently – Betsy, the grumpy lead mare of the herd, pushed the other horses away. Alpha mares are not usually so polite. Normally, if she had wanted the herd to move out of her space in a hurry, Betsy would have rushed at them with nipping teeth or maybe spun around with a hard kick: the very behaviour I was so afraid of. Yet instead she nudged them gently with her nose and – even more surprising – they moved away without the usual bucking, stomping protest that subordinate members of a herd usually display when the dominant one bosses them around.

Then Betsy lowered her head towards Rowan, still lying there in the grass laughing delightedly, and began to lick and chew with her lips, half closing her eyes. When a horse does this, it's a gesture of submission and acceptance – not dissimilar to when a dog rolls over and shows its belly. Horse trainers use various techniques to get to this stage with a horse. But I'd never seen a horse spontaneously show submission to a human being before. Much less a babbling, non-verbal, autistic toddler lying on his back in the grass. Something was passing between them, something magical. Clearly, Rowan had the same kind of connection with horses that I had. Probably more so, for Betsy's behaviour was way, way outside the norm. This seemed to be something purer, more direct.

And I'll never share it with him, I thought. Because of his autism. And with that, I burst into tears. Fortunately, I turned out to be completely, one hundred per cent wrong.

So began the most radical and positive change in our lives. Every day Rowan wanted to go back to Betsy. Once next to her, he would raise his arms and jump up and down. So I began lifting him on to her, keeping one hand on him for safety while Betsy grazed, calm and contented, as stable as a great big old couch. Laid on his tummy along the length of her brown back, his legs stretched out behind him, Rowan would explore the smooth softness of her coat with his fingers. When he lay on her like this there were no tantrums, only stillness. A stillness, a *pleasure* I had not seen in him before. All his self-stimulatory behaviour or 'stimming' – the flapping, rocking, chanting and other repetitive noises and movements that accompany autism and are usually a reaction to the neurological stresses of living in the human world of man-made stimuli – all this would fall away. He was a different kid. And I was back with horses – with *a* horse, anyway – even if I wasn't riding. Suddenly, life was a whole lot better than it had been.

Then the penny dropped. Betsy was a quiet riding horse (quiet with people, if rude and domineering towards her fellow equines), not the kind of hot-tempered sport variety that I was used to. What if I got up there with him and rode her, like the cowboys on the local ranches did with their kids? She would be perfect for this! The large Western saddles they used in Texas would be perfect for the job too: plenty of room for parent and child riding together.

Rowan was clearly getting a lot out of just being with Betsy. Might actually riding her maximize the effect? Surely it would be worth trying? Besides, it would be an adventure. An adventure that Rowan and I could share – father and son together.

I went to talk to Stafford about it. He already knew of the good effects that Betsy was having on my son. And he knew something of the stresses we were under as a family. When I told him what I wanted to do, Stafford handed me the key to his saddle room. 'Have at it,' he said. 'I hope the old girl works out for you.'

Stafford was taking an enormous risk. In today's litigious society – in the US, at least – many people would have considered the situation and thought: *Autistic kid, my horse, potential accident, get sued – sorry, but no way!* Just as our neighbour on the other side had done. He had recently built a swimming pool right up against our boundary fence. Worried that my uncannily agile son might climb the fence and fall into the pool, I had approached this neighbour with the suggestion that I teach Rowan to swim in that pool, so that should he climb over one day without my knowledge, he would at least be able to swim his way out of trouble. 'No,' the neighbour had replied. 'I can't risk the liability.' Instead, he posted a big 'No Trespassing' sign on the fence. For Stafford to just hand me the saddle-room key like that and say, 'Have at it,' was a gesture of unusual selflessness. Of faith.

So I found myself, one humid afternoon, alone in Stafford's saddle room looking at the biggest Western saddle I had ever seen. Hefting the thing off its rack, I puffed and panted it over to Betsy and swung it up on to her back, almost displacing a disc in the process. Clearly I would have to get fitter. I mounted and no sooner had I put my heels to her sides than she shot forward, yanking the reins from my hand, then, spinning with a vicious twist designed to unseat the rider (which it didn't – not this time), she headed firmly for the barn. I hadn't encountered a horse quite this rude in a long, long while. Clearly no one had ridden her recently, and she wasn't of a mind to suffer fools – or perhaps anyone at all. Was this really such a good idea?

But I'd learned to train horses – and more difficult horses than this: retired racehorses that had to be retrained for eventing or fox hunting. The old Leicestershire farmers who'd taught me the trade had taught me well. Within a few minutes, I had Betsy in hand. But I could tell from riding her that she had never had any real training. She was unbalanced, her gait unrhythmic, her mouth heavy on the bit and her centre of gravity so far forward that stopping and turning were a problem. Before riding her with Rowan I would have to work with her to ensure a safer, more balanced ride.

So, over the next few weeks, when Kristin was watching Rowan, I began to show the ornery old mare how to cooperate better with her rider, and soon she began to enjoy the attention and to accept a softer way of going, easier on both horse and rider. She also got fitter, more supple. As hot June turned to roasting July, I felt ready to attempt the first ride with my son.

And so the day came. Rowan was delighted to be swung up into the vast bathtub of a saddle, and I climbed up behind him, nervous as to how this would go. As I slotted myself neatly in behind Rowan, I could feel at once how he and I made one body together. More striking was that his almost incessant fidgeting had ceased: now that he sat in front of me he had a physical stillness that I had never felt before. I nudged Betsy forward into a walk, and stared around, looking for inspiration.

Now, although Rowan had almost no expressive language, I had always talked to him as if he *had*. As we walked the trails together, I had talked about everything around us: the trees, the birds, the sky, the atmosphere, oxygen, the pulmonary system, the fact that the sky was blue, and what *was* blue in any case, and the colours of the spectrum. One-sided monologues, maybe, but ones that I hoped were seeping into his consciousness and might some day come cascading out of him in words. I'm an optimist, as you'll no doubt have gathered.

But Rowan did have a language of his own, what in autism jargon we call 'echolalia', in which the child tends to echo, or repeat – often obsessively – things that he or she has heard: an advertising jingle, a snippet from a *Thomas the Tank Engine* video, a snatch of song from *The Lion King*. But they can't say 'Mummy, I'm hungry', 'Mummy, I'm thirsty', 'Mummy, I need the toilet', 'Mummy, I love you.'

So there I was, up there with my son, wondering where to go next. My eye fell on the wooded creek at the lower end of the pasture and the pond right in front of us.

'Do you want to go to the woods or the pond?' I asked, almost rhetorically, more voicing my own thoughts than expecting an answer.

'*To the pond!*' Rowan chanted back to me in a sing-song voice. Classic echolalia: repeating back the last three words you have said. Not real speech. Still, better than a kick in the face, I thought, and down to the pond we went. As we approached, a great blue heron lifted from the water and flapped away towards the west.

'Heron,' said Rowan.

I didn't know he knew the word.

Oh, my God. He was talking!

I started giving him choices: this way or that way? Faster or slower? Stop or keep going? And got responses. *Responses!*

Only a week or so before, his speech therapists had given up on him, said there was nothing more they could do, that my son was unreachable. And now here he was: bloody talking! And I noticed something else – the faster we went, or rather the more we went at the canter, the more speech I got.

We finally dismounted and I washed Betsy and fed her while Rowan ran around in circles laughing and crying, '*Horse! Horse! Horse!*' Excited beyond measure, I rushed back home to Kristin, busy writing up some research in the quiet time she had while I was looking after Rowan, and shouted: 'He's talking! He's talking!'

My wife looked at Rowan, by now back in his own world and lining up his toys in classic autistic fashion. Never a great one for horses herself, she was none the less tolerant of my own obsession. 'That's nice, dear,' she said, and went back to her psychology research paper.

But he had talked – he really had! And the next day, back in the saddle with me once more, he did it again. The door into his world had opened a crack and I was going to follow him through it. On horseback.

This was adventure, right here in my own backyard. My experience of autism began to change. And my son, more and more, began to talk in response to the things I pointed out to him. 'There's an oak tree,' I'd say as we rode towards it. 'O-A-K, oak!' We'd pick edible plants as we rode by, identify them – hackberry (you can eat the leaves and the berries, which are sweet like caramel), greenbriar tips, mustang grapes hanging from the vines between the trees. We'd point out the animals and birds – the flash of a cottontail across the path or the brilliant red of a cardinal bird: 'Cottontail! Cardinal!' We'd track as we rode, seeing here five-toed human-like handprints left by raccoons in the dirt – 'Raccoon hands!' – there the more tapered, clawed spoor of a possum: 'Snuffly wuffly possum-possum!'

We were exploring and making sense of the natural world, and Rowan was beginning to emerge from his shell. Derived from *auto*, the Greek word for 'self', 'autism' effectively means 'self-ism' – to be locked within the self, unable to relate to the exterior world. Betsy was carrying us into this world together without resistance, father and son.

About six weeks after we had begun to spend our days together in the saddle like this, Rowan's speech began to graduate from the horse and into the home. 'Wow!' cried Kristin, the first time he said 'Elephant' and held out one of his toy animals to her. 'So this is what you were talking about. Wow!'

That same year, 2004, at round about the same time that Rowan was diagnosed with autism, another strand of my life took off and developed in a strange and fortuitous way. My work with the Bushmen of the Kalahari.

Although I was born and brought up in the UK, I had been going to Africa on and off since childhood and, as a journalist, had naturally gravitated there to follow stories. During one such trip, I had discovered that the non-white side of my family (most colonial families have a white and a non-white side, though few acknowledge or even know their relatives across the colour bar) was related to the last group of Bushman hunter-gatherers left in South Africa, the Xhomani, and that this group – who had been living by the side of the road in complete destitution for the past thirty or so years – had decided to reclaim their old hunting territory. A tall order, you might say, considering that the land in question was now the second-largest national park in the country. I had began to follow the story in the late 1990s – taking me on a strange journey that led me to meet the Bushmen's trance healers, or shamans – up until 1999 when, against all odds, they won back their land, including half the national park. I ended up writing a book about it, *The Healing Land*.

Soon after this landmark victory, a second group of Bushmen, up in neighbouring Botswana, had launched a similar, but much larger claim, after their government forced them off their land to make way for diamond mining. I was approached by the Bushmen to help get this new group – the Ganakwe and Gwi of Botswana's Central Kalahari Game Reserve – to America so that they could protest at the United Nations and US State Department. Needless to say, I couldn't resist the challenge.

So the same year that Rowan was diagnosed, and met Betsy, I brought the Bushmen to America. It was an extraordinary journey: from Los Angeles on the west coast to New York and Washington on the east, staying with Indian tribes in between and attracting as much media attention as we could to highlight the Bushmen's plight. Some of the Bushmen in that delegation were trained healers in their own culture, and during the journey they met Rowan and offered to 'work' on him a little.

I had witnessed quite a few of these Bushman trance ceremonies over the years, seeing sick people, sometimes really ill, get remarkably better. Once I had seen a woman, her legs horribly red and swollen from rheumatoid arthritis, emerge from an all-night trance dance with the swellings inexplicably gone. I had observed stranger things too: leopards called out of the dark to the fires where the healers danced; healers bleeding from the nose and mouth as they laid hands on someone with cancer (the person then reporting, months later, that their tumour had gone). I'd seen people treated this way for snakebite, broken limbs, even depression – and I had seen these people recover. In each case, I couldn't help but notice that the patients got better without any, or at least very little, access to Western medicine. Whatever your views on shamanic healing, when you've been in Africa for a while you stop insisting that everything conform to the rules of rationality, because it just doesn't. So when the Bushmen offered to 'work' on my autistic son, I thought, *Why not?* It was just prayer and song after all; the worst thing that could happen was nothing.

But to my surprise, during the four or five days that Rowan spent with them, he began to lose some of the worst of his obsessive traits. That, plus the language gains he was making with Betsy, gave me pause. We'd been trying all the orthodox therapies – applied behavioural analysis, chelation to cleanse his bloodstream of heavy metals like lead and mercury (which can cause autism symptoms), the herpes medication Valtrex (on the basis that herpes might cause autism in very young children), occupational, speech and play therapies – though we never, ever used any kind of mood-altering medication. Compared to Rowan's radical and positive reaction to both the horse and the Bushmen healers, they seemed to be having little effect, however. So was there somewhere we could go that combined shamanic healing with horse riding?

This set me thinking. Where did horses originate? It was in Mongolia that *Equus caballus*, the horse as we know it, evolved and was first domesticated. And I knew – because of my experience with tribal peoples and shamanism – that they had a strong system of healing there too. In fact the word 'shaman' – meaning 'he who knows' – comes from that part of the world. I also knew that Mongolian shamans used the horse as a totem animal. A gut feeling, strong as a punch to the solar plexus, hit me. We had to go there.

Kristin had also seen and been impressed by the effect the shamans had seemed to have on Rowan, even though he'd fallen back into the depths of his autism when they returned to Africa. And so when the Bushman trip was over, I fielded the idea of taking Rowan to Mongolia for healing. 'We could ride from healer to healer!' I said excitedly. 'It would be such an adventure!'

'Rupert,' she said, 'that's a terrible idea. You must be mad. No way! Absolutely no way!'

It might seem naïve but I was shocked by her response – this, after all, was a woman who was no stranger to adventure. I had met Kristin in India, where she had been studying for her PhD in comparative psychology and I had been researching a guidebook. We had trekked the leach-infested rainforests of Kerala's mountains together, then the following year she had gone with me to Africa and we had hitchhiked across the Kalahari and gone to Bushmanland to meet the hunter-gatherers for the first time. Granted, she wasn't really a horse person but she could ride well enough – I had taught her. And she had seen what being on Betsy had done for Rowan. But she wasn't having it.

'Let me get this straight,' she said, when I pressed the matter. 'We're going to somehow keep our incontinent, tantrumming son on horseback across *MONGOLIA* while looking for some kind of healing? No way! Just going to the supermarket is totally stressful! I can't believe you'd even suggest such a thing.'

To my mind, precisely because it *was* so stressful just going to the supermarket we might as well go to Mongolia! But the force of Kristin's reaction was not something to set myself against . . . yet. So we both backed off, each hoping the other one would forget about it. Yet the gut feeling wouldn't go away, the feeling that if we *did* go there, if we did make this leap of faith, pursuing the two things that Rowan had responded to above all else, then something – though I did not know exactly what – would happen. I couldn't shake it.

Still, in one respect, Kristin was right: Rowan was too young yet, at two and a half, to withstand the rigours of such a trip. I was planning to try it later, when he was bigger, but still small enough to fit comfortably in the saddle with me. And as the next two and a half years passed, Rowan and I virtually lived in the saddle together: taking books with us for learning to read, dismounting for Rowan to write his first letters, then words, in the mud; learning to track, identify and classify animals and plants; and just revelling in the sheer, singing bliss of experiencing the world like this as father and son, together in the saddle on the amazing Betsy's broad brown back. And all the while the feeling that I had to make this trip, this journey – pilgrimage, you might say – only got stronger. In the meantime, my human-rights work with the Botswana Bushmen was gathering pace until finally in 2006 we – myself and my fellow activists – helped them win the largest land claim in African history. Suddenly that pressure was out of the way, leaving me free to do other things. Meanwhile, the various therapies we tried for Rowan continued to have little effect, none of them addressing the fundamental problems that still persisted.

In fact, for a while, they had got much worse, with Rowan becoming increasingly sad as he went into the special-needs classroom at the local school – a room with no windows, that gave out on to a playground that, despite the 100-degree-plus Texas summers, had no shade. He even began to cry a little sometimes when I drove him in. The teacher seemed nice enough but Rowan, who I knew was intelligent – it wasn't his intellect that was the problem, but how he processed information – seemed to be retreating further into himself. One day I arrived early to pick him up and saw why: the teacher was not in the room. Instead, the three teaching assistants were there, sitting eating junk food and chips, drinking Coke, and batting away the hands of the kids when they tried, quite naturally, to help themselves. To drown out the noise of the stims, the assistants had put on *Toy Story* and turned the volume up loud. We pulled Rowan out of school that very day, but had no idea what to do, no experience of homeschooling. So in the absence of any answers, I started with a question: what would be my ideal model if I had my own school years to do over again?

The Sword in the Stone, of course! The wizard Merlyn comes to the castle and teaches you by turning you into various animals and sending you on quests. Complete fantasy, of course, but was there anything in reality that I could think of that approximated to it? Yes, there was actually: *My Family and Other Animals* by Gerald Durrell – a man who had gone on to become one of England's leading zoologists, and who had helped reinvent zoos as repositories for the gene pool of endangered species, not just places where you went to gawk at animals in cages. Durrell's family, when he was a boy, moved to the island of Corfu and for several idyllic years the young Durrell did not go to school. Instead he had a boat, some dogs, the freedom of the Greek islands and coast, and – crucially – a mentor in the person of a local biologist. Together, armed with test tubes, microscope and an irrepressible sense of curiosity, they roamed at will, and Durrell learned the natural sciences, not to mention history, languages, Greek culture and, through navigation, maths.

Both stories – *The Sword in the Stone* and *My Family and Other Animals* – had something crucial in common: one-to-one mentoring out of doors, with a constant sense of adventure and exploration inspired by nature. That, surely, I could do. I'd been doing it already, after all. The worst that could happen would be that the schoolwork itself might take me a year or two to work out properly, and that I might have to cast around to find other mentors – for a whole tribe is always better than a single person. But if it did, so what? At least my son's sadness, the dimming of his soul, the damage and regression that was happening in that windowless room with the television that they called school, would be stopped. At least no more harm would be done.

So up there in the saddle, Rowan continued to learn to spell and read. We took Dr Seuss up there and flash cards, too; we counted Betsy's footfalls and began basic maths. Yet at five, despite the gains in language and cognition he had made, my son was still impossible to toilet train, he still tantrummed with an epic force that could (and once did) silence the machinery of a construction crew, and could not make friends. And all the time that deep gut feeling, that we needed to go to a place that combined both healing and horses and make a journey, a pilgrimage, just would not go away.

Finally, unable to brush it aside any longer, I said to Kristin one day: 'Look, I realize that this Mongolia thing is my gig. I know you don't even like horses – you're off the hook, you don't have to go. But I think I have to do this. The feeling won't go away. In fact, just keeps getting stronger. But you don't have to do it. Truly.'

It meant a lot to her to be let off the hook. We agreed I would go alone with Rowan. Then two days later she came to me, grinning wryly. 'Like I'm going to miss out on the greatest adventure our family will ever have,' she said. 'But,' she added, dark eyes twinkling, 'for me it's win/win. If it all goes to hell in a handbasket, I can say "I told you so" for ever, and if it works – well, all the better!'

So off to Mongolia we went. The story of that extraordinary journey into what – for us, at any rate – was the true unknown is told in *The Horse Boy*. Suffice to say here that we spent a month travelling from shaman to shaman, by 4x4 and on horseback, exactly as that original gut feeling had dictated. To say there were many setbacks and slips along the way would be an understatement. We had no idea if anything would happen, if any change or any healing would even occur. As a leap of faith it appeared crazy. But even if nothing happened, I reasoned, then at least the diagnosis of autism would not have stopped us from having the most incredible adventure together as a family.

But healing did happen. More than we could have predicted in our wildest dreams. I stress the word 'healing', though, not 'cure'. By the time we boarded the plane at Moscow's grim post-Soviet airport to take us to Ulaanbaatar, the equally grim post-Soviet capital of Mongolia, I had accepted that Rowan's autism was for life, that there was no cure. But could Rowan at least stop his terrible, self-harming tantrums, which we now knew were due to intense neurological discomfort. Could he at last become continent? Could he finally begin to make friends? Despite his autism, could he become a successful, happy, productive human being in his own right?

The first day in Mongolia, our guide Tulga – having put out the word about our arrival some months before – led us to a sacred mountain just outside the capital, where nine shamans, some of whom had travelled hundreds of miles to come and help this small Western boy who needed healing, performed a ritual that lasted hours. At first I thought I'd made a terrible mistake. Rowan hated the noise, the drumming, the overstimulation. Kristin and I were whipped at one point, to drive the 'black energy' out of us, and Kristin (I thought she would divorce me after this!) was made to wash 'the part of her where Rowan came out' using a sacred vodka to cleanse it. But midway through that long afternoon, as the shamans – in their feathered headdresses and masks and their coats hung with ribbons, fur, antler, bones and strange metal charms – danced and prayed to the 'Lords of the Mountain' and the 'Lords of the Forest', something shifted. Rowan began to giggle, laugh and play with his healers. The humidity lifted. Rain came down – a very good sign, said the shamans – and then suddenly Rowan turned to a small boy who was there at the gathering, a boy perhaps a year older than him, and – out of the blue – hugged him, calling him 'Mongolian brother'. He had never done anything like this before. The boy – Tomoo – turned out to be our guide Tulga's young son. At Tulga's suggestion, Tomoo came along on the journey with us. There in that first ritual, on the first day, Rowan had made his first friend.

We travelled north by stages, stopping at a sacred lake, so remote that even Tulga, a professional guide, did not know of it, where we washed in water that, so Mongolian legend has it, once carried the first horses down from heaven to earth. As we travelled across that green vastness, Rowan's friendship with Tomoo blossomed; he became a different boy. Finally, we reached the utter north, where the great rolling steppe gives way to an immensity of trees, hard by the Russian border, where the mountains of Siberia come down to meet the plains, and the forests of the great taiga, which stretches from Norway to the Pacific Rim, take over. The land of the Tsataan or Dukha – the reindeer people.

Just to make the ascent into those mountains took three days – on horseback, across rivers, through bogs deep enough to swallow a horse, and finally over a high pass on to the tundra just below the snowline, where the summer temperatures are cool enough for reindeer to thrive. Before man tamed the horse, he rode the reindeer: meeting these people, the Tsataan – who live in teepees and ride, as well as herd, reindeer – was like going back forty thousand years in human history, like entering a dream. Ghoste, their shaman, worked on Rowan for three days. It was on the last morning, as we were making ready to ride back down the mountain, unsure whether it had worked or not, that Ghoste told us that Rowan's spirit had accepted the healing, but that we would have to make three more such journeys – journeys like this, to healers – over the next three years, to complete the process. In the meantime, however, the stuff that really drove us crazy – the incontinence, the tantrumming – would end now.

I was surprised: in my experience with the Bushmen, it was unusual, unheard of even, for a shaman to make such an unequivocal prediction. Not unlike those of a Western doctor, their prognoses are usually a little more qualified than that. But Ghoste was quite adamant. And as we rode back down from the heights, through mountain meadows awash with purple wildflowers, to the river at the mountain's foot, that indeed was when everything began to change.

At the river, on the evening of the second day out from Ghoste's camp, Rowan did his first intentional poo and cleaned himself! It was like watching England win the World Cup: better even. And two days later, my son used the toilet for the first time. Kristin and I were over the moon.

From that moment until we finally got home to Texas, we counted perhaps six tantrums of any note. Normally that would be a day's or even half a day's worth, if things were going particularly badly. And that was that. Changed. All those years of despair, frustration and shame – of being the family whose normal-looking son would always shit himself in public – suddenly those years were gone. It seemed incredible. Incredible in its literal sense – i.e. unbelievable.

When we got home, Rowan immediately began to make friends with all the kids in the neighbourhood. Not quite on the level of riding his bike to their houses and saying 'Come out and play', but through playdates I began to offer informally from home that included rides on Betsy and Taz and Chango, quarterhorses lent by my kind neighbour Stafford. There were a few other families in our area with kids on the autism spectrum, and they and their siblings began to come out to see us. A little time on the trampoline, a little walking in the woods or splashing in the paddling pool, a little play with the pygmy goats and the dogs. Rowan interacted as much, if not more, with the non-autistic kids as with the autistic ones. I was amazed, and also curious. Partly I was running these playdates to see if Rowan really would keep playing with other children as he had with Tomoo. Partly I did it to provide him with a social life. Partly I did it to see if it was just my son who had this reaction to Betsy, and to horses in general, or if it was something more universal.

And it was. Pretty much all the kids on the spectrum calmed down, ceased to 'stim' and flap when laid body to body on the horse's bare back. And when I rode with them in the same saddle, just as I had done with Rowan, they would react just as he did. When I put Betsy into a slow, easy canter with the child in front of me, I would often witness a rush of euphoria from the child: peals of laughter followed, often, by proper words.

Of course, we were terrified that, back home, the three key dys-functions that Rowan had left behind him in Mongolia might return. After all, when he had met the shamans before – back in 2004, when I brought the Bushmen over to the USA – he had lost some of his more obsessive behaviour. And then when the Bush-men returned to Africa, he had fallen back into a state of profound autism. Would the same thing happen now?

But it didn't. Slowly, tentatively, as that hot Texas autumn began to unfold, we began to have faith in Ghoste's predictions. The tantrums did not return. Some bad days here and there, yes, but nothing like before. Nothing like. And the toilet training: '*Flush! Flush!*' Rowan would sing, hopping off the bowl after – amazingly – wiping himself! Then skip across the floor to the sink – '*Wash! Wash!*' – like a little bathroom elf. We could scarcely allow ourselves to believe it. And now, not just when we were running playdates with the horses, Rowan had friends over. Like a normal kid – almost. It was strange because, not unlike when he was playing with Tomoo out on the open steppe, there was no real conversation: something between repeated scripts from cartoon shows, easy-to-follow directions like 'Let's go play with the rabbits!' and games of chase that seemed to originate spontaneously; but it was miles ahead of the distant parallel play we'd seen only a month before.

And for me, his horse-obsessed father, the moment of high parental ecstasy came one warm October morning in 2007 when we'd come back from riding Betsy and, on a sudden inspiration, I'd dismounted for the final quarter-mile back to Stafford's barn. Walking beside Betsy, leaving Rowan up in the big Western saddle, I said, my heart in my mouth, 'Just pull the reins a little and say, "Whoa, Betsy!"'

He did. Betsy stopped.

'And now, give her a little kick with your heels and say, "Come on, Betsy!"'

'*Come on, Betsy!*' His voice was light, like a little bird's in the damp autumn air. She moved forwards as directed, me walking backwards a little to the front and side, wondering how much distance would be safe to put between me and her. Good as she was, like any horse she couldn't be trusted not to just take off back to the barn, given half a chance.

'Okay,' I said, deciding to take it one step further. 'Now pull on the reins a little and say, "Whoa, Betsy!" again.'

'*Whoa, Betsy!*'

She stopped. I couldn't believe my son was taking clear direction like this. It had never happened, never. Until now.

'Okay,' I said, wondering if this would be pushing things too far, and trying to keep the excitement out of my voice so Rowan would not feel pressured. Pressure, being put on the spot in any way could make him freeze, shut down completely. 'Okay,' I kept my tone level, 'take the reins in one hand like this and turn her back towards the gate – yes, like that . . .' I moved around in front of the mare, fluttering my finger to keep her attention, encouraging her to move in the desired direction. I was now a full six feet away – close enough to leap forward and grab the reins if necessary, far enough to not interfere. Rowan turned her, keeping his body straight, his inside leg acting as the pivot around which she moved, his hand light on the rein. As if he had been riding all his life – which in a way, I suppose, he had.

'Okay, now turn her again. That's right, so she's heading back towards the barn . . .' I skipped in front, making sure I could block Betsy if she did decide to take off, walking backwards, keeping my eyes on hers, willing her to behave. She did.

In the final few yards I said, 'Okay, now give her another little kick and say, "Trot on, Betsy!"'

'*Trot on, Betsy!*'

She went forward into the gentle jog trot I had taught her. I kept walking backwards, quickening my pace. Ten steps, fifteen, twenty, twenty-five, Rowan sitting up there on top of the movement, easy and graceful, like a seabird atop the rolling wave – effortless, at ease.

'And now say, "Whoa, Betsy!" again.'

'*Whoa, Betsy again!*'

But he stopped her. By himself. Right there on the barn's concrete aisleway.

I could barely speak for joy.

'You just rode!' It came bubbling out of me like champagne from a bottle. Pure happiness, pure delight. 'You just rode!' I reached out for him, took him in my arms and snuggled him. 'You just rode! You little scubby, ubby, wubby, nuggy, yuggy. You just rode!'

Next to us, Betsy snorted.

I turned to her, Rowan leaping down to caper happily on the aisleway. 'Thank you, Betsy,' I said, and kissed her.

For Kristin and me, the change in our lives applied to night as well as day. Suddenly, for the first time, Rowan would accept babysitters. And with him now being toilet trained, and actually enjoying playing with other kids, suddenly we could . . . go out. A strange new concept. The first time we had gone out on an actual date in, what, three years? Four? At a Mexican restaurant on Austin's funky East Side, we sat across from each other, looking at our margaritas and each other, almost not knowing what to say.

'So is this where we start acting like normal parents and go out on a date and talk about our kid?' Kristin quipped. Then she kissed me. We clinked glasses. God, but she was beautiful, dark eyes glinting in the candlelight, long brown hair falling to her shoulders. She had turned heads as we walked into the restaurant, as she always did.

Back home, with childcare suddenly available, I sat down to begin writing the book of our adventure in Mongolia that would become *The Horse Boy*, and to sort through the footage we had taken out there for a documentary of our trip.

Kristin also began compiling the results of her ten years of research at the University of Texas on the nexus between Buddhism and mainstream psychology, specifically the practice of self-compassion and how it affects people's mental health. Her work had been curtailed by Rowan's autism crisis. *Our* autism crisis. But now – with childcare a possibility as never before – Kristin could begin to put together her first book. It was as if the wellspring of happiness, so long dammed up, had burst out at last, and now we – all three of us – were quenching our thirst at the source.

We also decided to share what we had been given. We used the money from my book advance to purchase a plot of land some fifteen miles from our home, complete with 1900s ranch house, a broken-down ruin standing stark on the rich blackland prairie where once bison and the Comanche had roamed, and where mesquite trees now competed with grassland and cotton fields. There we began to plan out a centre where we could bring horses and autism families together free of charge. We were so close to the city, it made perfect sense. A line of mature cedar elms cast shade over the old homestead, while a set of fruit-bearing mulberries grew right by the fallen-down front porch. There were coyote runs through the mesquite; in the far back pasture were highways for wild boar. The shooting stars and meteor showers at night leapt like the thoughts and dreams of old gods across an illuminated sky. I could just picture the happy kids that would run across the ranch land. All we had to do was fix it up. Its address was 151 New Trails Road, so we called it the New Trails Center. It seemed fitting. We had no idea what we were in for – yet. For now, the success – for us miraculous – of the journey to Mongolia still lapped around us like a warm sea, rocking us gently after the storms and alarms of the last four years.

But Rowan was still autistic: his conversation still not real conversation; his nervous system still subject to sensory overload that made him flap and stim (less and less but he was still prone to it on a bad day); his diet still limited to a very few foods. He was still obsessive about his routines and about as flexible, despite his travels, as a Victorian grandfather. And what if the gains he had made left him? Never far from the surface of my mind were Ghoste's words – that we still had three more journeys to make, over three more years, to make the healing complete.

I was tired. Bone tired. All special-needs parents, all *parents* know this utter, resigned fatigue. It had taken so much to get to Mongolia, pull it off, make it happen, travel across that vast, free steppe and up into the Siberian mountains with my suffering son, my bemused and frazzled wife. As quests went, it had been the journey of a lifetime. Could we not now put up our feet and rest?

The kinds of journey that Ghoste would have us do are not undertaken lightly. So as autumn turned to winter, as the heat disappeared from the land and the rains came, I began, once more, to plan.

2. The First People

Ghoste had suggested the Bushmen, and he was right. Now that the horse shaman journey to Mongolia was done, I felt – gut feeling again – we needed to go back into Rowan's own ancestry, which meant Africa. But where to specifically? Most of the healers I knew, especially an old Bushman called Besa, to whom I had become very close – so close in fact that he and the other Bushmen had named me 'Little Besa' and I had given Rowan 'Besa' as his middle name – most of these healers lived in Botswana. But since 2006, when we had helped his people win their land claim, I and sixteen other human-rights activists and journalists, including the BBC's John Simpson, had been banned from Botswana for life. If Botswana was out, where could we go?

The answer was Namibia. It was in fact where I had first met the Bushmen back in 1995 when travelling with Kristin across the Kalahari. My grandfather Robbie, my father's father, had also been born there, so the ancestral connection was strong. And the Bushmen of the Nyae Nyae region in the remote northeast – the same ones that Kristin and I had first met together over a decade before – still lived in the most traditional way, hunting and gathering, of any of the Bushmen across the five countries of the Kalahari. It was the obvious choice.

So it was in July 2008 that, Kristin, Rowan, my mother Polly (who had accompanied me to Africa before to participate in the Bushman healing ceremonies) and our film-maker friend Michel found ourselves flying south to Windhoek, capital of Namibia, where my grandfather had lived as a little boy in the 1900s. Closing my eyes, the hum of the engines loud around our cheap seats in the rear of the plane, I was back on top of the sacred mountain with

Ghoste. 'Well,' I said to him in my thoughts, 'here we are – making the first of three journeys, just like you told us. I hope I've chosen right.'

Rowan turned to me from his seat, grinning his little-boy grin as Africa, land of our fathers, passed, brown and vast, thirty thousand feet below us.

'Mr Boy!'

His laugh was infectious. I 'scubbled' him – squeezing and tickling him and playing on his nickname, 'Scub' – then sang the song as directed.

> Mr Boy is a . . .

'BOY!'

I knew the lines well: we had been developing these songs – 'Scubby songs', Rowan called them – for the past few years. It was our private language, a private language of joy. I sang the next one:

> Mr Boy is a . . .

'BOY!' Rowan responded, all delight.

> He was a little . . .

'BOY!'

> And he was a little . . .

'BOY!'

> And he was a little, little, little . . .

'BOY!'

> Little . . .

'BOY!'

The first Scubby song had bubbled up spontaneously – the way these things so often do between parent and child – one day as I was driving him back from school, in the days when he had still gone to school, when I had first noticed that it was making him sad, dimming the brightness that was his normal, natural state except when the neurological firestorms, demon-like, came raging through his body.

I had turned to him in the little red truck that we had then, still have now as a farm truck, leaned over to where he sat next to me on the bench seat, and poked him for a tickle. The sad look passed as quickly as cloud dispelled by sun, and a little belly laugh came bubbling up from the depths of him. Next thing I knew I was singing, squeezing him in time with the words, as he grinned and squinted to the side with pleasure, his lower jaw thrust out slightly as only happened when he was really happy. The song – with a squeeze of the leg on every syllable – went like this:

> Because you're . . .
> My little boy,
> My little boy,
> My little boy, boy, boy . . .

I paused. He looked at me, grabbed my wrist and made me squeeze him again, saying, '*My little boy!*'

And so the first true Scubby song was born. Now they tended to bubble up semi-spontaneously. 'Mr Boy is a Boy' was something of a masterpiece, however – at least in our opinion.

'Squint at the eyes of that!' Rowan grabbed my head and brought it right up to his, just inches away, squinting up his eyes and half turning his face from me. A classically autistic reaction to something loved: to bring it close – so close it distorted the vision, causing the squint, eyes averted to look at it sidelong. One day, I hoped, he might explain to me why this seemed so good to him – and to others like him. One day, I hoped, we might converse, like fathers and sons usually did. One day.

'Mr Boy!' he commanded.

So, dutifully, I began again, sneaking a glance – as I sang – across Kristin's sleeping body at my mother, Polly, where she sat sketching me and Rowan, our heads together, as we shared our song. She beamed when I caught her eye. The further south we flew, the more relaxed she was becoming. I remembered this from ten years before when she and I had flown out to the Kalahari at the South African Bushmen's behest as part of the healing ceremonies they were conducting for the land claim they subsequently won. She had been a different person – at home, relaxed, not over-anxious as she could be in London. Africa was in her, Africa *was* her. Always, when in London, she grieved for longed for the land of her birth. England was a low-level constant source of stress for her. I sometimes wondered why she had never moved back to South Africa. But life, family, my dad's career as an architect had never allowed it. So many times people find themselves living lives that are not quite their dream. It takes its toll. Whereas in London our relationship could be strained, it was not, I remembered, in Africa.

My father, Laurence, loved London, despite his own boyhood in Zimbabwe. When we were children, Polly had regaled us with stories of her African girlhood that revolved around the beauty of the bush and the sea, along with the sheer physical force of the place and its passionate, often violent people. By contrast, my father used to snort and say, 'The bush? Not for me. When I first felt concrete beneath my feet and smelled the scent of traffic fumes, I knew I was home!'

For my dad this rejection of the romance of Africa was really a reaction to his own father – my grandfather Robbie, an unusual man by any standards but also, unfortunately, a tyrant of the first order. Born into a Jewish family in Namibia, when it was still known as Sudwest Afrika, Robbie had grown up to find the German-dominated colony too anti-Semitic for him to get ahead and so had moved east, in the early 1920s, to what was then Rhodesia and is now Zimbabwe. Here he first sold shoes, then joined an auctioneering firm, married the boss's daughter, to whom he was foul for the rest of her life, and finally became a cattle rancher or, more accurately, a kind of latter-day feudal *seigneur*, on a series of vast farms just to the east of the capital Salisbury, now Harare.

Kristin and I had experienced the old man's meanness when we had travelled there, back in 1995. The wretched car I had been able to afford on the guidebook money that had taken us out there had broken down in a remote corner of Zimbabwe, endangering the whole project.

'Call your grandfather,' Kristin had urged. 'He's got loads of spare vehicles on his farms.' I had just laughed, knowing what Robbie would say. When she insisted, I agreed but only if she would listen in, so she could understand the nature of what we were dealing with. I rang him and told him that the car was kaput and we were stranded.

'Well, my boy, car hire's expensive,' had been his response.

'Yes, it is,' I'd agreed.

'It is indeed,' he'd confirmed.

And that was that. I put the phone down.

'I can't believe that!' Kristin was indignant. 'I mean, he's your *grandfather*, and you're – *we're* – stuck here in his country and he has more trucks than he knows what to do with. I can't believe it! What are we going to do?'

I made some calls and finally managed to contact two old friends who owned a self-drive-safari company and who, as luck would have it, had a fully equipped Land Rover that needed to be delivered from its reconditioning garage in Windhoek, Namibia, to a new set of clients a thousand or so miles away in Victoria Falls, Zimbabwe. It was a more expensive vehicle than I could ever have dreamed of hiring. I could take my time to make the delivery, said my friends: months, if needed, as long as I looked after the vehicle in the meantime. It was a lifesaver. The only catch was that we were about two thousand miles away from Windhoek, the pick-up point, with a third of Zimbabwe, all of Botswana and a goodly chunk of Namibia to cross in order to get there. So I got to find out just how brave Kristin was.

'We're going to do what?' she asked, when I told her what our options were.

'Hitchhike,' I confirmed, a little less confidently than before in the face of the growing disbelief on her face.

'Across AFRICA?'

'Well, only a bit of it, not the whole thing.'

'You're serious?'

'I hitched the same route myself a few years ago,' I tried to reassure her. 'It's easy – a straight shot across the southern Kalahari. And they've been improving the roads since then. Shouldn't take more than a few days. And we can use the money we save on the transport for fuel once we get the Land Rover.'

'You're telling me we're going to hitchhike across the Kalahari Desert.'

'Um, well, I guess, um . . . yeah.'

'You must be crazy. No way.'

So across the southern end of the Kalahari we went, sticking out our thumbs on the Bulawayo road west of Harare and making it by easy stages to Gaborone, the bright, new, paid-for-with-diamond-money capital of Botswana. We crowded into the back of small pickups with up to twenty other locals, trying not to get catapulted off the flatbed as the *buckies*, as pickups are called in that part of the world, leapt and bounced over the ruts and potholes of the then untarred Trans-Kalahari Highway, the vast tawny immensity of southern Africa's arid interior stretching away either side from flat horizon to flat horizon – the sheer, uncompromising *thereness* of hot, unrelenting Africa. But not to exaggerate: it was easier than hitchhiking across Europe or – God forbid – the gun-crazed USA. In many parts of Africa hitchhiking runs a bit like an unofficial bus system. You, the hitcher, are expected to pay something towards the fuel for the trip. The more people the drivers pick up, the fewer expenses for them and maybe they even make a little cash on top. So because of this system, you're unlikely to get stranded: if someone has room in their vehicle, they are going to stop.

All the same, though, it was a massive act of faith and courage for Kristin, a suburban girl from Thousand Oaks, California, to stick out her thumb and cross Africa like that, and I was impressed. We only got seriously stuck on one portion of the trip, down where the bony, skeletal mountains of the Namib begin to take over from the red sand dunes and dry grasslands of southern Namibia, near the town of Keetmanshoop. Desolate country – hundreds of square miles of bare shale and black rock, baking under a pitiless sun – where we worried about our water supply, and spent the best part of a day clinging to the thin shadow of a straggly roadside tamarind tree, waiting for cars that never came. But at last, towards the red African evening, a *buckie* finally pulled over and drove us the last few hours up to Windhoek, where we picked up the Land Rover with its amazing roof tent (to keep you safe from lions), refrigerator (cold beers in the evening) and ability to go anywhere, through anything. We were set to go.

It was this vehicle that had enabled me to meet the Bushmen for the first time, in the very area – Nyae Nyae – to which we were now heading with Rowan. I had grown up on the myths and legends of the Bushmen, as told to me by my mother. White African cousins had talked of them as a kind of elusive fairy folk, living in far-away places you'd never go to, and even if you did, they would hide, wary of strangers, because they were people of peace, living in a land riven by aggression and war, and would allow contact only with the select few able to penetrate the remote back of beyond where they lived and win their trust. It was as if, somehow, for my extended family – themselves riven by apartheid and the guilt of conquest and horror at the atrocities the black tribes visited upon each other seemingly without a second thought – the Bushmen represented a kind of pure unspoiled Africa that existed before the present hell that defined most people's daily lives. Needless to say, I had become enamoured with these stories and, over the years, had spoken with anthropologists and old Kalahari hands, gleaning information that, if I could only find the money to mount an expedition, would take me exactly to where I wanted to go.

And now I had the vehicle that would take me there. So it was that Kristin and I found ourselves driving the new Land Rover deep into the baobab forests of Nyae Nyae, where the Kalahari experts had told us the most traditional Bushmen still lived. We made camp under one of those enormous trees and – sure enough – two Bushmen wandered out of the bush to say hello.

I had not been misled. On that and subsequent journeys into Nyae Nyae, I discovered that what people were saying about the Bushman culture – confirmed by anthropologists, archaeologists and palaeontologists, with a few geneticists thrown in – was true. It was the oldest on the planet and also the most civilized. I saw a culture, albeit threatened, albeit changing, in which women and men had equal power. In which children had rights and a voice in decision making. Where there were no chiefs, but people were deferred to by their areas of experience. And where the entire community came together every ten days or so in shamanic trance dances to wash their psychic dirty laundry. And it seemed that they were the ancestors of us all.

And so my long adventure – or perhaps romance would be a more honest term – with the Bushmen had begun and led to what had then developed into my desire to help them get back to their ancestral land. Back in 1998, Dawid Kruiper, their spokesman, knowing it was my mother's stories that had led me to his people, told me that I must bring her out to be part of the rituals they were conducting in readiness for the political battle ahead of them.

She had come out and – neither of us had had any forewarning about this – the Xhomani Bushmen had stripped her naked on the red dunes, had covered her in *saun*, a sweet-smelling pollen used to help bring shamans out of their trance, and celebrated what she had done for them. 'You kept us alive with your stories while we were dying here in the Kalahari! You sent your son to us to help us when we were without a voice! You!'

And then we drove up into Botswana together and there the healer Besa, whom I had met the year before – a man respected, loved and even feared by some (for it was whispered he could turn himself into a lion or a leopard at will) – had danced for the return of the Xhomani's land in South Africa. And – amazingly – precisely a year and a day later, Dawid Kruiper had sat down with President Thabo Mbeki of South Africa, Mandela's heir, and signed the document that brought his people, finally, home.

And now, ten years later, my mother and I were flying out to them once more, bringing my son to them for healing.

So really I had my grandfather's tight-fistedness to thank for this. For without his having forced us into the situation where we had borrowed that Land Rover back in 1995, we would never have met the Bushmen at all. And now we were flying out to seek healing from the First People, whom he had inadvertently sent us to in the first place. You never know what hidden blessings there are in the most seemingly adverse situations.

There is, incidentally, a funny postscript to my grandfather's story. About a year after Kristin and I returned from that fateful first Bushman trip, my grandfather was back in London, spreading joy around the family once more, and over dinner told me, 'You know, Rupert, when you and Kristin were out in Africa last year, you really hurt my feelings.'

'I did?' I asked, incredulous. 'How so?'

'Well, when you wanted to buy a vehicle to get around, you wouldn't even let your old grandad buy you one, or give you one from the farms.'

I did a double take. 'Hold on,' I said. 'If I remember correctly, we spoke about it right here at this very table, and you told me to go down to Johannesburg and buy a car, which I then did. And then when that car died, and I rang you to tell you what had happened, you told me that car hire was expensive and that was the end of it.'

'Ah yes,' he said, holding up a finger. 'But you had to ask!'

As we deplaned at Windhoek airport, I thought of my grandfather, dead now, who had lived here for most of his boyhood. With Rowan sitting on the piled bags as we wheeled our way our through the arrivals lounge, I could smell that Africa smell even through the air conditioning of the modern terminal hall: dry air, wood and dung smoke, earth. A scent that wakes the senses, puts you immediately on the alert for adventure.

'I want to *scoof*!' Rowan turned his blue-green eyes on my mother as we stood getting our bearings, realization dawning that the car-hire people had failed to turn up to meet us. Africa being the family stomping ground, as it were, we had organized this trip ourselves. There was no Tulga and his well-oiled guiding machine to pick us up from the airport and waft us through the logistical side of things. Which meant, of course, that everything immediately went wrong: not only had no one from the car-hire place come to pick us up, as had been arranged, no one was answering the phone at the lodge I had booked us all into.

'*Pigs Might Fly!* I want to scoof!' Rowan went whizzing around the dusty arrivals hall, the early-morning sun streaming in through the plate-glass windows. He was pretending to be Pint Size, the piglet character from the latest book – *Pigs Might Fly!* by Michael Morpurgo – that he had latched on to, and which he had made both Kristin and my mother read aloud to him over and over during the flight down. The piglet in the story, envious of the flying ability of the barnyard birds, tries to build a flying machine, which he then launches off the farmhouse roof and dive-bombs ('scoofs') the rest of the terrified animals, time and again, until they finally prevail upon him to remain a terrestrial pig, and learn to enjoy life as it is. Now while I tried to sort things out from the arrivals hall payphone, Rowan went around 'scoofing' the various waiting people, seated sleepily on the uncomfortable airport benches, as my mother shadowed him, embarrassed, and Kristin broke out the toy bag, hoping to find animals to distract him. Still, hyper as he was, at least it was a good-humoured hyperness. Then came the telltale smell as he whizzed past me for the umpteenth time. He'd soiled his pants. I felt a chill pass through me. All those gains he'd made during and after Mongolia. Would this healing – all the healings – really work? We were doing what Ghoste had told us to do, but who knew? So many people thought we were crazy, deluded.

But the *only* things that had worked in any kind of radical, positive way, were the horse riding and the shamans.

And the fact, the scary fact, of this trip was that, in the last few months, Rowan had started to regress. It had begun with a few accidents. But by May he had started refusing to go the toilet again, four or six times out of ten. And his tantrums were coming back, stronger and stronger, like a rising tide, no longer something one could ignore or explain away by tiredness, 'coming down with something' or any of the other things that put children in grumpy moods. He was slipping. The hard-won – so very hard-won – gains he'd made in Mongolia were steadily evaporating. Yet I had faith. Ghoste had told us we'd have to make three more journeys to complete, to confirm the healing. And here we were, good pilgrims, making the first of those three journeys. But I was terrified. And so was Kristin. With autism, as with anything, there are no guarantees, after all.

We spent half a day getting logistics together, putting through calls to try and ascertain that my Bushman friend Jumanda was in fact bringing Besa over the border from Botswana – no mean feat – that my old South African friend Belinda Kruiper, who had worked on the land claims with me, was coming to join us as she had promised, that another activist friend, Megan Biesele, up in Nyae Nyae had been in touch with the healers there. So many strands of my old life coming together. But Africa is like that – despite the huge distances, the difficult logistics. When things need to be done, people rise to the challenge.

That night, having secured our equipment in the Nissan 4x4 we'd rented, with two roof tents that popped up side by side on top, we decided to camp, and drove west out of Windhoek into the jagged mountains of the Khomas Hochland – just outside the city but for all that, still untouched, Africa in its primordial state. As in Mongolia, where one is either in the city or on the steppe, there is no suburb, no farming zone, before the great 'out there' begins. Emptiness and silence are the two defining characteristics of this huge corner of southwest Africa. Just a million or so people spread out over a country four times the size of Germany. Most places you go, you're the only one there.

We made a fire, put up the roof tents and cooked dinner over the flames as the winter stars came out overhead. 'There's the Southern Cross,' said Michel, the first to spot it.

'The Bushmen call it the "Giraffe's Head",' I remembered, looking over to where Rowan lay – quiet now, the long, long day having caught up with him at last – with his head in Kristin's lap, her fingers playing gently in his hair.

'It does look a lot more like a giraffe's head than a cross, come to think of it.' Michel looked upwards. 'Over to the right, I think that's Taurus – if they have that in the Southern Hemisphere.'

'And there's Orion's Belt!' he added, spotting the familiar constellation, which rises in the north as well as in the south of our planet's skies.

'The Bushmen call them the "Hungry Stars",' I said, a little pompously. 'And that star behind them there to the left, that's supposed to be an arrow, fired at three zebras – each of those stars below Orion's Belt is a zebra, I guess, that escaped because the hunter fired too early. And now every night he has to track the three zebras across the sky till dawn, waiting for another chance to shoot, to slake his hunger.'

'A lesson in patience?'

'Maybe.' I looked over to where Rowan and Kristin sat by the fire. My mother, exhausted, had already turned in. The night was chilling down rapidly. It would go below freezing by morning, for sure. 'Maybe that's what I need.'

'Patience?' Michel snorted. 'Dude, I was with you in Mongolia. You've got your faults, all right. But I wouldn't say impatience is one of them.'

'I've learned to hide it.' I paused. Michel knew the score as well as anyone, but even so, it was so hard to talk about this. 'I still worry. I mean, a month or so ago I'd have said he was doing so well. Brilliantly, even. Now he seems to be going backwards to where he was before Mongolia. I just . . .'

'Worry? You're a parent, man. It's your job to worry.'

'Yes, I do. I mean, even with all the leaps he made last year, he's still way behind – he's going to be seven years old soon. He's still not really conversational. It's not that I don't want him to be autistic, I just . . .'

Just what? Just wanted him to be normal? The unasked question hung there in the cold night air between us. No, it wasn't that. I didn't want him to be normal. But I did want him to be happy, and to learn to survive. Yet what if he couldn't, and one day I wouldn't be around to protect him? What then? The thought scared me.

'Well,' said Michel, 'from what I know of Rowan so far, if any kid can pull that off, he can.'

I shivered, suddenly very tired and very cold. 'I hope you're right, Michel. I really hope you are.'

3. Into Africa

Rowan's first morning in Namibia, land of his fathers, dawned bitterly cold. Ice – even here in these semi-desert mountains of the Khomas Hochland – froze the zippers of the tents so firmly shut that Kristin and I had to rub them from the inside for a few moments before they would give. And rub we did, because Rowan was suddenly eager, desperate almost, to get out.

I had slept in my clothes, so as soon as I got the tent zipper undone, I skipped down the ladder, its metal freezing to the touch, so that I could receive Rowan into my arms as he came barrelling out.

'AFRICA!' he yelled, his face alive with delight, squirming out of my arms. He hit the ground and set off running across the campsite towards the closest hill, its thorny trees and scrub bare with winter. I followed: automatically, as if programmed, I stuck to his shadow.

'Shadowing' becomes an instinct, a skill that every autism parent learns. You have to: autistic children, especially the young ones, when they set off running, will *run*. And they move so fast; if you're not within grabbing distance, anything – literally anything – can happen. So you learn to run too, shadowing or marking them just as one football player marks or shadows another. After a while shadowing becomes instinctive – something you do without thinking. So now, in that freezing Namibian campsite, off I went, after him. Rowan on his first day in Africa, too excited to think – who knew what he might go blundering into? Excitement makes any kid less aware of danger; with autism everything is amplified. You can't let them out of your sight, out of your reach, even. At the same time, you don't want to prevent them exploring, because that is the only way they can learn.

Off Rowan went, cruising at a fast clip, hugging the side of the steep hill through thick bush, the trail winding off towards where I could glimpse the waters of a small lake glinting in the cold air. Too cold, also, for snakes on the trail this time of year. Too high here in the mountains for crocodiles, but water is its own hazard. So along the path we trotted, towards where the dry woodland gave out at the small lake's margin. And then we saw them. Dark shapes, human-like, huddled, squatting and scooping water into their mouths. One of them spotted us, turned a grizzled head, bared dog-like fangs and let out a shout like a man's.

'Baboons!' Rowan shrieked with delight, while the baboon troop, alerted to humans by their leader's shout, bounded back up the wooded mountainside, the females scooping up wide-eyed babies on to their backs as they went. Rowan turned a serious face on mine. 'Chacma baboons from southern Africa, not hamadryas baboons, which live in the Horn of Africa, or Ethiopia,' he announced, as if reciting directly from a wildlife encyclopedia, which he probably was – photographic or near-photographic memory being a gift of autism that still leaves me speechless. 'They belong to the genus *Papio*, and the West African version is called a mandrill and has a blue nose and a reddish-pink bottom.'

The shouts, so human-sounding, and crashing branches faded into the morning stillness. 'You're right, Scub!' I said, somewhat stunned – I'd had no coffee yet, after all. 'You're dead right!'

And he was – in a burst of lucidity that made him seem almost normal; one of those rare, teasing liftings of the veil, before it dropped once more. I'd followed, given up control, shadowed him to see where he would lead me and – as so often happened – he had rewarded me. Why did I not do this more often?

'More Africa!' he was suddenly back in his little-boy voice once more, and off he tripped, down along the shore of the lake, startling a group of shrilly protesting stone plovers, back towards the campsite. 'Tracks!' he said, looking down at the criss-crossing of waterfowl web-prints. I recognized the print of a Cape clawless otter, the humanoid spoor of baboons and the neat double-leaf imprint of a . . . 'Small antelope!' Rowan was there before me. 'What kind, Daddy?'

As always when out in the natural world, his brain was just more alive. I wasn't good enough as a tracker to know all the various species of small antelope from each other. 'I'm not sure,' I admitted. 'But up here I reckon it would be either klipspringer, steenbok or maybe a grey duiker.'

'*Klipspringer, steenbok or maybe a greeeeeeeeey duiker . . .*' he repeated it over and over, somehow getting the inflection of my voice just right, as he trotted back to the tents, branding it into his consciousness. '*Klipspringer, steenbok or maybe a greeeeeeey duiker . . .*'

Rowan rushed up to Kristin and rugby-tackle hugged her round the waist. '*Klipspringer, steenbok or maybe a greeeeeey duiker! Pigs Might Fly!* I want to *scoooof*! WOW, LOOK! WARTHOGS!' and off he went again, top speed, this time towards a small group of warthogs, the ubiquitous wild pig of the African bushlands, which – seeing him coming – all turned from their grazing of the short-cropped grass of the campsite to go scurrying away with their tails held up straight in the air like car aerials. Kristin was busy with coffee. Rowan had already gone five or so paces when I opened my eyes wide at my mother and inclined my head.

'Rowan! Come back here, darling!' she shouted.

'No, you have to physically go after him! Go!'

She shot me a look, then took off. 'Now Rowan, darling . . .' Michel, taking a cue from me, took off after her as backup.

I watched as Rowan went tearing around the perimeter of the campsite, outstripping my mother by yards, until Michel swept him up on to his shoulders and galloped him back to the fire – the warthogs being long gone by now – to where Kristin had his bacon ready.

'I want to scoof!'

'What a good idea,' said my mother, panting after her recent exertions as she went to his toy bag and pulled out a book. 'Let's read.'

Rowan plumped down in her lap, his first morning burst of energy spent. So strange, this mix of language and memory, of sharp intellect and clouded perception, that made up his autism.

The imagination was alive and well, the intelligence keen, yet the conversation was still not there. And he was slipping, slipping. I pushed the thought away.

I watched his grandmother read to him. It would all be okay; it had to be – had to. Kristin handed me a coffee.

'Everything all right?' she asked.

I shrugged, not quite knowing what to say. 'I know, darling.' She sipped at her own coffee. 'I know.'

Having packed up our camp, we headed back down the mountainside to Windhoek. We wove our way slowly through the city, past the colourful craft markets, where tourists were gathering in the rapidly warming sunshine to buy souvenirs – hardwood and stone carvings, beaded jewellery, decorative spears – and then northwards, past the big, four-chimneyed power plant, incongruously industrial against the backdrop of Bushveld and dry rocky hills. More baboons scampered across the good tar road we were now on. Built by the South African army back in the bad old days before Namibian independence in 1990, it was designed to take their tanks north to the war – South Africa's Vietnam – in Angola.

The road north stretched long and blue-black. The day had warmed to T-shirt weather by now, causing the horizon to shimmer. Next to me, Kristin slept. Behind me, my mother and Michel slept too. Rowan sat unusually quiet, unusually still, but alert, watching the bush pass by, vast and silent, outside the car window.

From the moment we passed the park gate of Etosha National Park, hours north of the capital, we began to see wild animals. Animals on a scale you almost never see outside of Africa. In the Americas, only Yellowstone in Wyoming and the Pantanal marshes of Brazil have herds on this sort of scale. In Asia, only certain parts of Mongolia and northern India have herds of a comparable size; yet Africa still has a staggering amount of game. As we drove, black-and-white zebra began to appear, first in little clutches of three or five, then more and more until one realized that the road was merely a black ribbon through a vast herd, tens of thousands strong, spread out into family groups, clans, tribes, extended federations of tribes. A universe of stripes. Rowan, wide awake suddenly, pressed his nose to the window.

Back in the States, we virtually lived at the zoo, and Rowan had been saying for some time, even despite his lack of real conversation, that when he grew up he wanted to be a zookeeper. We read him zookeeper stories. Sometimes when we addressed him by name, he said (at least on the days he *did* respond to his name): 'I'm not Rowan! I'm a zookeeper!' But no zoo had anything on this! Too stunned to speak, he merely watched, awestruck, as we drove slowly through that world of hoof and mane and muscle, all in black and white – dazzlingly exotic to Northern Hemisphere eyes – under a sky of azure blue.

We camped at Okaukuejo, a safari site the size of a large village where I had stayed years before. On that occasion, three lions had crawled over the high wire fence separating the viewing platforms from the floodlit waterhole just outside the camping area and had devoured two Germans who had been sitting up all night game watching. Which just shows how illusory any health and safety measures really are, especially in Africa, even in the most tried and trusted locations. The lions were old and starving, it turned out: it must have required a Herculean effort for them to climb that fifteen-foot fence, its upper part bent forward to make climbing near impossible. But made it, they had, and secured a last meal of man-flesh before the rangers shot them. Rangers led, coincidentally, by another distant cousin of mine, who was the main vet at the national park at the time.

Family: I sneaked a look behind me in the rear-view mirror. Back on the road again the next day, my mother and Rowan both had their eyes peeled, looking for more animals, leaning closely together, grandmother and grandson: a beautiful sight.

'When I was a little girl,' she told him, 'we lived for a time in a town called Pietersburg, up in the Transvaal, and in the dry season it looked just like this. Yellow grasses. Dry, dry air that made your lips crack. Here, would you like an orange, darling?' She passed him a segment.

'No, thank you.'

'You really should eat fruit, darling. Kristin, dear, does he eat much fruit?'

'Not as much as he should. We have trouble just getting calories into him, he's such a picky eater.'

My mother tutted. 'Try a carrot,' I suggested. 'They should be in the box at your feet. He'll usually eat carrots.'

'*No no no no no no more talking!*'

I reached behind me, fished for a carrot from the food box – we were travelling so slowly on the dirt road that it was safe enough – pulled one out and presented it to Rowan, saying in a commanding voice: 'WUB!'

He giggled. It was one of our scripted jokes. The way I got him to eat vitamins and fibre – relying on humour where logic failed. He took the carrot, saying, 'A wub is . . .'

'. . . a word that has two meanings,' I replied, knowing my part.

'One meaning is the carrot itself . . .'

'The other being the imperative command that tells the receiver of said carrot that he must chomp it forthwith!'

'WUB!'

'WUB!'

He giggled again, and took a bite. Parental attempt, through use of humour, to get healthy food into offspring: one. These small triumphs, how absurdly pleased they make us. Even if it's just a carrot during a long hot drive with tempers beginning to fray.

We rounded a bend and stopped the car, all of us taking a collective breath; we had arrived at a waterhole. A riot of animals were crowded around the muddy pool. Gemsbok with long, straight black horns and faces striped like silent-movie bandits. A spiral-horned kudu bull and his harem, elegant and aristocratic, their grey-brown hides marked by delicate, thin white stripes. Springbok by the score, their tan-coloured backs and black side-stripes rendering them almost invisible in the heat shimmer of midday, lyre-shaped horns atop narrow heads with liquid eyes, tails flicking at the flies. A file of zebra marching in from the bare thorn bush, a scarred old stallion leading the mares, one of whom limped, her quarters scored by deep red claw wounds from where a lion had tried and failed – wounded but still living, protected by her herd. A lone wildebeest bull, outcast, standing apart from the bustle at the water's edge, patient, still, waiting out his days. In the middle distance an elephant family cruising slowly in, like great, grey ships, dust clouds puffing skywards from their soft-footed progress, for their evening drink. I switched off the ignition, cut the diesel-chug of the engine, rolled the windows down a little so that the snorts and stamps, bleats and whinnies – the sounds of primordial Africa, as it was, as it still is and hopefully always will be – drifted in at the window. Rowan climbed forwards from the back seat, upsetting my mother's neatly balanced water bottle and landing squarely in Kristin's lap.

'It's the circle of life!'

We laughed, watching the animals as they milled and drank, scratched and jostled under the blue, dry-season sky, completely ignoring us. July in Namibia – midwinter and no rain for another six months. Water is life.

'Oh, I just can't *wait* to be king,' I began.

'NO NO NO NO NO NO NO NO SINGING, DADDY!'

Not conversation as such. But still, a credible response to a prompt. Would I one day actually converse with my son? Really converse? Rowan clambered across me to get a better view of the elephants now shuffling into closer view. Perhaps I should reverse the vehicle, make a discreet withdrawal in case their mood was cantankerous today. As I turned the key, the smell hit me. I caught Kristin's eye. Caught her despair. Could the leaps forward of last year be regained or were they lost for ever? Was he slipping? Would the healing we had come here for actually work? Would we ever be free of this ever-present sense of suspense, of wondering when healing and normality, a sense that *everything is all right now*, would arrive in our lives. Would it ever happen?

4. The Dawn of Logic

We camped at Halali, another huge tourist camp, set below that rare thing in the Kalahari – a tall hill. Etosha is vast, the size of maybe Wales, or a chunk of New England. Perhaps wisely, tourists are corralled into just three camps, leaving the hinterlands free for wildlife to roam. There are immense pans of baked white clay that, in those rare years when rain falls, fill with water, shimmering into infinitude like great inland seas. The past year's rainy season had been unusually good. The pans shone bright, streaked here and there with smudges of pink: flamingos that had migrated in from the Skeleton Coast to feed on brine shrimp released from the clay, the little crustaceans having lain dormant for years – water creatures buried in the bone-dry desert, waiting for the reviving rain.

Were we, too, waiting for rain? If so – as the flamingos and the brine shrimp knew all too well – it could be a long time coming.

We set up camp. Unlike the nature reserve outside Windhoek, which we had had to ourselves, the Etosha camps have hundreds of people camping in them. Stupidly, I hadn't considered this when planning the trip: no sooner had we claimed our spot than Rowan was off at a run. Before we could grab him, he was already inside one of the neighbouring tents. Kristin rushed in after him, to find him happily scoffing potato chips in front of an astonished Dutch family – at least, we soon found out they were Dutch as apologies were made, embarrassed introductions done, and the family's two boys, more or less Rowan's age, rose to the occasion and graciously let him examine their travelling toy box.

Thank God they were nice people. This kind of thing had happened before with Rowan, not always with such a good outcome. We had become used to being the parents with the kid that runs up to someone else's birthday party in the indoor play area or at the park and tries to eat the cake right in front of the outraged birthday child, then has a massive tantrum as he is manhandled away. That kind of thing had become much rarer lately, but, somewhat short-sightedly, I hadn't take account of the fact that in Etosha we'd be camping in such thickly populated spots, with no way of controlling whose space Rowan, and therefore we, invaded.

As the two very sweet Dutch boys sat down with Rowan on the floor of their family-sized tent and let him play with their toy cars, trying to engage him but with limited success, I chatted with their mother. Yes, she said, she had a few friends who had kids on the autism spectrum – more and more in fact. Why was that?

I took a deep breath. 'It's true: when I was a boy, autism was a rare thing. Two children in ten thousand is the official figure they gave for it back then. Now it's one child in eighty-eight over the age of eight, and one boy in fifty-six. Over the age of eight! So that doesn't even account for all the kids being born now who are probably affected. They say that the rate of autism is going up at a thousand per cent and rising.'

'But why?' she persisted.

'Honestly,' I told the lady, still thanking my lucky stars that she had been so cool about my son busting in on her and her family, 'we don't really know why. The science is lagging behind while the numbers are galloping along at a hundred miles an hour, and we on the front line aren't scientists – we kind of just have to deal with it.'

'Better diagnosis maybe?'

'Maybe,' I looked at Kristin, she – a professor of psychology, after all – was the scientist in the family.

'A thousand per cent rise is too much to put down to better diagnosis,' she shrugged. 'And if that were the case, you'd see a corresponding drop in numbers of related diagnoses to do with the brain and nervous system – but those are all going up at the same rate too. The science is pointing towards the environment.'

'Environment?'

It was a hard one for people to understand; how one environmental factor might affect one kid, and a different one might affect another, while a third kid might not show any symptoms at all, but Kristin had a go. 'As far as I can make out, it's basically a case of the world getting generally more toxic, and therefore people who didn't show up as reacting to these toxins half a century ago are now showing up because the amount of toxins in the environment in general has increased so much. There seem to be some toxins that affect the brain specifically. These include industrial heavy metals like aluminium, mercury, lead, cadmium, tungsten, found in things like cell phones, paint, cars . . . Then there are plastics that break down in the environment and act like hormones on the body, pharmaceuticals that leach into the water supply through human excretion . . .'

'What about vaccinations? What do you think about that?' said the mother. 'I heard that the guy who said that vaccinations were to blame was totally discredited.'

'You mean Andrew Wakefield and the measles, mumps and rubella vaccine?' said Kristin. 'They did go after him, yes – hard. He even got struck off the doctors' register in the UK. But what's strange is that he never actually said that the MMR vaccination causes autism – he just noted that a lot of the kids that he was working on who had autism had had the MMR vaccination and that their parents had reported a massive regression after the vaccine, following a fever and terrible gut problems. Yet they went after him with such a vengeance.'

'So what do you think?' the mother looked at me. '*Do* you think vaccinations cause autism?'

'Honestly, I don't know,' I said.

'So would *you* vaccinate?' The mother offered me a glass of water, which I gulped down gratefully. She added: 'I spaced mine out when the boys were little because I was worried.'

'That sounds pretty sane.' I handed her back the cup. 'I'd probably do the same thing if I had another kid. Space out the vaccinations, see what their reactions are.'

'Ru,' said Kristin, tapping me on the shoulder, almost whispering. 'Look!'

Rowan was reading a book with the two Dutch boys, spelling out the words. It was some official literature, or guidebook, on the national park. He spoke slowly and sonorously: '*Etosha National Park was founded in 1907 . . . the name of the camp Halali comes from a French and German term for the end of a hunt, when the hounds make a noise that sounds like "Halali". Some say the name was given by German hunters because it was known as a good place for hunting, others because of the noise of the spotted hyenas who frequent the hill and the waterhole, whose laugh at night sounds a little like "Halali".*'

'Wow,' said the elder Dutch boy, 'you really read good!'

'Hey!' said his younger brother, not the least interested in reading. 'Let's play hide and seek!'

I thought of saying something: sure, Rowan did play with other kids now in a certain kind of way – basic chase-me games, bouncing on the trampoline together, wrestling – but a complex activity like hide and seek was still beyond him. He'd certainly never played any sort of rule-based game like that before. But then, you never knew. I caught Kristin's eye as Rowan got up and followed the two boys out of the tent.

'He may not be able to follow the game exactly,' Kristin explained.

'Don't worry,' said the mother. 'They have a couple of kids at their school who are on the autism spectrum. They'll understand.'

'Perhaps I should go with him to help.'

Outside we could hear the younger Dutch boy counting: 'One, two, three, four, five, six, seven, eight . . .'

'Come on,' said the older boy to Rowan, holding out his hand. 'Let's hide.'

Kristin made to follow – I put up a hand. 'Let them do it.'

We watched as they ran behind the vehicles, crawled up the ladder into one of our roof tents and disappeared from view.

' . . . nineteen, twenty! Here I come, ready or not!'

And off he went, scooting around the immediate area – behind the family tent, peering under the 4x4s. From the roof tent where he was hidden, I heard a Rowan giggle. The younger boy's head shot up, trying to locate the sound.

Another giggle. 'Are you hiding in the tree?' The boy went under the large acacia that shaded the two adjacent camping spots. Not there. He looked around, just as Rowan's grinning face shot out of the roof tent's unzipped front. 'Here I am!'

'Found you!'

Kristin raised an eyebrow. 'Well, that was his first real rule-based game . . . even if he broke the rules. That's kind of a developmental milestone in child psychology, you know that?'

I didn't: I should have, given how much autism dominated my life – but truth be told, I tended to leave the science to her. I made a note to be more conscientious from now on – this stuff was important to understand.

'Let's play again!' Rowan shouted, delighted.

And so passed a long, hot but rather wonderful hour. The two Dutch boys were total sports, letting Rowan put them through round after round of his own version of hide and seek. Despite their attempts to get him to wait until he was actually *found*, Rowan had decided that game consisted of hiding, giggling uncontrollably for a minute or so with his hiding partner, then bursting from cover shouting: 'Here I am!'

Their patience worn thin at last, the boys announced they were off to the campsite's pool for a swim. 'Good idea,' I said. 'Come on, Rowan, let's go too.'

'Swim!'

So we followed them, the Dutch boys immediately joining a group of kids to dive-bomb and race with in the deep end, while Rowan and I splashed in the shallows. He loved water, would play in it all day, but I'd had no luck actually teaching him to swim. In fact even this love of playing in the water was something recent: for the two years before that, he'd refused to go near water at all, which was weird because in his really young years he'd been a total water baby. Then suddenly, right before setting out for Africa, he had been okay with it again. What was going on in his head? Why these strange reversals and gains? Would we ever know? Would he ever swim? The world was so dangerous for those who couldn't. I was worried that one day he might fall into water somewhere – it weighed on me constantly.

But hide and seek with the boys was something. And we were on a healing journey after all.

Suddenly Rowan went up on his toes in the water. The Code Brown look. Christ! He was going to poo right there.

'Okay!' I tried to hide the panic in my voice, keep it light. 'Code Brown! We have to get out. Now! Let's go!'

I swept him up in my arms, his body rigid. '*No no no no no no no!*' he wailed, making people's heads turn. God, they'd think I was abusing my kid, so I headed quick time – feet slapping on the poolside tiles, hoping not to slip, hoping that the cubicles wouldn't be occupied – for the men's changing room. Thank goodness a stall was free. In we went. I sat him on the pot. He hadn't pooped on the toilet for over a month now. '*No no no no no no no!*' He squirmed, trying to get off the toilet, eyes wide with alarm.

What to do? I searched for inspiration. When in doubt – use humour. I put on an evil Godzilla voice: 'GREAT. BIG. POOPY!!!!!'

'*No no no no no no no no no no no no no!*'

Silence.

'GREAT! BIG! POOPY!' I roared.

God, the people outside would think I was nuts. I decided to push my luck. So I roared it once more at the top of my lungs. More silence. Then a giggle. 'Do it again!'

I took a deep breath, screamed it again, loud as I could.

A torrent of laughter.

And then – oh, my God – he went in the toilet.

'Again, Dad!'

Damn right, I'd say it again. Anything, if it got him using the toilet once more. Who cared if the folks outside thought we were nuts?

I came out of there beaming, despite the odd looks. When I got back to the campsite, Kristin was taking a break, reading, and my mother was painting the great hill above us. 'Success!' I whispered, hoping it wasn't just a one-off.

'You don't mean . . .'

'I do.'

'Oh, thank God!'

'Thank God what?' my mother looked up from her sketchbook.

'*Rowan went in the toilet!*' I whispered – not wanting to embarrass him.

'Well, so he should,' said my mother. 'Has anyone seen my book? I'm sure I left it on the back seat of the truck . . .'

Any other day I would have reacted, but nothing could spoil my mood.

'Going to see the Bushmen! Going to see the *shamans*!' said Rowan suddenly, apropos of nothing.

'Yes, we are!' said Kristin. 'Yes, we are!'

The camp at Halali had one more surprise for us – a good one. As sunset approached, touching the hill with its bare thorn trees and its great, jutting boulders first pink, then orange, then red, we took the dirt track towards the waterhole, with its viewing platform overlooking the unthinkably vast expanse of Etosha. The first pale stars began to show against the dark blue of the sky.

We weren't the only ones on the path to the waterhole. In ones and twos, little family groups, people were strolling up from the campsite, enjoying the languor, the luxury, of the cool evening air. Kristin and I walked with our hearts in our mouths.

For I had made another miscalculation when planning this journey. Just as it hadn't occurred to me that we would be camping cheek by jowl with so many other tourists in such a vast area of national parkland, I also had not allowed for the fact that the game-viewing platforms at these camps had stringent rules. You weren't allowed to talk loudly, shout, scream or run about grabbing people's snacks and frightening off any game that visited the floodlit waterhole throughout the night. People who did cause a disturbance were sometimes escorted out by the camp's staff.

Would Rowan be able to handle this? Would his energy bubble over and end with us being shushed and shamed and having to leave? He was so excited: would he be denied – through my oversight – his chance to live out his dream of finally seeing African animals in the wild? I wracked my brains for a way to prepare him.

There was another complication too. This was the wild, not a zoo, and so there was no guarantee that one would see anything. Maybe animals would show up at the waterhole to drink, maybe not. You might see the entire range of Namibian fauna in the space of an hour or two, or you could sit all night and spot no more than a warthog and a few guinea fowl. It was pure luck. What if Rowan was disappointed? What if he tantrummed? Was I a complete idiot for even thinking that this might be a good idea?

Then I'd remembered a story we had read aloud earlier that year while riding together on Betsy. A Dr Seuss story about sounds and letters that had a particular phrase that had pleased Rowan: *Like the soft, soft whisper of a butterfly*. It came to mind now as I ransacked my brain for a strategy to impress upon him in some meaningful way that we would have to sit still, possibly for hours, and whisper while at the game-viewing platform, where we might or might not see anything at all.

'We'll have to *whisper whisper*,' I kept saying – a kind of mantra – as we walked up the path. '*Whisper whisper*, like butterflies.'

Rowan giggled. Then shouted, '*Pigs Might Fly!* I want to scoof!' A few heads turned. I winced.

'*Whisper whisper*,' I repeated, somewhat lamely. 'And it might take the animals a long time to come. We'll have to sit very still and very quiet and *whisper whisper* like the soft, soft whisper of a butterfly.'

'What animals will we see?'

'Well, I don't know exactly. It all depends what animals feel like coming. They're wild, not like zoo animals. You know that. They make their own decisions about where to go and what to do. So it'll be a surprise.'

His face lit up. 'A surprise!' Again, he boomed it out at a zillion decibels. More heads turned. This was going to be a disaster. How would we deal with it? The shame of setting him up for failure, his grief at not being able to see his long-cherished animals, and the public disapproval.

'We're getting closer, Scub, so we'll have to *whisper whisper* now. If we shout people will get cross with us and tell us to leave, and we don't want that. But if we *whisper whisper* and wait for the animals to come and sit as still as we can . . .'

But he had already taken off ahead of me. And here was the entrance to the game-viewing platform. A few people were already there, looking down on the waterhole below, where the floodlight had now come on, illuminating the large brackish pool. Rowan was darting about already like some manic woodland elf, running up and down the bleachers and giggling as we hurried through the gate to catch him up.

'Now, Rowan, darling . . .' I heard my mother begin.

Rowan turned a mischievous face on her and said, in the first whisper I had ever heard him enunciate: 'Shhh, Granny, we have to *whisper whisper* . . .'

Then he came and sat down next to me, laying his head on my lap and his feet on Kristin's. 'Dad,' he whispered, 'we have to sit quiet and wait and see what animals come! It's a surprise!'

I couldn't believe it. I almost cried.

What followed was pure and utter magic. One of the rarest large land mammals in the world is the black rhinoceros. Aggressive, short-sighted and therefore very easy to kill, they are an endangered species, with maybe two thousand of the beasts left in the wild. That night, between six o'clock and maybe ten or eleven, we saw nine of these supremely rare creatures emerge from the darkness at the edge of the waterhole. A mother with her baby. Males interested in the mother. Males challenging each other, standing stock still and screaming at one another, emitting weird, eerie-sounding yowls of apparent fury before coming together, clashing their long, sharp, sometimes double horns, then circling away once more. Something which, in all my years in Africa, I had never seen before – a real privilege to watch.

And throughout, Rowan lay across our laps, always moving some part of his body, but the quietest, stillest and most focused I'd ever known him – off a horse, at any rate. He remained riveted, as the benches filled and his tiredness grew, yet even as he yawned he kept his eyes on the rhinos. He knew how rare they were. Autism is no bar to knowledge; he had read up on the black rhinoceros. And every time one or other of them would amble off into the darkness once more, occasionally leaving the waterhole deserted, he'd turn to me and whisper, 'Dad, what's next?' and then, 'It's a surprise!'

It took the best part of a morning to drive the forty miles from Halali to the third and last of Etosha's camps at Namutoni. We went slowly, taking in the sheer scale of the place, the distant pans still filled with the shimmer of blue from the previous season's rains. It was strange to think that what looked like a mirage, away in the distance, was in fact no mirage at all. Often the blue was streaked with pink where flamingos waded. But closer, much closer, there was so much to see. A lioness, stalking in the grasses, eyes intent on a group of gemsbok grazing on an unusually green patch of knee-high pasture. We waited, Rowan keeping his voice down to an absolute minimum even inside the vehicle, to see if she would make a rush. For some reason, after almost half an hour and watching so intently, she abruptly got up and walked away. Was there a pride waiting for her off in a thicket somewhere? Was she merely scouting, going back to report?

'Maybe she isn't hungry yet,' said Rowan, echoing our thoughts. I looked at him. When he talked like this, it was so normal-sounding. And yet the easy back and forth, the exchange of thoughts and emotions, even at a basic level, still wasn't there. It was as if it was *almost* there, unseen, latent, tantalizing, on the tip of his tongue, or his consciousness, but always – at the last – unexpressed. Was it simply that he didn't want to converse? Couldn't? Such an enigma: always, every day, an enigma.

Later, as we rounded a bend, we found our way blocked by a

large bull elephant. I stopped the vehicle, waited to see what his intentions were. Nine times out of ten when you meet elephants on the road you can drive by them without incident, as long as you do it slowly and cautiously. One time in ten, however, the elephant takes exception. He can open a car like a tin can with his tusks, or roll it over and stomp it to the ground. Mostly it doesn't go this far – usually just a mock charge, in which the elephant flaps his ears at you, lifts his head so that he seems to grow to twice his actual size. You freeze in that moment – especially if you happen to be on foot. But usually it's just a warning, telling you to beat a measured retreat. If the head goes down, however, you're really in trouble.

I've been charged like that only once – by a matriarch who came hundreds of yards out of her way to try and pluck me and a friend of mine from the open-top vehicle in which we were travelling through the highlands of northern Zimbabwe. It's something you never forget, having an enraged elephant speeding along behind, trunk poised to coil round you, lift you up and then crush you out of sheer ire. Luckily, after a few short minutes' sprint, the old cow elephant was out of breath and gave up. We kept going, putting as much distance as we could between us and her. Then, perhaps two miles further on, we came upon the reason why she had charged us. An adolescent elephant, its leg caught in a poacher's snare designed to catch a buffalo: a loop made from steel hawser. He must have walked into it weeks before. The steel cable had cut so deep into his flesh that the knee hung on by a few threads of gristle around the bone. The wound squirmed with maggots. He stood, head down, in absolute despair, unthinkable agony. Abandoned by his herd – the worst fate for this most sociable of animals, the most human-like in its intelligence. They must have only just made the heart-breaking decision to abandon him: no wonder the old matriarch who had had to make that decision was mad. Elephants are like us – they live seventy years or more, have incredibly complex social structures, a language like that of dolphins that carries over vast distances at frequencies too low for the human ear to register.

They mourn their dead and bury them with branches. They destroy their environment, vandalize it, when too cooped up or stressed. Young males without the benefit of older males and females to keep them in line run amok and have even been known to rape and kill rhinos for the sheer dysfunctional sport of it — which is why when elephants are culled they now take out the whole family group, tragic though that is, rather than leave young-sters to grow up without proper socialization. I wasn't surprised the matriarch had tried to kill us. She was right — in the world of wild elephants, humans are bastards.

We had looked at the poor, suffering adolescent awhile, and radioed for the ranger — another friend of ours. He had arrived, taken one look, turned away to hide the tears of anger at what had been done, and gone to fetch his high-calibre elephant gun from his vehicle.

If you have never seen an elephant shot, I hope you never do. There is a sense of tragedy to it that defies description. I accept that in game reserves population control has to be carried out. But I can't imagine wanting to do it. It's a harsh fact that in southern Africa most game conservation is actually funded with money from people paying to hunt legally. A licence for an elephant that is going to be culled anyway can exceed 100,000 dollars. And then on top there are the trophy fees, the fees paid to the professional hunters and guides and trackers, the meat to the local villagers and so on. I accept that it's a necessary evil. But I can't imagine *wanting* to do it. I can't imagine waking up one morning and thinking: *I know what I want to do this year! I want to go kill an elephant!* I can't imagine it at all.

The magnificent grey beast had crumpled, fallen. Its great heart stopped, its precious life extinguished. Gone.

So now, in the car with my son and family, I approached the great lone bull with extreme caution. So much so that, as I inched closer, and he kept approaching in his unhurried, swinging gait, I stopped, and put the vehicle into reverse.

'What are you doing? Why are you doing that?' Rowan was

immediately distressed. Any reversal or unexpected change of direction while driving, any U-turn, wrong turn, always upset him. It was part of his autism, the distress at the unexpected. But there was no choice.

'The elephant's ahead, Scub. If I drive by him and he's in a grumpy mood, he might squash the car, and us in it! I have to back up to show him I'm no threat.'

'No back-up! More straight! Going to see the Bushmen!' His voice rose to the beginnings of a wail. This was regressive language, even for him. Something in his internal logic system was thrown. The distress was genuine. I looked at the others for help.

'But he has to, Scub!' explained Kristin. 'Otherwise the elephant might get mad.'

'Mr Elephant might get very mad if we're in his space!' agreed Michel.

'Daddy's just doing what he needs to do to keep us safe!' my mother added.

The wail stopped. I sneaked a look behind. Rowan appeared thoughtful. I'd never known anything cut a tantrum off before, except cantering together on Betsy.

'Daddy's keeping us safe!' he repeated.

'Yes, that's right!' Kristin was as surprised as I was.

'Daddy's keeping us safe!' It was as if the thought was something new and wonderful.

'Yes,' said my mother. 'Daddy's backing away from the big bull just in case he makes a charge.'

'Like a charging Pumba!' Rowan's thoughts were never far from *The Lion King*.

'Yes, but much, much, much more dangerous.'

'And not a cartoon . . .' he said, slow and sonorous. 'But real. Not a cartoon, but real.'

'Yes, exactly.'

We were all so amazed, this sudden dawning of logic – the first time we had seen it so clearly and explicitly – that we were surprised to look ahead and find the road suddenly empty.

'Oh,' I said, 'I guess we can go forward after all.'

So forward we went, very slowly, in case the big bull elephant was still close by and might step out suddenly from the thorn and mopane trees. And sure enough, as we passed a small opening in the branches, there he was, just a few feet away. Enormous, his skin yellow-grey with dust. He regarded us with a neutrally assessing eye, as a businessman on his way to a meeting might vaguely eye a pigeon or a piece of litter or some other object of only marginal interest.

'Don't get too clo-ose!' Rowan said in a sing-song voice. 'We don't want to be squoosh-squooshed!'

'That's right, this is a squoosh-squoosh-free zone.'

'Bye bye, Mr Elephant, thanks for not squooshing!' Rowan waved as we sped up marginally, continuing down the dirt road toward Namutoni.

Using the toilet again, modifying his behaviour at the waterhole, and now the dawning of logic. Amazing! And we hadn't even seen the shamans yet. What would follow next? I remembered Rowan's whispered words in the rhino-haunted darkness the night before, his eyes wide: '*It's a surprise . . .*'

Namutoni Camp occupies an old German fort left over from the early days of colonization, when my grandfather was a boy. Complete with battlements, guardhouse and a central courtyard with a little restaurant and a resident tame mongoose. The little creature came to beg charmingly for food, putting its paws together, sitting up, cocking its head to one side and flashing its long-lashed, liquid brown eyes. Rowan was enchanted, running around as the mongoose dived and darted around the trees growing up through the courtyard flagstones. It was playing chase: always diving just out of reach, then coming back to tease again, just as a puppy might.

The sense of enchantment continued throughout the afternoon. Rowan read in the park literature that Namutoni had a museum on the history of the place. We went to it and found it closed for repairs. He grumbled, but without the tantrum he

usually threw when plans were thwarted, and then allowed me
to take him into the camp swimming pool. He even allowed me
to carry him into water that was out of his depth, his fear of
deeper water having seemingly evaporated in the dry desert air.
While we set up the roof tents, Rowan, shadowed by Kristin,
wandered calmly through the campsite – and other people's
camping spots – but without invading their tents, stealing their
snacks or otherwise causing mayhem. Was it the effect of just
being out in nature for so long again? I remembered the year
before in Mongolia, where gradually, out on the wide, wide
steppe, his hyperactivity had calmed to the point of almost non-
existence.

Here, almost a week into camping in Africa, he had achieved a
deeper calm. Camping as a family seemed to be the key. Why
didn't we do this more often? Then again, at home we were surrounded by nature: so was it the radical change of environment?
Who could say.

But the real surprise came later, at Namutoni's waterhole. The
previous evening had been amazing enough, but there had been a
constant procession of ultra-rare black rhino and other animals to
excite the soul and delight the eye.

Tonight there was nothing. Once, after we had waited in the
game-viewing shelter for perhaps an hour and a half, a group of
elephants had filed past in the near distance, ghost ships drifting
by, glimpsed for perhaps thirty seconds. Then nothing for another
hour, until, eyelids drooping from the long, warm day, we headed
back down the track towards the roof tents and bed. Rowan had
sat, or rather sprawled, across our laps, and whispered, and waited,
and made no sudden movements, no stims. Who was this patient,
normal-seeming child?

'I've never seen him so calm like this.' Michel – who had been
across Mongolia with us after all and knew Rowan pretty well –
echoed our thoughts.

But the next day, it all began to fall apart once more.

It happened slowly, gradually. First, as we drove out of Etosha, out of the magical realm, Rowan began to whimper: 'More animals!'

'Don't worry, Scub,' Kristin reassured him. 'There'll be more animals when we're with the Bushmen. Lots of them. I've been there before with Daddy and we saw all kind of things: elephant, hartebeest, gemsbok, kudu . . .'

Rowan's whimper became a wail. 'MORE ANIMALS!'

'Now, darling,' my mother intervened, 'let's read. Would you like *Pigs Might Fly!* or *Sharing a Shell*?'

'MORE ANIMALS!!!!' A deep breath, then: 'WAAAAAAAA AAAAAAAAAAAAAAAAAAAAAAAAH!'

Suddenly he was three again. What was going on? Things had been so good, so calm! The noise filled the small space inside the vehicle to bursting. I could tell he was just getting going. We hadn't witnessed one of these since Mongolia. What was up with him? I fought down the urge to give in to anger, to turn around and scream at him to be quiet. Like fighting down demons – the noise, the fear. No matter how many years you go through as an autism parent, you never quite lose the shameful, guilty desire to give in, to scream, even to hit your impossible, endlessly draining child. So you just set your eyes on the road in front of you and keep driving, as I did now.

It lasted a good hour. Long enough to take us almost to the towns of Grootfontein and the strange, mining settlement of Tsumeb, set among dry rocky hills. As Rowan screamed and screamed, his shrieks rising steadily in volume, obliterating all thought, all feeling other than pain, I breathed deeply and let my mind go numb.

When the screams finally stopped, a hundred or so miles further on, I realized I was grinning with a rictus-like intensity. I had been fantasizing about throwing Rowan, my beloved son, out the car window, flushing him down the toilet, hitting him until he stopped this torture.

'Penny for your thoughts?' asked Kristin softly. We were far east of Tsumeb now, heading for the final leg of the long journey into Bushmanland – where the tar highway ended and dirt road began again – the last few hundred miles to Nyae Nyae.

I shook my head. 'I should be better at this by now.'

'We're only human, love.'

'Yeah. I know.'

'Do you want to try a self-compassion technique? I've been doing it myself this past hour. It really does work.'

No, I didn't want to try a bloody self-compassion technique. I wanted to scream, hit something, have a drink, indulge in all my usual dysfunctions – anything but submit to her hippy bullshit crap. Except it wasn't hippy bullshit crap, I knew. And just stifling the emotions never helped either. I knew she was right – I'd watched her conduct the research into self-compassion, had read some of the studies of the other scientists she collaborated with. They had found that meditation can, astonishingly, control pain, even, it seemed, enabling the immune system to boost itself. 'It's amazing,' Kristin had told me when we were first looking at this stuff together. 'It used to be the accepted wisdom that the brain was hard-wired at the age of five. Now we know it can be re-patterned, rebuilt, at any age, any time of life.'

Was that what had been going on with Betsy and Rowan? Was that, in some way, what went on during the shaman ceremonies? Kristin and I had used to meditate together earlier in our marriage and I knew the benefits, but had found it hard to do, being such a restless, physical character.

'That's the thing about the self-compassion techniques,' she'd pointed out. 'You don't have to sit on the floor cross-legged for hours. Even just putting a hand over your heart, and saying, "It's okay, you're trying your best, this is what everybody goes through", talking to yourself as if you were a good friend and not letting your inner critic kick yourself to pieces, it helps amazingly.'

I knew it, had tried it, and – in my more conscious moments – used her techniques. But when the shit really hit the fan – as it had now, reducing the car to a tortured sound box of high-pitched screaming – it seemed so hard. Even though I knew it would do me good. Like turning down that drink and taking mineral water instead: you know it will make you feel better now, and certainly tomorrow; you know you're plenty buzzed enough and don't need any more booze to feel any better. Yet you hold out your glass for the refill you don't need, which you know will only make you feel worse. It was like that now.

'I'm fine,' I said, eyes fixed on the long, straight road ahead, knuckles white on the wheel.

Kristin said nothing. I sneaked a look at her as I drove. She sat, eyes closed, a hand on her heart, breathing evenly. I knew she was saying the words to herself, knew it was helping. Why did I find it so hard to do – ego, pride, some strange deep-seated embarrassment?

I sighed, annoyed at myself. Why didn't I just give it up? Here I was embarked on a three-year healing journey – four, if you counted Mongolia – and yet I couldn't, wouldn't, do anything for myself. Too much British stiff upper lip absorbed too young, perhaps? Maybe, but I surely needed to do something if I was going to last the course.

Slowly, I put my hand on my heart, breathed. I felt the shift almost immediately: the good feeling as oxytocin gradually replaced cortisol, the stress hormone that had been flooding my body, making me want to lash out, flee, dive down a hole.

It's okay. I started to say the words Kristin had taught me, a technique she had used during her training workshops and which had proved so effective that universities around the world now recognized it. It was only her stupid, self-absorbed husband who seemed to resist, as he seemed to resist all things that were good for him and would help him be a better father. *It's okay,* I repeated to myself, holding the wheel steady with my left hand, my right still over my heart, the road stretching off into the distant blue. *You're doing your best. You're just experiencing what everyone on the planet experiences when these things happen. It's okay . . .*

5. The Shape Shifters

The long road from Tsumeb and Grootfontein into Bushmanland is one of the great drives in Africa. There is a very real sense, once the tar surface gives out and the dirt takes over, of truly leaving civilization behind. No more farms or ranches. The wire fences disappear. Unconfined, herds of cattle and goats begin to drift by or wander across the ribbon-straight road, tended by waving Herero boys, naked but for a loincloth or pair of old shorts and a wide, bright smile. Occasionally you might see a Herero man on a horse, riding between cattle stations, or the incredible Herero women, who despite the heat wear long heavy dresses, sometimes complete with bustles, and headdresses tied into two great, starched flaps either side of the head to represent cattle horns – cattle being the ultimate symbol of status for the Herero, as for almost all the warrior tribes of southern Africa. The women, sweating in the thick fabric of their missionary-era dresses, cruise by like stately, painted ships. Then the emptiness takes over once more.

You drive on, and notice that now even the livestock has disappeared. Occasionally a small duiker or steenbok – a small antelope the size of a little goat – darts across the road. Or a leggy, impossibly elegant grey-brown kudu, the females in groups, the spiral-horned males usually alone. Lilac-breasted rollers flash iridescent purple as they tumble aerodynamically after flying insects, swooping across the windscreen in an acrobatic flurry of wing beats. Elephant dung starts to appear along the roadside. If you drive this road at night – which is inadvisable because suddenly there are a lot of eyes on the road and dark forms flashing across your headlights, which if you hit you're dead – you'll glimpse hyenas and, if you're lucky, a leopard, possibly even a lion.

And you're not in a national park, a game reserve or an otherwise protected game area. You're just in Africa: Africa as it always was. You're in the territory of the Bushmen. The First People.

Taller trees begin to emerge from the mid-eye-level scrub. Hardwoods like marula, ironwood, leadwood, rise through the heat haze like stately green-canopied buildings. And then the real tower blocks appear: baobabs, which the Bushmen call 'upside-down trees' because their upper branches are so disproportionately small compared to their vast elephant-skin-resembling trunks. Odd trees in other ways, too: they're pollinated by fruit bats attracted to their flowers, which, though beautiful, smell of rotting fruit and meat. And their fruits, smooth like velvet on the outside, a hard, wooden pear within, yield a white, dry but chewable flesh that forms the basis of cream of tartar. Elephants, in times of great drought, will bore into a baobab with their tusks, gouging vast holes, yet the tree survives. Until, after a millennium or two, its time is up and it simply implodes, collapsing in upon itself like an old industrial chimney demolished by dynamite. Strange place, Africa.

We stopped at a small Bushman settlement, a collection of round clay huts with conical thatched roofs, where the local San people had set up an attempt at community tourism. I remembered, from visiting the region years before, that if you pulled off the road here, someone would appear who spoke English, more or less, and you could then go for a guided bush walk, having the medicinal and edible plants pointed out to you. Or you could buy crafts: animals and birds carved from dark ironwood or red-and-white tamboti wood; beaded pouches made of antelope skin or soft jackal fur; little tortoise shells filled with *saun* – that pollen-based powder used in healing ceremonies – strung on rawhide strips for wearing around your neck; little bows and spears such as a child might use to practise with. We stopped the vehicle and pulled off the road by the huts, grateful for the chance of a leg stretch. As we got out, we were immediately swamped by children.

'Bushman kids!' Rowan was as delighted with them as they were with him, and went off at a sprint into and around the huts. There wasn't an adult in sight – highly unusual when a people's economy is largely financed by travellers like us stopping to buy crafts and dispense much-needed cash. But what followed was a magical hour. A young girl and boy immediately adopted Rowan and – in the absence of any common language – a riotous, noisy game of chase began and without any apparent need for either preparation or communication. In and out of the huts, popping out to startle each other, child laughter filling the warm African air with heart-gladdening joy. We adults lumbered after, torn between feeling we must keep an eye on Rowan and a desire not to interfere, not to break the spell that he and these children of the wilderness had conjured into being.

Two older boys broke away from the group rushing from hut to hut and disappeared into the trees. Perhaps ten minutes later they reappeared leading two donkeys attached to a cart. Rowan whooped for joy.

'Take a ride! Take a ride!'

So on we hopped, he and I together, and the two grinning teen-agers whipped up the reins and away we went up the dirt road, bumping and rattling at a surprising lick, the cart bouncing us this way and that, Rowan's laughter like silver bells, nourishing me, his father, as only the laughter of one's own beloved child can do.

But when we finally got ourselves reluctantly back into the vehicle, Rowan's earlier tearful, whiney mood returned. 'More Bushman children!' he wailed.

Was another tantrum brewing? God, it made one jumpy. But no, this time it was okay as we drove the final three hours east-wards to the little frontier town of Tsumkwe. The government administrative centre for the surrounding area, it consisted of service offices, shanties and ramshackle shops selling anything from truck tyres to party dresses to cans of pilchards – the edge of the utter wild. Rowan was smiling, then came a powerful waft from his seat. So familiar, so soul-destroyingly familiar.

Fatigue made Kristin's voice small: 'I thought we were past this.'

Tsumkwe had a new lodge – new since I had last been there, anyway – where travellers could stay: a few pleasant wooden chalets clustered behind a tall, electric fence whose current was strong enough – in theory anyway – to deter the local elephants from ambling through and raiding the lodge's kitchen. And here, in the softening late-afternoon light (and after I had taken Rowan off to the ablution block, trying to sound cheery while I cleaned him up), my friend Megan was waiting for us.

Doctor Megan Biesele is a legend in the anthropological world. A former professor, she had turned activist back in the early 1990s and began helping the local people secure their hunting grounds as a government-sponsored conservancy. Now, twenty-plus years on, her organization, the Kalahari Peoples Fund, worked on everything from alcoholism to education to tourism. A humble, easy-going woman in her late sixties, Megan was well loved in the Kalahari. We were lucky she had agreed to come to translate for us and facilitate the healing, knowing the shamans personally as she did, as friends.

Wearing round glasses that gave her face an owlish look, her grey hair falling to her shoulders, khakis blending with the green/grey of the darkening bush, she came out to meet us, arms spread wide. 'Welcome back to the Kalahari!' she said. 'Welcome home!'

And indeed, whenever you return to the world of the Bushmen, to their purer way of being, to the wilderness around them, to their way of relating to that wilderness, to its animals and plants, to each other, to God, the heart, the body, mind and spirit, there is always a sense of homecoming. To the source of what it means to be a human being. To the home of the heart.

The sun set over the bare branches of the vast marula tree just outside the lodge's fence. Somewhere out there a leopard coughed – harsh, clipped, like someone briefly clearing their throat before getting down to brass tacks. Rowan ran off down the sandy pathway to the camping area, then joyfully hurled himself into the soft, grey-white sand, revelling in its fine texture, Michel filming him discreetly from a few yards off.

I stood watching, the long drive done, letting the peace of Nyae Nyae begin to wash over me.

'Hey, love, I thought you might like one of these,' Kristin's voice was warm/cool like the evening.

'Yes, indeed, perfect!' agreed my mother and I heard Megan's laughter. I turned; they were clasping nicely chilled cans of Windhoek beer. Kristin offered me one. Namibia, being an ex-German colony, brews good beer. I cracked mine open, cheers-ed and took a sip, letting the ice-cold bitterness bite at the back of my road-dusty throat. I sighed with satisfaction.

'To healing!' I said.

'To healing!'

Next morning, in the cold crisp dawn, I climbed down from the roof tent with Rowan to pee. I went first, one rung at a time, slow with early-morning stiffness. As I dropped down on to the soft sandy pathway, reaching up to receive an incoming Rowan, my eye fell on a long, smooth shape just to the left of my foot. I froze.

'Don't pass him to me just yet!'

'Why not?' Kristin was bleary-eyed, still half immersed in dream. Rowan struggled to get to me. 'Get down! Down!'

'Look by my foot.'

Kristin looked. 'Oh, my God. Okay, okay, what are you going to do?'

It was a puff adder, one of the great hazards of southern Africa. Thick-bodied, triangular-headed and venomous enough to kill a child or land an adult in the hospital for quite a while, it had emerged from a hole to lie in the narrow patch of rapidly warming sunlight. Unusual for this time of year: it was generally too cold for them to come out of hibernation. But step on one and you'll know about it. I stood stock still.

'Want down!' wailed Rowan, his bladder no doubt full to bursting, as was mine. '*Doooooooown!*'

Ignoring him, I took a carefully executed step to the right, picked up a large stone and threw it on to the ground hard, next to the snake. It stirred but did not move – normally a large vibration on the ground is enough to get a snake to move, but this one still clearly wasn't warm enough.

'It's a puff adder!' Rowan suddenly understood the reason for the delay; frustration turned to interest – his encyclopedic, obsessive knowledge of animals bubbling to the fore. 'Poisonous! Careful, Daddy!'

Logic again. Was Rowan back to his normal, post-Mongolia self? I picked up another rock, admiring the beauty of the patterns on the snake's scaly back, and threw it again. This time the snake moved, reluctantly. I threw a third and a fourth. It slithered under a large log.

'You don't think you should have killed it?' Kristin was worried.

'No.' I reached up for Rowan, took his compact, almost seven-year-old body into my arms. 'I always feel it's unlucky to kill snakes.'

'He was a beautiful snake!' said Rowan, and pulled down his pants to pee against the nearest tree, as did I. We agreed on so many things.

I have kept a lot of animals. When I was eight or so, I remember people asking me what I wanted to be when I grew up and replying, 'A herpetologist.' I wasn't trying to be precocious. I genuinely loved reptiles and amphibians, was fascinated by them. I found them beautiful, the strange juxtaposition of smooth and dry of their scales almost hypnotic. I had a garter snake, a chameleon and a series of lizards, including a slow-worm – a legless lizard that looks like a snake – which broke out of her cage, disappeared and then rematerialized one morning three months later in the kitchen, double her previous size, and then promptly had babies when we put her back in her terrarium.

A chip off the old block, Rowan by now had – back in Texas – a couple of fat-tailed leopard geckos, a corn snake, a tree frog and a horned toad that the cat had brought in and we had rescued, and couldn't believe its luck to be installed in a tank and fed crickets all day with zero worries about predators.

At night when Rowan couldn't sleep, he and I would go on animal-find walks in the woods close by the house, taking a torch and looking for Houston toads (endangered, it turns out, due to deforestation and urban development) under the stones in the front yard, green tree snakes in the foliage of the hackberry trees, copperheads (dangerous!) in the leaf mould of the forest floor, not to mention Mexican free-tail bats, fireflies, raccoons staring wide-eyed and bandit-masked down from the tops of the cedar elms, a grey fox or a coyote occasionally flitting across the dry creek-bed below the house. Once we even glimpsed a bobcat sitting on a fallen log before, with one smooth bound, it took its amazing ghost self off into the outer darkness.

Even when we were in London visiting my parents – where Rowan would soon start to become agitated after exposure to endless concrete, traffic thunder, the tube – we would escape to the thousand-acre haven of Hampstead Heath, go under the spread of the old oaks and watch the magpies swoop and chatter, and the grey squirrels scamper up the trunks of the plane trees to get away from the pit bulls being walked below, along the tracks where I had once ridden my bicycle as a boy.

The natural world. It had always saved us; from those first months after Rowan's diagnosis four long years before, when I realized that he simply did better, tantrummed less, when out in the woods, to being on Betsy, to going across Mongolia, to now . . .

Father and son in nature – as it should be.

'See more snakes!' trilled Rowan hopefully and trotted off towards the lodge, following the scent of bacon and toast from the kitchen. My mother and Megan – peers and old friends, both – were already there, talking over their second cup of coffee. I got bacon for Rowan – he always improved with animal protein in him – and sat down next to them.

'Nervous?' asked Megan, reading my thoughts. I was. Whenever I had come to the Kalahari before, or interacted with the healers there, my role had been as a bringer of hope, a helper in the quest to get their land back. Now I was coming as supplicant, asking for healing for my son, for myself, because there can be no real separation between a parent and a child: one love, one heart, always and for ever. And always the same questions when one goes to see a healer – will he or she even be there, and if so, will they agree to, will they be able to handle the healing? Will it work? And if it works, will it continue to work or will there be regression?

'Yeah,' I admitted. 'I am.'

'Well, there are never any guarantees, as you know.' Megan sipped her coffee, her kind face thoughtful. 'But I've known /Kunta thirty years, more. If he wasn't reasonably sure he could handle it, he wouldn't have told me to bring you.'

/Kunta was an old, old friend of Megan's and known in the Nyae Nyae area as a healer of great effectiveness. I had worried, when organizing this journey, that something might prevent Besa and Jumanda from making it. So I had asked Megan to see if any of the more senior healers in Nyae Nyae might be prepared to step in as well. She had immediately gone to see /Kunta, the most experienced healer she knew, and he had provisionally agreed, though he wanted to meet Rowan first, and had been honest enough to say that this was something outside his usual remit. He might or might not be able to take it on.

'What do they understand autism to be?' my mother wanted to know.

'Good question. Well, as in any kind of shamanism, things are looked at ancestrally, and also in terms of ill-wishing – as in someone ill-wishing or cursing someone else. /Kunta's likely to look at it from both points of view, so we'll just have to see. One thing's for sure: it's the Bushmen, so me and Kristin won't get whipped like we did in Mongolia.'

'Or have to wash out our privates with vodka.' Kristin appeared at the table. She wagged a mock-angry finger at me. 'You still owe me for that one.' I blushed, acknowledging the debt.

'Yes,' Megan chuckled. 'At least that won't happen.'

'I don't know how you put up with the things Rupert makes you do,' said my mother.

'Nor do I.' Kristin smiled. 'But he puts up with some stuff from me too, you know. And remember why we were in that position – we didn't travel all the distance just to chicken out when it got uncomfortable. And look at all the good things that happened as a result.'

'If you choose to believe that it was the healers, yes.'

I sighed. 'That doesn't make me feel any better.'

'Just expressing my opinion, darling.'

'Indeed you are.'

'Well,' said Megan, cutting through the awkward silence that followed. 'I know /Kunta is anxious to meet you all. So when we're done eating, maybe we should go say hi?'

Twenty minutes or so later, we all piled into the car, me, Kristin, Rowan, Michel, my mother and Megan all squeezing in as best we could, and out we drove. The deep sandy tracks required every ounce of 4x4 the Nissan had, through the thick bush of acacia and butterfly-wing-leafed mopane – the two trees that support the majority of the Kalahari's browsing antelope – through glades of golden-yellow grasses, waist high from last year's rains, to Dau Post, the village where /Kunta's people lived.

At first glance, these straggly Bushman settlements appear to be farmer or herder villages, rather than hunter-gatherer camps. Over the decades, numerous foundations, organizations, government institutions and other groups have tried to wean the Bushmen from their wanderings and turn them into farmers. The Bushmen never argue, so most of their villages, when you drive into them, have a few mangy cows, maybe a horse or two, some chickens scratching about, a half-hearted patch of melons or beans, grown almost for appearances' sake. What livestock survives the depredations of lion, leopard and hyena tends eventually to be eaten by their owners, and the melon patches often die, until the next round of do-gooders come in and offer replacements. Meanwhile, the beloved hunting equipment – the straight-handled spears, the deceptively small bows that look more like children's toys than serious hunting kit, the quivers of arrows tipped with poison from a beetle larva (a toxin so deadly that it can knock out a giraffe), the leg rattles made of moth cocoons filled with chipped ostrich eggshell used to help shamans go into trance – all this is stashed discreetly away in the huts, or hung in the branches of the village's shade trees. Because of this, casual visitors to the Kalahari sometimes think that the old life has gone. But any attempts to please the outsiders that want to turn them into farmers are lip service at best. As one hunter once famously told an American anthropologist: 'Why should I plant when the world is full of mongongo nuts?'

The people were sitting in the shade of a thorn tree, grouped around a smouldering low-flamed fire on which steamed a kettle. The women wearing bright-hued *duks* (headscarves) and dresses or animal skins with beaded designs on them – the colours loud against the yellow/brown of the winter bush. The men barechested, in dusty dirty shorts or, in a couple of cases, skin loincloths. A few wore baseball caps. Kids played and chased in the fine white sand around them. As we parked, and Rowan barrelled out of the car shouting, 'Bushman children!', an old man got stiffly to his feet from the little circle of villagers and walked over to greet us.

'/Kunta!' Megan's face registered the same delight as his, the old man with his bright, mischievous eyes, close-cropped peppercorn-grey hair on a honey-coloured scalp, and the accumulated wrinkles of decades around his eyes and across his broad forehead.

'This is Rupert and the family I told you about,' Megan explained to /Kunta in Ju'/Hoansi, before translating for us. 'And that wild thing running around over there is, obviously, his son, Rowan!'

Our eyes followed Rowan as he went tearing around the village, scattering chickens, rib-thin dogs, a few grumpily protesting goats and a pair of emaciated cows who lolloped away into the bush in disgust. At once the rest of the children were up and running with him, immediately accepting him into their pack, grins and laughter bright in the morning sun.

/Kunta smiled, and made the very courtly greeting typical of the Bushmen. A slight bow, left hand holding the right wrist, right hand extended, and shaking three times, not looking the other person in the eye, gently respecting their space. It occurred to me, as we shook hands, that this would be the perfect way for autists to greet neurotypical people, or vice versa. No forcing of eye contact, keeping the emotional pressure light.

He was introduced to each of us in turn, as was his wife, N!ae, their faces that strange mix of wry and respectful, knowing and kind, that is unique to the Bushmen. Small in stature, yet so elegantly proportioned that they don't appear short, economic in their movements as people always are who must use their bodies every day of their lives.

'Let's meet your boy,' said /Kunta simply, through Megan, once the introductions had been made.

Easier said than done. Rowan was now in full, laughing chase-game flight – in and out of the little huts and chicken coops once more, the other children trailing behind him in a laughing, happily yelling parade. Only one girl, an anxious-eyed little thing of perhaps five or six, held back, clinging close to her mother in the circle of adults who watched the laughing game playing out with tolerant, patient gazes. Rowan came running into the circle, and reached out for the little girl. She screamed in terror, went into hysterics, hid behind her mother, who laughed but did not stop her. Rowan came trotting back to me. 'Why doesn't she want to play?'

'I don't know, Scub. She hasn't met you before. Maybe she's shy. Here, this is the shaman. His name is /Kunta.'

Rowan looked at him doubtfully. /Kunta said something to Megan.

'He asks if he can lay hands on him, to get an idea of what is going on.'

'Um, sure . . .' I hesitated. 'Rowan's not very happy about being touched by people he doesn't know – just so you're aware. Can you explain that to /Kunta, so he won't be offended if Rowan doesn't like it?'

'Don't worry. I already did. /Kunta says that's the way it should be with children and adults they don't know. All the same, it would be helpful.'

'Okay, sure . . .' I scooped Rowan up in my arms, he letting out a kind of grumpy burp as I did so, and held him out – a good sixty or so pounds of him – towards /Kunta's open arms.

'*Nooooo thank you! Urgh! Arrrrrgh!*' Rowan twisted in my arms. N!ae had come up now, concern on her lined, high-cheekboned face. Both she and her husband laid their gentle but rough-skinned palms on Rowan's temples, his head. His wails rose to a shriek. He twisted in my arms as if he'd been burned. I let him go immediately. The wails stopped and he rushed straight back to his game with the waiting, grinning children, who had gathered around as if they saw this kind of thing every day. Which probably they did.

/Kunta turned to Megan and said something gently in Ju'/Hoansi, the phonetic clicks coming thick and fast, his tone grave, his eyes no longer laughing. Megan hesitated a moment before translating.

'He says this is serious. More serious than he had thought, more difficult than he as a healer alone can manage. He says he'll need the help of another healer to do this.'

'Does he have someone in mind?'

'He does. But he hasn't seen him in quite a while. He thinks he's at his village. But it's far from here.'

'How far?'

She and /Kunta exchanged a few words. 'On foot, two days. Maybe three. And the paths between here and there are full of elephant. In your vehicle, a few hours. He can show us the way.'

I looked sceptically at Rowan. Would he be up for a long journey through the thorn scrub to meet a man who might not be there? I conferred with Kristin. No – they would go back to the lodge and chill; it had been a long journey here, after all. Instead, just Megan, /Kunta and I would make the trip.

So, once Rowan and his new friends had finished their game of chase, back to the guest lodge we went, Megan and I then returning to Dau Post, where we picked up /Kunta, his wife and a couple of other lads from the village and set out on the long ride to see his friend.

Deeper into Nyae Nyae we went. To the untutored eye it all looked like trackless bush. In fact we were passing between one *n!ore*, or hunting territory, and another, each with its own complex boundaries, each passed from generation to generation, even millennium to millennium, without the people ever needing to go out and look for more land, because they never over-populate. I remembered how, years before, I had hunted from one *n!ore* into another, tracking with Bushman hunters, who had explained that the rules of hunting allowed hunters to go into each other's territory if the animal took them there, but that hunters could not start hunting the animal in another person's *n!ore*, even if it was just a spear's throw inside. Conflict between villages was something that was avoided at all costs. War, organized violence, was a concept known to the Bushmen – after all, they were surrounded by hardcore warrior peoples, both white and black. But still it was alien to them, not the Bushman way.

Now, as we bumped and bounced down the long sandy tracks, keeping a watchful eye out for any elephants that might casually, suddenly, step out from the bush and into our vehicle's path, I remembered the first Bushman tracking expedition I had participated in, during which I had been shown that, for the Bushmen, hunting was no macho pastime of man conquering beast. Instead, it was connected – very closely connected – with healing.

It was back in 1997, in Botswana, during my first few forays into the world of the Kalahari, in a part of the country unprotected by any kind of conservation laws. Because more aggressive cattle-owning tribes had come in and killed off the game on which they had traditionally relied, the Bushman villagers were now beginning to try their hand at cultivating arid-land medicinal plants for sale – devil's claw for arthritis, hoodia (a cactus-like succulent and an appetite suppressant) as a slimming aid, marula and moretlwa juice for the immune system. A cousin of mine had been instrumental in getting these projects off the ground, but the people's hearts still lay with hunting. One day, while I was staying with them, two of the younger men took me out tracking. They were no longer allowed to go hunting: game had become so scarce due to the depredations of cattle herders, and the government, in an attempt to make the Bushmen into farmers, to 'modernize' them, had taken their hunting rights away, so as to speed up the process.

The two young men, Cera and Opi, wanted to show me their tracking skills, they said. Always up for watching master trackers at work, I readily agreed. Out into the bush we went and soon picked up the spoor of a big gemsbok bull. Probably an old one that had been pushed out of the herd and was now living out the rest of its days alone. He was some distance ahead of us, which I was secretly relieved about, because the gemsbok is one of several antelope species that will hunt *you* once it realizes you are on its trail. I had once seen an irate gemsbok attack a game ranger who had been trying to save it from being stuck in the mud of a waterhole. The animal had slashed and slashed with its long, spear-like horns as the poor guy attempted to free it. Giving up eventually, the ranger got back into his truck to radio for more help, only to have the now incensed beast wrench itself from the sticky goo unaided, charge the (thankfully) closed vehicle door and plant its right horn straight though the metal, missing him by inches.

So I wasn't grief-stricken when we finally caught sight of our quarry some distance ahead of us on a lowish rise, perhaps three hundred yards off. The hunters were not carrying bows or spears, so the chance of getting too close for comfort seemed unlikely. We were just tracking after all. Then Cera, the older of the two, turned to me, gave a sly grin, pointed to himself and announced, in English: 'Senior doctor.'

Then he pointed at the ground. There in the red sand lay a single fresh dropping – gemsbok, a bull's. Dropped there just a few minutes before. Meanwhile, the bull in question had just sauntered over the distant rise where we'd first spotted him, disappearing from sight once more. Carefully – very carefully – Cera picked up the still wet, glistening dropping and placed it inside one of the back hoof prints that the gemsbok had left in the sand. Then he covered it over.

Cera stood. Took first his friend and then me by the shoulders and turned us, his hands light, not forceful, through 180 degrees, so that we were looking back down the trail the way we had come. Next his fingers sought out our eyelids and closed them, first Opi's and then mine.

We stood thus, eyes closed, for perhaps ten breaths. Then, very softly, he whispered, 'Okay, okay . . .' and turned us around. 'Look!'

There on the trail right in front of us, a mere bowshot away, stood the gemsbok bull. Broadside on, offering his shoulder to the arrow.

As one, the two hunters each plucked an imaginary arrow from an imaginary quiver, set it to an imaginary bow and let fly. The big bull stood there for the long second it would have taken the arrows to arc their way to his shoulder and pierce the heart and lung, before he spun abruptly on his haunches and thundered away in a cloud of red dust.

Cera turned to me. 'Ah, Rrru,' he said, using the nickname they had given me. 'This was our way.'

Later that night, having ignored or laughed off my demands to know how he had made this extraordinary thing happen, Cera said, 'I think it's time you met the healer.'

So off we went to a hut in the middle of their settlement, accompanied by my half-Batswana, half-white interpreter. The healer, a gnarled, kindly man, as Bushman healers usually are, welcomed me in and showed me what he had in his hut – these roots for menstrual cramps, this herb to be placed in water if your livestock had diarrhoea, another type of root that you ground up for headaches. 'But all this stuff – if you haven't got it, or if it's not growing – you can do without, as long as you have a good trance healer,' he said. 'If you have a good trance healer, you don't need any herbs at all.'

How did trance healers heal, I wanted to know. Did it have something to do with what I had seen on the trail that afternoon, the gemsbok bull somehow, inexplicably, manifesting there, on the trail, ready for the arrow? Was some kind of magic involved, whether for hunting or healing? Was that it?

'Hunting magic? Yes, it has to do with that. There are many ways to hunt. Animals, plants, a sickness, a spirit, an answer to a question.' He smiled to himself, shaking his head. 'I'm sure you will be invited to a trance dance soon, and then you will begin to understand.'

He had been right. That next full moon, in another Bushman camp near the rough little town of Ghanzi, I had been invited to attend a dance called for an old woman afflicted with rheumatoid arthritis. The healer, when he fell into trance, had screamed, fallen to the ground, then danced, moving in slow, stamping circles around the outside of where the rest of us, myself and the villagers, sat hand clapping and chanting (me trying to follow the complex rhythms and chants without much success). He laid hands on us all – fragile, moth-like movements that made you feel strangely calm when they touched you. Whenever he went back to the old woman for whom the dance had been called, he would pull at her legs, sobbing. Time after time he went back to her, dancing, singing, suffering, healing under the silver moon, the sand around him lit up like a field of liquid silver. When the first rays of dawn came, he was still dancing, and the old women's legs were no longer swollen or red.

The healer slept all day after this. 'A hard healing,' I was told. When I asked the old women if she thought it had worked, she had shrugged. 'Undoubtedly,' she replied, indicating her much-improved legs. 'But it doesn't last for ever. I'll have to call the healer back in in a year or so, just to keep it under control.'

'So it's like regular medicine, you have to have regular treatments?' I asked, and she nodded – it seemed so.

'Here, turn here,' Megan's voice broke into my reverie, and I turned off the track we had been on and proceeded down another, narrower trail, one that took us suddenly out of the thorn scrub into a large open area in which sprawled another straggling Bushman village. We had arrived.

The two old men greeted each other the classic Bushman way – with mock insults that concealed the deep affection they had for each other.

'Face like an old, dead spirit!' said /Kunta.

To which his long-lost friend responded: 'Death to your penis!'

It took me a while to pick myself up from the ground when Megan translated this.

So this was his friend. An older healer, too, but with something more youthful about him; his name was Gwi. A small man with an upright, elastic bearing that belied his years, and a blue baseball cap set at a jaunty angle on his balding head. Their insults done, he and /Kunta went off into one of the huts to confer, Megan accompanying them. It took a couple of hours, during which time I went for a short walk, a small procession of curious, doe-eyed children trailing behind me. Which was a good thing: it's all too easy to get lost in the bush, especially in the Kalahari, which is really just one big thicket with gladed areas in between that all look the same. I had made that mistake before, wandering off from camp, and had had to shout to my fellow travellers to make a noise so that I could find my way back – and I have a good sense of direction. But it is impossible to overemphasize how disorientated you can become in the bush.

Another time had been at night right here in Nyae Nyae, several years before, a potentially lethal situation. Just at the moment when I realized I was hopelessly, stupidly lost, I heard a soft but powerful sigh to my right. I froze. I knew what that sound meant. Elephant! I sank to my haunches and squatted there in the dark, wondering what to do. So close, it must know I was there. Now, letting my eyes focus on the darkness around me, I could make out the huge creature's darker, slightly moving form . . . then another. And then from behind me I heard the tear of a branch and a rich, rippling fart. I had blundered inadvertently into the middle of a small group of them. It's a classic way to get duffed up by elephants, this, accidentally bumping into them in the dark, because they make so little noise most of the time. Drunk people wandering around in the bush sometimes get caught this way. Startle an elephant by stumbling into him and you're going to find his trunk whipped around you at full force, enough to break your ribcage. And that's just for starters. Why had I done this? Stupid, stupid, stupid. Too scared to move, too scared almost to breathe, I simply squatted there in the warm, quiet night and waited. They knew I was there. They were tolerating me, as elephants often will – for the time being. For what felt like hours, but was probably a little under an hour, I waited, growing sore in my limbs, until it seemed they had moved off. At least the tearing and slow munching of branches faded gradually from earshot. It took an age to find the camp. Having wandered into the bush unescorted at night a second time, I would never do it again.

So now, as I waited for /Kunta and Gwi, I was glad of the little escort of children who had followed me into the bush. They would keep me safe, as children often do if adults only did but know it. Some carried sticks, and began to play a game I'd seen before. Deceptively simple, it consists of a *xane*, or shuttlecock, made from an ostrich or kori bustard feather with a wild bean tied to its nether end with a strip of rawhide. One kid loops the rawhide over a stick and flips it up in the air. The other, also holding a stick, watches the *xane* keenly as it comes helicoptering down, and intercepts it at the last possible moment, just before it hits the ground, flipping it back up into the air once more with his stick. It takes enormous skill and dexterity to do this – a kind of cross between badminton, Hacky Sack and . . . well, I don't quite know what. It's mesmerizing when done well. So I watched, marvelling at the children's skill, until the sun rose higher, making it hard to look up and focus in the harsher light. The game suddenly over, the kids began trickling back to the village, and I followed.

Megan was waiting. Gwi had agreed to help with the healing. Together we drove back to Dau Post, with even more people stuffed into the vehicle than had been before. The healing, which would take more than one attempt – /Kunta and Gwi were both certain – would begin tonight.

There is a special tension that leads up to a trance dance. The healers need to rest: they might be dancing for two hours or for twelve – once they are in trance they have no choice in the matter. Once the *nxum* (the Bushman word for spirit energy) takes over, it makes its own decisions about how long the healing will take, whom among those gathered there the shaman targets for healing, or what ancestor or other spirits the healer must bargain with for the soul of the sick one. The experience can be ecstatic for the healer – a closeness to God, an intimacy with the divine that anyone with a bent for the spiritual craves. Equally, it can be terrifying, as healers battle with every nightmare manifested by the tortured spirit of the one they are healing. They say it can make you feel shot through with arrows, impaled with spears. They say you can die.

'What – it feels *as if* you die?' I had once asked old Besa. (Would he be able to make it? I hoped so, suspected that without him the healing here would not be complete.) He had been speaking to me about healing – one of the rare occasions on which he spoke in a direct manner rather than almost impenetrable riddles. 'No,' he replied. 'Sometimes you actually die. It's a known risk: it can happen if you encounter something more powerful than you in the spirit world.'

If Besa suspected that it was going to be a hard healing, such as when someone had ill-wished or cursed another person, and hence

1. Rowan and Betsy just after coming back from Africa, 2008.

2. Hurray for zoos! A hot day at Dallas Zoo, 2009.

3. When you ride with a child, you are a voice in their ear and can insinuate yourself into their thought processes, tailoring the conversation to their interests. The results can be extraordinary.

4. When I first met the Xhomani Bushmen in South Africa in 1996, they were reduced to living by the side of the road and had constructed an ironic sign for passers-by. It reads 'Bushmen for Sale'. Dawid Kruiper is in the centre.

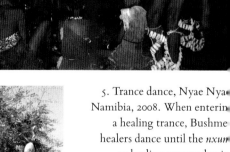

5. Trance dance, Nyae Nyae, Namibia, 2008. When entering a healing trance, Bushmen healers dance until the *nxum*, or healing energy, begins to boil inside them.

6. Villagers in Nyae Nyae. The old hunting and gathering way of life still holds strong in the face of attempts by various organizations to modernize it.

7. Michel at the huge baobab tree, Nyae Nyae, 2008.

9. Rowan, me and Kristin inside the huge baobab tree.

8. The three Besas: Old Besa, myself and Little Besa (Rowan).

10. N!ae, the healer /Kunta's wife, and Rowan share a private moment.

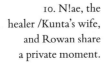

11. The initial diagnosis: Rowan's hair showing in the centre, /Kunta in cap, N!ae, Kristin and me.

12. Healing by the fire: Kristin and me on the right with Rowan lying across us.

13. The women and children provide a chorus of singing and hand-clapping that helps the healers dance their way into a state of altered consciousness.

14. My mother Polly's watercolour of the healers dancing.

15. The Daintree Rainforest clings to a long narrow stretch of country between high mountains and the sea in northern Queensland, Australia. It is the world's oldest rainforest.

16. Harold, the Kuku Yalanji healer from the Daintree Rainforest.

17. Harold preparing paperbark for a smoking ceremony to purify; Rowan was 'smoked' before his healing sessions in 2009.

18. The sacred pools in the forest where Harold told us to swim with Rowan to help confirm the healing.

19. Rowan loses his fear of water.

20. Rowan becomes a water baby at last.

he, as the healer, might get hit by the full force of the ill-wishing and die while in the spirit world, unable to make it back to his own body, then he made sure to have another healer with him, two even, to bring him back.

'How often does that happen?' I asked.

'Not often. But the cattle-owning tribes, they use a lot of black magic, a lot of ill-wishing. Which is a bad idea because the curse always comes back to consume the one who wished it. Black-magic witch doctors tend not to live long, and in the end the people who use them suffer more than the people they try to hurt. But it never seems to stop them trying,' he sighed. 'Some people just aren't right in the head: the black-magic witch doctors and those who use them are too crazy to think about the consequences of what they do, and in the end it destroys them. Every time.'

Such were the thoughts that went through my mind as we whiled away the last of the warm afternoon before the evening's healing ceremony began. To help pass the time, we drove out to Nyae Nyae Pan, a vast expanse of grassland occupied by a shallow salt pan similar to those of Etosha, its expanse so broad that, looking at it, you could swear the slight curvature of the earth was discernible in its surface. But where the great pans of Etosha had been away in the distance, far from the road we were travelling along, this one was close at hand. Its waters reflected the pale azure sky, the flamingos that stalked across its surface so near that as our car rumbled out of the tree line they took off as one in a flurry of dazzling pink, whirring across the shallow waters to land again further out, surprised by the intrusion but not panicked, for this was a spot where few people ever came.

'They're scoofing! I want to scoof too!'

'I guess Pint Size from *Pigs Might Fly!* is pink like the flamingos,' my mother mused. We were all in a good space. Rowan had spent a peaceful afternoon being read to, and playing with his animals in the sand, enjoying the downtime in the quiet lodge – we were the only people staying there and had the whole camping area to ourselves. While I'd been away there had been one poop accident, Kristin reported, but he hadn't been upset. No tantrums. My mother had spent the time sketching and painting. So a good day, even if one that was regressive by our post-Mongolia standards.

But the same thoughts kept swirling around in my head. Would /Kunta and Gwi be able to repair what was damaged? Would Besa make it here sometime in the next few days, to complete the healing? The same questions – round and round, endlessly. Would Rowan be fully healed in the end, as Ghoste had said he would? Was it even right to hope for this? Did it mean that on some level I still hadn't really accepted Rowan's autism, still hadn't really accepted him? The autism wasn't the problem after all: I had met quite a few successful adult autists by now, including the renowned scientist and author Dr Temple Grandin. But going in your pants at nearly seven years old was a problem. No one wants to be friends with a child, let alone an adult, that is incontinent and tantrums at the slightest provocation. Back at Halali Camp, all had seemed to right itself once more – yet now it was, if anything, worse than before. Would it ever end?

'Oh, wow!' said Michel, shifting his camera immediately into action through the open window, through which the soft breeze blew. 'Elephants!'

There they were – a family group of five or so, moving like slow grey battleships, like houses on legs, out of the tree cover, towards the shallow waters of the pan, to drink and cool off after the heat of the day. There is always a special magic in seeing big game outside of the accepted confines of game reserves and national parks, as if the rules are being broken somehow.

'Elephants!' Rowan was delighted. 'Go closer!'

Dutifully, I put the car in gear and began to chug-chug slowly out towards the elephants, making sure not to startle them with too sudden an approach. When I was at the minimum safe distance – for these were not game reserve elephants habituated to vehicles driving up to them, and I had no idea how they'd react – I stopped. A hundred yards or so – enough to fly into reverse if necessary and make it out of there in one piece should one of the herd take exception.

'Closer! Get closer to the elephants, please!'

'This is about as close as I can get, Rowan. These ones might possibly attack us if we bother them and we don't want that!'

'CLOSER TO THE ELEPHANTS, PLEASE!'

There was such a plaintive note to it. Of course I wanted to satisfy his desire to commune with the great, beautiful beasts. But no way would it have been safe.

'Scub, I'd love to, but . . .'

'ELEPHANTS! ELEPHANTS! ELEPHAAAAAAAAAAAAAA AAAAAAAAAAAAAAAAANTS!'

It was amazing that the pitch of the shriek didn't shatter the glass of the car windows. It certainly shattered our frayed nerves. I tried to force down the urge to shout . . . and failed; turned around in the driver's seat and roared, at the top of my lungs:

'SHUT UP!'

There was an abrupt pause. Then the worried eyes, not understanding. Then the sobs. Floods of them.

'Just give me a gun and I'll go shoot myself right now,' I said to Kristin.

'Oh, it's all right, sweetie,' she was busy comforting Rowan, his body shaking, terrified by what I'd let fly. 'Daddy didn't mean it, he was just trying to keep you safe.'

But I had meant it. I was nearing the end of my tether. In an agony of embarrassment, shame, guilt at having lost control in front of everyone, at what I'd done to Rowan, I put the car into reverse and began to back away, for the elephants had noticed the noise and were putting up their trunks, testing the wind, testing our scent, deciding if we were friend or foe. Or rather whether we were foe they could ignore or foe that they needed to do something about. I turned the car around on the first piece of level ground I could find and drove slowly back over the wide grassland, back through the thick thornveld to Dau Post, where the healers were getting ready, the sound of my son's sobs loud around me.

6. Boiling Energy

A Bushman trance dance never begins formally. It's not something that is ritualized in a churchy sort of way. There's no hushed silence, no enforced sense of reverence or awe. Instead, people just start to gather in an area where, some time before, enough camel thorn wood – which burns hotter and longer than other kinds of wood – has been piled to meet the demands of the coming ceremony. There's a kind of happy expectation: people aware that healing is going to happen, anticipating a good outcome, whatever the night ahead may bring. There is laughter, villagers chatting together, kids playing. Rowan, recovered now, immediately went chasing around with the others as before, making sure to make a grab at the little girl who thought he was so terrifying (she duly burst into tears and started screaming as he put his hands on her head, then 'scoofed' away, laughing). There were greetings. Everything was informal. Michel could film the proceedings, agreed /Kunta and Gwi, who between them would be doing the bulk of the healing. It would be no problem. He could even come right into the centre of the circle, by the fire, where the spirits were strongest, if he wanted, but he should watch out – the force of the *nxum* might shut his equipment down.

'That happened to me in Mongolia last year,' laughed Michel. 'As soon as the healer went into trance, the light I had set up went out suddenly and everything I filmed ended up completely dark.'

Megan translated. 'Yes, that can happen,' said /Kunta. 'You aren't the first person to ask to film a healing – we don't mind but you never know what the equipment will do. Just so you don't get cross with us if it shuts down! We can't control it, you see. Once the *nxum* takes hold . . . it takes hold.'

'I understand,' said Michel.

/Kunta turned to me. 'Tell us again about the journey you made last year, and the healer who sent you to us,' he wanted to know. I had given him the bare-bones version, and no doubt Megan had too, but now, as we sat in the sand while the younger Bushmen built up the fire and people began to gather – some standing and chatting, some sitting where the circle would form around the fire, the women deftly pulling their skirts in under their backsides and settling comfortably in the soft sand, the men squatting on their haunches, some of them smoking, others flirting – I told /Kunta the full story.

While we talked, the fire was lit. One by one, as the light faded and the flames began to crackle, the rest of the villagers began to gather and Rowan, to my surprise, consented to cease rushing around and to come and lie quietly in my lap. 'Time to see the shamans,' he said. I was relieved: after he had twisted out of my arms when /Kunta and N!ae had tried to touch him earlier that day, I didn't hold out much hope for him seeing out the ceremony. As always, I was fully prepared to just leave if Rowan really didn't like it. But this was a perpetual worry: what if we had come all this way just to have to shut it all down before any healing could occur? *If* any healing could occur . . .

Night falls fast in southern Africa, being so close to the Equator. Both sunrise and sunset are brief, if spectacular, affairs. One moment the light was glowing, gold and pink – on the skin of the people around us, the sand we were sitting on, in the sky itself, against which the thorn branches were etched black like precise illustrations in an old picture book – then it was dusk, with flitting bats and the odd winking star, and then, abruptly, night, the whole southern firmament now ablaze with stars and the firelight bright in the centre of our circle. There were between thirty or forty people, not counting children: Kristin and I sat together, Megan and my mother a little way off to the right, the rest of the villagers in between. /Kunta and Gwi weren't in sight, but I could hear their low voices from the darkness somewhere outside the fire circle.

A snatch or two of song – the beautiful polyphonic chanting that evokes Africa itself come alive in the night – a snatch of rhythmic hand clapping and then the music would die, like a fire not quite getting started, and conversation took over once more.

Little by little, the brief phrases of song became longer, perhaps with a male bass note easing underneath the soprano melody, the hand clapping becoming more complex, before fading out again. And then, almost like the unconscious glide into sleep, where you are unaware of where waking ended and dreaming began, suddenly there was nothing but song and rhythm. It had begun.

The song swelled like a wave. Rowan sat up in my arms, looked around at the faces in the firelight. 'Bushmen!' he sighed and nestled back into my lap. I hugged him. How I loved him: his compact little body solid in my arms, the scent of his hair in my nostrils. The visceral, animal love which binds parent to child, father to son. The song lapped around us like a warm and gentle sea. So strange that he would just lie like this. He never usually did.

When the healers finally entered the dance, it happened softly, without warning, without theatre or ceremony. Suddenly they were just there. Dancing a slow, stamping dance, first around the inside, then the outside of our circle, their cocoon leg rattles shaking in counter-rhythm to the hand clapping and chanting of the villagers, their voices booming softly like the song of ostriches heard deep in the night.

The rhythm was complex: if you try to dance behind a Bushman healer – as occasionally I have been invited to do – you'll find it isn't as easy as it looks. Just as trying to follow the cross-rhythms of the hand clapping or the organ-pipe chanting is far from straightforward. But the dance is beautiful to watch, as the song is to listen to. Mesmerizing in fact, hypnotic.

/Kunta danced over to me. His hands touched my head. Gentle, fragile movements fluttering around the edges of my scalp, my brain, my mind. They travelled down the back of my head, on to the knobbly bit where the spine almost meets the skull – the place where your spinal cord gets ready to flow up your neck to the brain (Bushmen call it the *nxau* spot, where sickness is pulled from the body and healing is pushed in) – down my spine to my pelvis and back up again. Almost immediately, a deep calm came over me and I could discern a faint, pleasant buzzing in my spine, my heart, like a distant purring from some other place, some other person, felt dimly, at the furthest edge of sensation. Then his hands travelled to Rowan.

I braced myself for the inevitable scream. It came. But not from my son.

It was /Kunta. He went suddenly rigid, as if electrocuted. His scream rent the night, causing a momentary, shocked pause in the chanting song, then a moment later he was dancing again, but shouting at some unseen spirit, angry, his finger pointing, accusing. Then almost abruptly he laughed, sang a few snatches of some other song from whatever world he was in, and on he danced. It wasn't until he had moved on that I noticed that Rowan had gone limp in my arms.

I looked down. He was fast asleep.

Incredible. As the dance went on, and the chanting grew louder, the flames higher and hotter, the healing became more intense, the hands that touched him – /Kunta's, Gwi's – harder, their pressure deeper. These were things that would normally have freaked him out, yet through it all Rowan simply slept. Deeply, peacefully, the healing flowing over him like a river of caring, a river of empathy, a river of love; buoying him up, rocking him upon its surface while the current beneath ran deep and strong.

It washes over you, a Bushman trance dance, caressing you. Everything heals: the rhythm of the hand clapping and the counter-rhythm of leg rattles and foot stamping, the healer's touch, even the screams, rising to shrieks, and all you are required to do is simply be the recipient of the healing. For it was as much me as Rowan who received the healing from /Kunta and Gwi's hands – so rough-skinned yet the touch so gentle. Above all, it is kind: when you come for a healing among the Bushmen, the healer does the suffering for you.

Our first healing the previous year among the Mongolian horse herders had been somewhat different. Kristin and I had been whipped, we'd had milk spat in our faces, been laid under the pounding drums, and one healer had even drawn back his arm and hit Rowan with the ribbons of his drumstick to drive out the bad energy. It had been quite an ordeal, yet at no point had we thought that the shamans had anything but our best interests at heart and indeed it had transformed Rowan from a tantrumming, confused ball of distress to a happy, giggling child, playing with the shamans and making his first friend, Tomoo. And with Ghoste the healing had been equally effective, if a much more low-key affair.

But here among the Bushmen, despite the fact that this was clearly a hard healing for /Kunta and Gwi – both of whom, despite the rapidly chilling night, were shirtless and now bathed in sweat – for us, the recipients of the healing, the feeling was blissful. All the suffering was being done by the professionals on our behalf. And I was grateful. Because I was so used to being stressed. So used to everything being stressful. Everything seeming impossible, taking such monumental effort. All the things that ordinary parents could take for granted: a child speaking, a child pointing, a child playing with other children, a child getting toilet trained, a child who . . . Normal parents didn't know how easy they had it. How could they?

But to sit here, as the dance lapped around us like a warm, caressing ocean, and just let the healing come, to see how hard, so hard, the healers worked on our behalf – shrieking, screaming, laying on hands and occasionally going off on apparent scoldings and remonstrations with unseen figures in the spirit world – was oddly restful. And it wasn't just Rowan and me whom the healers laid hands on. They went to my mother, running gentle fingers over her head, her back, her neck, her chest. They went to Kristin and did the same and I saw the same blissful smile appear on her face, lit up in the firelight. They went to Megan, even Michel, filming, received some healing, and the villagers sitting at the fire.

But time and again, in between going to the others, /Kunta and Gwi returned to me and Rowan, sleeping so peacefully in my lap, no matter how loud their screams, their cries, no matter how hard the pressure of their hands. Sleeping as peacefully as if he had been at home, tucked up in his own bed.

Until, somewhere between one shooting star and the first sinister whoops of hunting hyenas from uncomfortably close by, the dance, abruptly, with a final stamp and handclap, as if by some invisible signal, was done.

/Kunta and Gwi were no longer in a trance. As suddenly as the dance, the song and rhythm, had ended, so they too stopped, sat down abruptly in the sand, each of them looking a hundred years old. Having given their all. And I, by contrast, felt loved, filled, replete, gently humming with the gift of being so cared for.

There was no need for words. As the villagers dispersed to their beds and my mother to hers, I took Rowan to our roof tent, hefting him in my arms, his heart against mine. Climbed the metal ladder with my son in my arms to sleep, nestled between me and Kristin, in the lullaby African night.

Dawn came without waking us. All three of us slept so soundly that it wasn't until the sun had risen high and was starting to beat down on the walls of the roof tent that we eventually woke, bleary with heat and ten deep hours of sleep.

And indeed, the day passed in a kind of dream. Around a slow fire and after a breakfast of tea, biscuits and – for Rowan – the inevitable bacon, /Kunta told us what he had discovered while in the spirit world. He knew about my efforts on behalf of the Bushmen in Botswana.

'They threw a bone at you,' he explained, 'which missed and hit your son instead. But don't worry: we see this kind of thing all the time. We will send it back where it came from.'

'What do you mean by "they threw a bone at you"?' I asked.

Megan translated, and I listened, as a very African story played out. Most powerful people, especially those in government, explained /Kunta, employed witch doctors to practise black magic – whether to increase their power, go after their enemies or try to influence others. 'It's always a bad idea,' he said. 'Witch doctors and the people who employ them always become sick in the end, and sometimes even die. Yet they never learn, they only see the short term. But don't worry: like I said, we see this all the time. We know how to neutralize it, how to send the curse back to the person who sent it so that it hits them with greater force.'

'I don't want anyone to be hurt,' I said. 'I only want healing for my son, for us. I'm not interested in revenge, or feud.'

/Kunta shrugged. 'If you wanted such things, I would not dance for you. It's not the Bushman way. But it's the way the universe works. When we undo a bad thing that was done intentionally, that bad thing travels back to the one who sent it and does its work there. There's nothing we can do about that. It's the way things are designed.'

I let this sink in. 'You really think the Botswana government hired a witch doctor to go after me when we won the Bushman land claim?'

'I'm just telling you what came through loud and clear while I was dancing for your son. I saw the witch doctor when I was in trance last night. A very bad man. And I could see who sent him, so yes. People in the government. This shouldn't surprise you: people like that do this kind of thing all the time. It always backfires on them. But it doesn't stop them trying.'

'I guess their attempts to dispossess the Bushmen in the first place backfired.'

/Kunta paused, pulled a newspaper roll-up from his shorts pocket, lit it with a stick from the little fire and took a deep pull. It never failed to amaze me how the Bushmen could smoke like that their entire lives, and drink all kinds of rough alcohol into the bargain, and yet keep going well into their nineties. Was it their healing? 'I guess you could say that it's true,' agreed /Kunta. 'Their attempt to dispossess the Bushmen did backfire on them. It always does: no matter what they do to us, we Bushmen endure. They can take our land, kill the game, evict us, do bad things to our women and children, make us fight in their armies, try to make us into farmers, herders, try to kill us off completely. Yet,' he shrugged, 'here we still are.'

We drove out that day to a grove of baobab trees, monolithic in size. Their bark was so smooth, almost like living skin – elephant or human, or something in between. There was one Goliath in particular that had grown out from a core that wasn't exactly hollow, more like a natural platform with living walls whose vastly thick branches had themselves hollowed out in their lower portions into smaller 'rooms'. A living treehouse – magical.

'Why don't people live in trees like these?' Michel wondered aloud, as he climbed up into the upper branches, Rowan scrambling a little way after him, me lumbering a bit behind, trying to steady him from falling. All day his mood had been great, totally calm. More than that, he'd pooped behind a tree, not in his pants, which for me, obviously, was a big deal. A huge deal. But did I trust it after all the recent regressions? Time would tell.

'I mean, this is like a natural fortress!' Michel was enraptured by this fairy treehouse, as we all were. 'You're safe from lions up here, hyenas, even elephants . . .'

'But not snakes,' said Megan, watching from below. 'In summer you get boomslangs, cobras, green mambas in these trees, hunting the small creatures – rodents, lizards, big insects. You have a better chance keeping those out of a hut on the ground.'

'I guess . . .'

Rowan was enchanted, scrambling around the treehouse (as it was winter, the snakes were all hibernating). 'I'm Pint Size on the barn roof! I'm going to scoof!'

Snakes in trees. It was true: danger lurked in the trees in Africa in the summer. One time, years before, I had been walking along the banks of the Kunene River between Namibia and Angola with two crazy German girls, and a huge rinkhals, a spitting cobra, had fallen out of the tree right next to me. We scattered, screaming.

Snakes in a tree, snakes in the grass – you never knew where poison might be lurking.

That evening the healers danced again. As before, it began casually: children chasing each other, villagers happily chatting and flirting. There were some new faces too: word had got around that two of Nyae Nyae's most senior healers were dancing for a little white boy from overseas, and more people had turned up – the shyly curious as well as those who came seeking healing for themselves. For when the *nxum* possesses a healer, he or she has no choice of to whom to go and transmit the healing – the energy itself directs them.

'What is *nxum* exactly?' Michel wanted to know. It was a question I myself had asked, many times, many years ago when I had first gone among the Bushman trance healers. It was liquid energy, they had told me. 'An energy that resides at the base of the spine, a sexual energy, life energy, the thing that makes us tick, makes us go . . .'

'You mean spinal fluid?' I'd naïvely asked.

'Perhaps,' had come the chuckling reply. 'It's energy first and foremost. We heat it, make it boil, draw it into our bellies to boil it there. It hurts, burns. Then we make it rise up, up our spines to our brain and out the top. *Poof!* And then when the boiling energy is steaming from the top of our heads, it is then we can begin to heal . . .'

So /Kunta and Gwi danced and danced. Their bodies, streaming sweat in the firelight, seemed to burn. It was cool, becoming cold in the winter night of the Kalahari. But the healers, dancing, suffering on our behalf, were hot to the touch – we could feel the heat from their hands as they placed them on our heads, our backs, our necks, our shoulders, as if they had put them in the fire before touching us. They were hotter than the night before. The cries of the healers, their screams, their shrieks intensified, echoing the sinister whooping of the hyenas – so close this night that the villagers had to jump up from the fire and chase them away, yelling and banging pots, while /Kunta and Gwi kept dancing, dancing. And in my arms my son slept, so peaceful, letting the healing wash over him like a hot tide.

Back from seeing off the hyenas, the villagers took up their chant and rhythm once more while /Kunta rounded on them, yelling, exhorting them to greater effort, more chanting, upping the tempo, and their voices swelled, rose to the challenge. For among the Bushmen the need for healing is always seen as collective, with everyone in the community partly responsible for everyone else. The true Brotherhood of Man principle: that your suffering is my suffering and vice versa. And so they rallied around Rowan – this little white boy from another life, another place, another world, yet the same world, connected. The song swelled, and my heart with it, because of their deep, loving kindness towards me and my son. My son.

Gwi danced over to us, began running his hands down us, singing, the sound beautiful, supplicating . . . then suddenly he stood bolt upright, shrieked a great rending shriek that sounded as though his soul had been torn open, and dropped to the ground as if shot.

Cries of consternation from the fire circle. Men rushed to where Gwi lay unmoving, picked him up, moved him closer to the fire. /Kunta bent over his friend, his lined face grieving, panicked. Megan, sitting next to me, translated as /Kunta screamed and cursed and gnashed his teeth, shaking his fist at the night.

'He's dead,' she said flatly. 'Gwi took the curse into his own body – it's a very generous but very dangerous thing for a healer to do. Now it's taken him.'

I looked down at my sleeping son, so peaceful despite the noise, the drama all around him. The hyenas that had ventured into the village so boldly – did that have anything to do with this? I had heard of shape shifting, though it was a concept I barely understood. Megan wasn't sure, but the concern on her face was real enough.

'Will he be okay?' Kristin asked from next to me. The singing and chanting, the clapping and stamping, had not broken rhythm. 'Have you seen anything like this before?'

'Very rarely.' Megan's eyes were fixed upon her friend as he tried to revive his co-healer.

'Will he recover?'

'Probably, but it'll take a while if he does, and he may not be much good after this. /Kunta will have to heal him before he can complete the healing for Rowan.'

'Will he be able to?'

'Well, /Kunta is one of the best. But I can see this has taken him by surprise. He's calling on God directly to intervene. We'll find out more tomorrow. For now we'll just have to wait.'

So we watched the healing within a healing unfold before us, /Kunta and N!ae, and some of the men from the fire circle, pressing their bodies to Gwi's unconscious form in order to channel all their *nxum* into him in a combined force – a kind of psycho-spiritual jump-start, you might say. It took a long time. /Kunta, dripping sweat, appeared to lose weight before our very eyes with the intensity of the dance, the healing, the suffering, one moment exhorting the singers to sing harder, more strongly, the next fighting for his friend, giving him his *nxum*, clawing him back from whatever place he was in, away from the dark forces he had gone to do battle with.

How long it took, I don't know, but the stars had travelled some distance on their axis by the time Gwi stirred. There was a joyful shout from /Kunta and his wife. An answering roar from the villagers, and gradually Gwi was brought up into a sitting position, head slumped, eyelids fluttering, mouth starting to move. /Kunta hugged his friend to him, stroked his head, caressed him, healed him. Then he and three others hauled Gwi to his feet and began dancing him in front of them, holding his still limp but gradually recovering body to /Kunta's as the senior healer moved his friend's body with his own, the other men steadying them as they re-entered the stamping, slow-moving dance. And the chorus of song and hand clapping swelled, rising heavenwards with a myriad sparks from the fire, drifting on the night wind, a song as old as the human heart itself. Perhaps older. Perhaps as old as whatever created us – the song of where we came from before we came here, and where we go back to when we depart.

Gwi's eyes opened. He took a stumbling step away from his friend, held himself upright a moment, then tripped and collapsed in the dust. /Kunta and his helpers scooped him up once more, began dancing him puppet like again, in front of them, until, a full round of the fire later, Gwi managed to take first one, then two, then three steps on his own. He was dancing again. Unsteady, but alive.

Had he actually died? Had he actually been brought back from the dead? What was reality and what allegory or psychic theatre? Were they the same thing? All I knew was that these people were working to an insane degree on our behalf, and I was grateful. Profoundly heart-grateful, for I could see with my own eyes their sweat, their tears, the fatigue, all being expended for the little boy who, throughout, slept on, undisturbed, breathing gently in my arms.

Shortly after this, Gwi danced over to us once more and laid hands upon us again, just as the sky began to lighten. Dawn was not far away, but the hyenas paid us one more visit, forcing the villagers to break off their singing once again and chase the predators – who can easily snatch a sleeping child – away into the bush. It was unusual for hyenas to be this bold. Was their raiding connected somehow to Gwi's 'death' and revival? I could only guess. But not long afterwards the song began to fade, the rhythm to slow, the intensity – like the fire at our centre – to die down. And suddenly, on a final handclap, a final polyphonic chord, the dance was done. I realized I was shivering with cold, Kristin too. It was time to sleep.

Just as we had the morning before, we slept until the heat building up on the side of the tent roused us. /Kunta and Gwi were nowhere to be seen when we finally woke, Rowan skipping off to play with the other children as if it was any normal morning back at home. The healers were played out, exhausted, Megan told us once we had found breakfast. /Kunta would no doubt report to us in the evening but most likely they would sleep all day. Gwi might need a couple of days to recover. It had been a very hard healing, and they would need to regain their strength.

As for me, I was feeling perhaps the best I had ever felt. Two nights in a row of receiving the best healing that humankind can offer. I had experienced this before in the Kalahari: a kind of quiet bliss, in which the usual anxieties, the usual worries, even the usual aches and pains – shoulders stiff from driving and worry, shin bones achy from old riding injuries – no longer bugged me. They would creep back, sure enough. But you could see how if you really lived this life, received this kind of healing on a regular basis – not just every few years when one was lucky enough to be down in the Kalahari – you might indeed live as long and healthily as these hard-smoking, hard-drinking, hard-living people clearly did, and experience the kind of quality of life (or perhaps quality of soul is a better way to put it) that was the human birthright and that, if everyone were to share it, would result in a kind of gross national happiness. Was the pursuit of life, liberty and happiness in fact no more than a desire to return to our most natural state – being happy? Was every human misery simply an aberration caused by having strayed so far from this original, authentic way of living, and no longer having access to healers who could set one straight every ten days or so when the mind and body started to get a little cranky?

Kristin felt it too. 'It's amazing,' she grinned. 'So . . . light. I can't describe it . . .' Even Michel, who both nights had shadowed the healers through their dance, through their crisis and out the other side again, and so had not received hands-on healing himself, beyond a few fluttering moments, even he was smiling. 'I think that what took place last night was the most beautiful thing I've ever filmed. Maybe ever seen.'

A young Bushman took us walking in the golden grasses.

Showed Rowan, normally so unresponsive to instruction, how to point and fire a small bow. Showed him the tracks of different animals: steenbok, duiker, the big hyena pads from the night before, the larger twin crescents of red hartebeest and kudu spoor. We painted ourselves with sandy mud at the new water borehole, put in by a development agency and ringed with a high stone wall designed to keep the elephants from destroying the pump in order to get at the water in the dry season. 'It doesn't work, they wreck it all the time,' the young man confided, through Megan. 'But it doesn't matter – we still know how to dig for water if we have to.'

It was only as the day wore on that my anxieties began to return. We had not been back to the lodge since the healings began. There was no way to find out if Besa and Jumanda were on their way from Botswana. And it mattered. Because later that afternoon, /Kunta and N!ae – Gwi was still out cold, recovering – told us that they had done all they could do.

'Gwi encountered the ill-wish, took it into himself and it killed him. We were able to bring him back. But it has taken all our energy. Your friend from Botswana will have to complete the healing.' /Kunta looked monumentally tired, as if he had aged five years, the lines on his kind old face deeper, his eyes more hollow in their sockets. 'We will need to rest now, replenish our energy. We have done the main work. The curse is lifted, sent back. The effect it had on Gwi will be much worse on those who sent it, but our work is done. Your friend from Botswana must come now and make the work complete.'

But would he? It had been such a tall order, to get an old man with no fixed address – a Bushman who lived under a tree – a passport and arrange for his travel across such vast distances not just of time and space, but of language and culture. Jumanda and I had been in reasonably regular contact about it before I had left the USA. But since being here, phoning and emailing had not been possible. We just had to have faith. As the afternoon wore on, the old tensions, old aches and pains, began gradually to return.

'It'll be all right, darling, I know it will,' Kristin tried to reassure me as we watched Rowan play, quiet and happy, in the dust with his toy animals, taking a break from his chase games with the other children. I hoped she was right.

As the sun began to set, we took our leave of Dau Post. 'I must rest again tonight,' said /Kunta. 'Tell your friend from Botswana to make the work good, strong. I will see you in a day or so when my energy is replenished. Go well.' And with that we took our leave.

Such a short distance in terms of miles it was, back to the sprawling shanties of Tsumkwe and the travellers' lodge on its southern outskirts. But it felt like a much, much longer journey from the world of the healers, the original human beings, back to the relative modernity of this town in the middle of the bush, where one could hear radios blasting African dance music and see litter drifting along the dirt roads. But when we reached the lodge, we found that friends had indeed arrived to see us.

My friend Belinda had driven two thousand miles up from South Africa to meet us. We hadn't seen each other in over three years, but we'd been close: not only had she been pivotal in the work with the South African Bushmen back in the 1990s – and still was, in fact – she had also helped me bring the Bushmen over to the United Nations. Suffice to say, we'd been through a lot together.

And just to make things more interesting, she had in tow an old mutual friend from the UK – a young Welsh girl who'd grown up with my niece and who was about to go to nursing school but had decided to travel South Africa first. I'd put her in contact with Belinda and her half-Bushman lover Tomas, who lived a wonderfully hybrid life along the dry riverbed marking the border between Botswana and South Africa. They occupied another border, too, one between modernity – they had a car, for example – and ancient times: they herded a few goats; lived in a house that was half grass shelter, half old trailer; gathered medicinal herbs; and produced art that ended up being shown in galleries in London and New York. A hybrid life, beautiful yet hard at the same time.

Because of the harshness that this way of life could entail, Belinda could be harsh herself. She was now: 'Rupert, you've got fat!' Half black, half white, she was a striking woman with hazel eyes whose feline gaze could sometimes lull and sometimes terrify you. 'You didn't tell me how far this bloody place was. I'm going to need all kinds of repairs to the car to get it home. Are you going to pay for them, hey? Give me a hug, you bastard.'

'Still your grumpy self, then.' I hugged her. 'No, I'm not paying for your bloody vehicle. I didn't hold a gun to your head to come here.'

'Touchy!' she grinned. In Africa, friends will drive miles, hours, days, to see each other. It's how it's done. Adventure is built into daily life here; it's not something you do sometimes, once in a while. In Africa, adventure *is* the day to day, the same old same old. One never feels so alive as one does here. So Belinda, when she'd heard that I was coming with my son to seek healing, had elected to drive up and join us, if only for moral support. 'I'll give you some bucks for the fuel, though,' I offered, knowing she and her boyfriend lived hand to mouth. 'And I appreciate you making the trip.'

'*Ja*, you'd better.' She kissed me. '*Ach*, but your boy has grown since I saw him last. And he's just like his dad, I see.'

I looked where she looked. Rowan was in Tayaba – the Welsh girl's – arms, clearly delighted with her. They had met before on trips to the UK, where she was a friend of the family. A tall, shy, dark-haired girl, more beautiful than she was conscious of, which of course only added to her charm, she had certainly charmed Rowan. He had pulled her down to lie with him in the sand, laying his head on her taut belly and making her flex and then relax it so that his head bounced. 'Say "*Hup!*"' he commanded, giggling. She flexed her belly, said '*Hup!*' and made his head bounce. He giggled. 'Do it again!'

'The apple doesn't fall too far from the tree, eh,' Belinda twinkled.

'I don't know what you mean.' Kristin, also smiling wryly,

came level with us. She looked at Rowan, giggling and 'hupping' away with Tayaba, both of them laughing together as they did so. 'How does he always get people to do exactly as he wants?'

'He's got no ego.' I had given this a lot of thought of late, Rowan's incredible, magnetic charm, the same charm I'd noticed in many young autistic children, so the words came out without my really searching for them. 'It's like, he doesn't want anything from you, doesn't want you to be anything other than yourself; it's like he allows you to just be you. Because he is just himself. And that makes you love him unconditionally, because that's what he gives to you, and he gives it first.'

'Kind of like being born enlightened.' Kristin tended to think in Buddhist terms, but it made sense.

'Yes.' I tried to follow the thought. 'Maybe that's how a deficit becomes a positive – I mean, if the autistic brain develops differently, is the lack of ego a part of that? And therefore the autistic child is happier, somehow, than the regular kids.'

'Or not just kids, grown-ups like us too . . .' Kristin finished the thought. 'It seems so.'

'The ancestors speak through him.' Belinda always liked to put a spiritual twist on things.

'But don't the ancestors speak through everyone, everything?' Kristin countered. 'I mean, even rock is sand, or ancient coral reef. We're all composed of elements that started somewhere else and will go off somewhere else when we decompose.'

We stood a moment in silence, considering this. Then Rowan, spotting me, suddenly stood up from Tayaba's 'hupping' tummy and ran over, eyes bright and shining, shouting: 'Wrestle with the Scub!'

Scubby games – or *geemz*, as Rowan liked to call them – were like the Scubby songs, a private language that we had evolved together over the years. New ones popped up every few months while the tried and tested ones endured alongside them. They would strike – like happy rays of sunshine through cloud – as random moments of joy at any time of the day, though often first thing in the morning. 'Wrestle with the Scub!' was one that had come back with us from Mongolia, where Rowan had seen wrestlers pushing each other over in contests on the open steppe. He and his friend Tomoo had wrestled all the time and he had taken to tackling me, too, as he did now.

We fell to the ground, him pretending to pin me, then me pretending to pin him – at which he'd shout, 'Let me go!' and I'd release him, which he found hilarious. The bubbling, happy Scubby giggle that made all things right with the world.

'Way jump!'

Scub was in full *geemz* mode now. I knew the drill. Stand up and pretend to look for him in a silly place. Like under a pebble, or in my pocket or shoe. It had to be absurd. 'Scubby! Where are you? Anyone seen Scubby?' While he giggled from his prone position in the sand. Then I pretended not to be looking for him at all, staring off into space, scratching my back, humming a little song. More giggles. Then without warning I launched myself into the air right at him, shouting: '*WAAAAAAAAAAAAAAAAAAAAAAAAAAAAA AAAAAAAAAAAAAAAAAAY!*'

Roars of laughter as I hung in midair and mid-yell for a full half second, then plummeted down right on top of him.

It's all in the roll. As you land, making it look as if your full weight is about to crash down on the giggling body below you, you actually take your weight on your elbows then roll to the side, allowing just enough pressure to make the giggle go up ten decibels then grab the giggling boy and tickle him, going: '*Scubbyubbywubbyyubbynubbylubbytubbygrubbynyubbyubby!*' The deepest happiness of life is in such moments between parent and child.

'Sing me a Scubby song!'

'Okay.' And I began:

> He was a Scubby boy,
> A little Scubby . . .

'Not that one! New Scubby song!'

I searched for inspiration – then it came to me, as these songs often did. A kind of reference to the sufferings of the past few weeks, made light, made healing.

> He was a whiney complainy boy
> Who was a little bit yelly . . .

Rowan collapsed into laughter. '*Yelly!*' he rolled the new word around his tongue, his mind. '*Little bit yelly!*'

> And on the ground he did a poo . . .

More laughter. From the adults this time too. I went on:

> That was a little bit . . .

I paused, wondering if he'd anticipate the rhyme. He did.

'*Smelly!*' he roared, delighted. 'Again! Sing it again!' And so I did.

'A masterpiece,' said Kristin, laughing despite herself. She looked at Rowan, shaking her head. 'Such a boy. Such a total boy.'

'The cutest little boy on the planet.' Tayaba, sitting up in the dust, held out her arms and Rowan, shouting, 'Charging Pumba!', tackled her and rolled her over. '*Hup!*'

She was right: he was. He was perfect. And there in that silly rhyme through laughter we had healed. Why was I so anxious to heal him? To change him? He was perfect as he was.

Late, late that night, with a steady chug-chug of diesel, Jumanda and Besa rolled in.

'You!' Besa said when he saw me emerge from my tent the next morning. 'You!' And he burst into song. 'Two Besas! Two of them! Count them! One, two! Two Besas!'

He meant me. Ever since I had first met him, he and his wife Katarina (as tall and lanky as Besa was short and compact, with his little round eyes that were part lion, part owl) had called me 'Besa' and so did all the other Bushmen I knew.

'Three Besas now!' I corrected him as I climbed down the ladder. And as if on cue, Rowan appeared behind me, yelled, 'It's Old Besa!' and came scrambling down, rushing past me and hugging the tiny yet powerful man before I could. Besa squatted down, eye to eye with his young namesake, and held his gaze. Rowan, usually immediately discomfited by such an invasive first-time meeting, held Besa's gaze without distress and laughed. 'Besa the Bushman shaman!' Then peeled away and went running towards the lodge kitchen and its inviting smell of cooking bacon.

Besa looked at me and smiled, nodded. We embraced. His body felt at once frail and strong in the way a young thorn tree is slender and strong. He seemed ageless. Though almost a decade had passed since we had last seen each other, I suspected it was I, running to fat, my beard streaked with grey, who was showing the years. The hunter-gatherer life seems to keep people young even when they drink as I knew Besa could drink, when he could get his hands on the stuff, and even when they smoked as I knew he smoked. As if on cue, he hawked up a great gob of phlegm and spat it into the dirt. 'Two Besas!' he shouted again. And with that, Jumanda appeared.

'*Ehe*, Rrru. Good to see you.' We hugged. 'Getting a little fat!'

'Don't you start! Anyway, you can't talk!'

It was true. He had put on some pounds since America. It suited him. So began a very happy day of reunion, remembrances, stories and song. Only Katarina, Besa's wife, held herself apart. Emerging only for the briefest of greetings before disappearing back into the shade of the tent that Jumanda had put up for her and Besa when they had rolled in late the previous night. Jumanda took me aside.

'I don't know what's wrong with Katarina. The last time I saw her and Besa she was her normal self. It's like something has happened to her. She's mad all the time, demanding money, alcohol. I'm sorry, man, it might be a little difficult.'

I was used to this. You never knew, when dealing with the

shamans, what the mood would be. Even Besa, sometimes when I had gone to see him, had been truculent, demanding booze, money upfront – even though the sums that change hands in shamanic transactions (it's not honourable not to pay, though a shaman will always treat you free of charge if you truly have nothing to give) are very small. In my early days working with indigenous peoples, I'd been shocked, had taken it personally when these sudden mood swings happened; when the person who had been my friend, had been so nice to me one week, turned surly the next, then, without warning, switched back again. It had taken an older Bushman to explain: 'Don't mind too much. It's part of our way. A lot of outsiders come in wanting things from us: our land, our knowledge of the plants and animals, to know how we heal. We test people to see how true they are. We need to see how you are when you fall out of love with us before we can trust you. Learn to take the rough with the smooth and we will open up our world to you.'

So the day was spent in a happy chaos. Everyone exchanging stories, catching up on what had been happening in our lives these past few years, joking, eating, drinking. We did a beer run for Katarina – not as much as she wanted (she wanted enough for oblivion), but enough for us all to share. Rowan played ecstatically with Tayaba and even my mother relaxed a bit more, as morning turned to afternoon and afternoon to evening. Jumanda, Belinda's boyfriend Tomas and I went firewood gathering. Enough for a trance dance. Megan had gone to fetch /Kunta, Gwi – who had recovered faster than expected – and their wives. It would be an intimate healing. Just a small group of friends, albeit very select – gathered from disparate corners of the subcontinent, the world. No villagers – or at least this time *we* were the village. Night fell, the fire was lit and we gathered around it, not quite knowing what would happen.

Because normally, to create a healing circle, you require a whole village, well versed in the polyphonic chant and complex clapping rhythms that the healers need in order to dance themselves into a state of altered consciousness – and we did not have that at the lodge.

There are no psychotropic plants in the Kalahari that can induce trance. To get his *nxum* boiling, to enter the spirit world, a healer needs the song, the rhythm, as a backdrop, or perhaps rather a portal through which to travel. Unless they are very, very senior healers, so versed, so practised in the art that they can slip in and out of trance at will. Ghoste, in Mongolia, had been that kind of senior healer. /Kunta and Gwi were that kind of healer. And Besa was too.

I had seen it happen to him before: once, when doing the final healing to help old Dawid Kruiper win back his people's land, Besa had fallen straight into trance long before the chorus had started, spontaneously bleeding from the nose as he began his healing song and the laying on of hands, without the need for any of the usual accompaniment. So now, with Besa, /Kunta and Gwi, we had three such powerful healers, at the very apex of their art, in our midst. What a privilege.

It was so intimate, this healing. Unlike anything I'd known among the Bushmen before, so quiet, so —what was the word – so *familial*. I sat in a chair, with Rowan in my lap – again strangely quiet after his rambunctious day, quieter than his normal restless self, not asleep this time but unusually still, in a way he simply never was normally.

That dance was strange, beautiful, sweet. As if a grandfather were healing his son and grandson. /Kunta and Gwi, and even Katarina – roused from her day-long grump – sang softly in the background but did not get up to dance or lay on hands. Besa danced alone, sang as his hands feathered our heads, our necks, shoulders, backs. He danced away from us, muttering and singing to the ancestors, to God, putting his hands on the others in turn, then danced back again, squatted down, pressed his head to our chests, our backs, once more. He moaned as if in pain, then the moaning turned euphoric, as if expressing the deepest possible pleasure. And there it was again, that feeling I had felt before at the best Bushman healings, that gentle inner hum, as if my body was producing bucketloads of quiet bliss and all my cells were drawing it in, slowly, like a sponge soaking in liquid love.

It lasted an hour, perhaps two, before, all of a sudden, Besa shook his head, shaking off the trance. He stood upright, smiled at me, patted me on the back, then his shoulders slumped, he looked immeasurably tired and, without a word, he and Katarina sought their beds. Quiet, happy, we sought ours too. Rowan, lying between Kristin and me, was out in a moment, snoring peacefully.

A few hours later, I woke to the sound of laughter. It was Rowan, giggling in his sleep.

Laughter in one's dreams. Could there be a better definition of human happiness? I turned over, warm, listening to the breathing of my family, until I too slipped back into the deep, dark pool once more.

The next day Rowan was strangely volatile. Up and down. One minute laughing, the next crying. He had another accident in his pants, threw a truly massive tantrum when Tayaba disappeared for a bush walk with Jumanda, Belinda and Tomas – a real, throw yourself on the ground, hit your head against things and have to be restrained type of tantrum. Yet in between these regressions were strange moments of unusual clarity.

'I need to learn to stop,' he said, when the tantrum was done. Kristin and looked at each other. Who was this child? We'd never heard him speak like that before. Then almost immediately, back he went into his scripted, more typically autistic way of speaking: 'I want to scoof! *Pigs Might Fly!* Charging Pumba!' and away he went, 'scoofing' all around the lodge's camping area. Then later, when the sun was going down: 'Wow, look at the cool sunset!' And then back to the scripted speech once more. Was this the healing working? Was real conversation about to break through the fog of autism mind at last?

My mother sat quietly, painting him, painting the others, as the day wore on. Such accurate portraits. Such a gifted artist she was. Such beautiful use of colour, mixing gouache watercolours and inks to capture perfectly the golden-brown of the winter grasses, the azure sky, the sunshine on Belinda's feline face, and Jumanda's dark skin flecked with amber light as the sunset deepened from gold to orange to red. She attempted some quick sketches of Besa too, capturing his owl/lion look, the strange penetrating, staring eyes, half sane, half mad, half of our world, half of quite another.

I sat with him for a quiet hour in peaceful, companionable silence. Besa rarely spoke, and when he did, it tended to be in snatches of song, riddle, rhyme. Occasionally he would say something fully lucid, fully coherent, but usually not. Often he would laugh, flap his hands, dance a few jigging steps as if to music in his own head. In our culture they'd have chucked him into the funny farm years ago. Yet here, in his culture, a culture where no human resources could afford to be wasted, he was a valued shaman, with a wife, children, grandchildren, a successful career. Was he autistic? It seemed so. Yet in his culture such a condition – one foot seemingly in the spirit world, one foot seemingly in our own – was regarded as a job qualification. Would our culture, currently experiencing such a massive rise in autism, one day learn how to harness the talents of our own autists, as the Bushmen and other indigenous peoples had? Only time would tell.

That night was the final dance. Like the previous night, it was gentle, easy, Rowan once again unusually quiet in my lap. It felt like being tended to by a father, a grandfather. Besa's song was sweet in the night. There were no jackals, no hyenas intruding at the edges of the firelight. /Kunta and Gwi had gone home earlier in the day. It was just us, the family and close friends, with Besa carolling to the stars in a low contralto. No pain, no screams, as if happy with what he saw in the world of the spirits, there on the other side of consciousness. And again, that peaceful hum somewhere in the dim recesses of the soul, Rowan lying back against me, so calm that both Kristin and I could do nothing but marvel. The song travelled around us, rising heavenwards with the sparks from the fire, everyone receiving their healing in turn, until, as the previous night, the song faded, the dance ended, Besa shook himself like a cat and, smiling, giving Rowan, Little Besa, one last caress, he disappeared into the dark.

7. Questions and Answers

Parting was indeed a sweet sorrow. Besa was ageing fast: would this be the last time I saw him? So much of my adult life had been affected by this man, despite the relative handful of meetings we'd had over the past fifteen years. It had been he who had first really talked to me of healing, in one of the only few lucid conversations with him I had ever had, when we had first met back in the late 1990s, under a tree in western Botswana. The tree – an acacia – had been in blossom after the rains, and the sweet, citrus-scented flowers had attracted clouds of flying beetles with the most amazing yellow-and-black-striped carapaces. Like flying humbugs. He had fixed me with his owl/lion eyes and told me how, when he wanted to heal, he would fly abroad as a bird, seeking the spirit of the sick one, and when he found it lying there in the sunlit bush, he would hop on to its back and sing the sickness out of it. Feeling the light bird's presence on its back, the spirit would smile, and when he felt that smile, Besa could go back to his body and rest.

Is that what he had done with Rowan, with me, with us all, these past two nights? The songs had been so gently joyous, guaranteed to make one's spirit smile.

Besa had been the healer that the South African Bushmen had requested to lead the ceremonies aimed at winning their land back in 1999. And then he had led healing for the return of the Bushman land in Botswana. And now, a decade and a half later, he had healed my son. Or so I hoped.

Life, family, career, it was all tied up with this strange, adult autist hunter-gatherer shaman who knew more than I would ever know, and who said so little, but whose influence reached out to hearts and minds across the globe. If all things human begin and end with the San Bushmen, then Besa, for me at least, personified this beginning and ending.

We hugged, and then he, Jumanda and Katarina chugged away in the diesel Toyota 4x4 that I had raised the money to buy them years before. Would I see them again, I wondered.

Megan was staying – she had work to do in Nyae Nyae for her own Kalahari Peoples Fund, and Belinda, Tayaba and co. were going to stay on a little longer too. So when the goodbyes were done, Kristin, Rowan, my mother, Michel and I all climbed back into our rented vehicle and headed west, starting the long road that would take us back to the real world once more. If it was the *real* real world – perhaps both were in their different ways.

We hadn't been gone long before Rowan suddenly became aware that Tayaba, with whom he had fallen deeply and firmly in love, was no longer with us. 'Tayaba? More Tayaba?' Rowan's voice had that querulous note that made me instantly cringe, or rather flinch, the solar plexus tightening. I was so conditioned – just the rise in tone of voice was enough. And then it came.

'TAYABAAAAAAAAAAAAAAAAAA! WANT TAYABAAAAAAA AAAAAAA! TAYABAAAAAAAAAAAAAAAA!'

The tantrum hit like a punch to the heart. The worst I could remember since before Mongolia. The car rang with it, our skulls rang with it, rattling our eyeballs in their sockets. Like emotional, sonic artillery going off point blank inside your head, all around you. There was nothing anyone could say. No way to fight it, avoid it, end it. We drove, the vehicle exploding with sound, anger, upset, rage, distress. Miles passing, the bush outside the window as tranquil as the explosions within the car were not.

A full hour, a seemingly endless hour, an hour of utter torture for the mind and heart; for as much as it was torture to listen to it, it was more torture for poor Rowan to suffer it from within. What parent, caught between rage and frustration, despair and compassion, would not feel their heart was being squeezed in a vice, in a fist, leaving them choking, gasping, raw?

And then, like a storm moving off the mountain, it passed. For a while we drove in stunned, shell-shocked silence. And then as if nothing had ever been wrong, a sweet, quiet voice from the back said, '*Pigs Might Fly!*?'

'Oh, do you want me to read to you, darling?' The relief in my mother's voice was palpable. 'Of course! Now, let's just see where I put the book.'

We drove in easy stages, down long, long back roads of red dirt, white sand, orange gravel, purple shale, the flat Kalahari bushland an ocean, stretching to infinity in every direction. My mother's reading voice, precise and calm, flowed over us, a healing balm after the jagged trauma of the previous hour. Rowan's mood continued sunny. We stopped to eat lunch by the roadside at a place where rugged, flat-topped hills of blood-red rock began to rise above the sea of leafless dry-season thorn. Rowan climbed up to the roof of the vehicle.

'A bird's eye view!' he shouted joyously, chomping on cold bacon. 'I can scoof from here!'

Was it just me, or was his use of language just a tad more lucid?

We camped up in those hills – hills that rose to small mountains with straight-sided crimson cliffs, on whose tops rose springs of precious water. The Waterberg Plateau, as it is known, is another national park – a protected area still rich in game. That evening we saw white rhinos – the more placid, larger, cousins of the ornery, nearly extinct, black rhinos we had seen in Etosha. Was that just a week or so ago? It felt like months, years. That same evening, Rowan asked where the toilet was. I walked him to the outhouse in the little private campsite we had found on a farm that let travellers pitch tents on its land. He shut the door on me, went in, did his business. Like a normal kid. Or at least like the kid he had been before the regressions set in. But would it last?

In the cool of morning, he and I took a walk together. 'Come on, Dad,' he said. I didn't need telling twice. Shoes discarded, we walked along, the cool red sand refreshing on the soles of our feet, baboons barking on the cliffs above us, strolling in companionable silence together, father and son, barefoot in the bush, as fathers and sons have done together since time immemorial. I loved him. I loved him so much.

Interestingly, the usual bickering between my mother and me dwindled almost to non-existence, and even – God be praised – a little humour crept in from time to time. Perhaps it was me – less reactive because Rowan was suddenly back to using the toilet once more, and because the tantrums, after that last mega-eruption in the car, had gone into abeyance. Or perhaps the healing had rubbed off on the dynamic between my mother and me, too?

The night before leaving Namibia, we had stayed in a lodge not far from the airport, where they had horses and you could ride out among the game animals. There was also an aviary in the main reception area, full of little blue and green parakeets that Rowan found entrancing.

'Get a parakeet?' he asked.

'Why not? When we get home. We can get two, because they like company.'

'Green one and a blue one?'

'Absolutely!'

Rowan's face lit up like sunshine. God, what would I not do to see that face happy? So we mounted up, one of the safari guides riding ahead of us, on a good, quiet horse, Rowan perched in front, leaning back against me as we rode out among the hartebeest, impala and wildebeest grazing quietly in the morning chill, both of us singing a song as our bodies – or rather one body, one heart – followed the movement of the horse.

I started:

Two little parakeets, two little parakeets, two, little, parakeets . . .

And he sang back in his turn: '*Two little parakeets, two little parakeets, two, little, parakeets . . .*'

Then me:

Two little parakeets, two little parakeets, a green one and a blue one.

And then him: '*Two little parakeets, two little parakeets, two little parakeets . . .*'

Leaning, reaching back and putting an arm around me – so casual. Enough to melt the heart. The horse snorted in the cold air, startling a group of zebra ahead of us, so that they bolted briefly, then stopped and turned to look back, watching the humans, man and boy, ride past them in the morning.

'Ride Betsy!'
  'You want to ride with me?'
  'Ride Betsy by myself!'
  'You really want to?'
  'Yes!'

We were back home, standing in my front field with Betsy saddled and ready for us to go on our daily ride together. Rowan, since our return, had been riding her solo more and more, mostly towards the end of the ride when we were just walking or gently trotting the last couple of hundred yards back to Stafford's barn. Today, though, was different. I had gone over to fetch Betsy, Rowan being engrossed in a morning cartoon show, expecting to venture out together as usual on one of our regular trail rides: to the climbing tree down in the Arbuckle pastures a mile or so away; to the splashy creek on the A and L ranch; to the 'dead armadillo' – a ranch a little further off where we had once found the decaying carapace of an armadillo in the tall bluestem grasses, and where one occasionally spotted a small pack of coyotes lying up; or to the 'deer bit' – a stretch of open woodland where we sometimes surprised does and their fawns, and even a wild pig or two.

But today Rowan wanted to ride by himself right away. He'd never asked for this before. 'Okay,' I said nervously, casting an eye around the small pasture. The gates were closed. What was the worst that could happen? If she took off, she couldn't go more than fifty yards or so, and I'd never known her do that if her head wasn't pointed towards home, which it wasn't as we were in my front pasture, not over at Stafford's. Anyway, I'd be right there within grabbing distance of the reins, and he'd been practising controlling her over this past year.

'Okay,' I said. 'Why not?'

So we walked together, the good bay mare, to whom I owed so much, snorting contentedly as we walked along the board fence, side by side.

'Take her for a little trot,' said Rowan.

'You're sure?'

'Take her for a little trot.' He was insistent.

'Okay – give her a little kick with your heels . . .' He gave her a bit more than that. She shot forward. He giggled. I ran beside Betsy, a gentle hand on the reins to regulate her speed. Rowan rode so well, the years of having sat there in front of me paying off – his seat was so steady despite the bounce of the trot, which can make most beginners fall or at least throw them around. His hips simply absorbed the motion, just like a trained rider's – which I guess he was in a way. I jogged next to them, sweating in the early autumn humidity. Then suddenly Rowan giggled again, saying, 'Give her a little kick!' and booted her properly with his heel. She surged forward into a canter. I couldn't keep up. Damn! Away she went from me. My heart in my mouth, my precious child on top of the great, cantering beast. And then, miraculously, he simply turned the reins against her neck, sitting back, as he had seen me do a thousand times, and turned her, in mid-canter, back towards me, loping back in a steady three-beat footfall to where I stood, heart racing, and stopped her. A rider.

I could have cried.

It had been like this since we'd got back from Africa. Adventurous, trying new things. He was just more . . . more *awake* somehow. The use of the toilet was back on schedule and the tantrums, after the final one over Tayaba, had faded once more, thank God. But after the regressions of a few months before, I was taking nothing for granted. And the easy, age-appropriate conversation I had hoped for at the start of the year still eluded us. But what *had* started, almost as soon as we had returned from Africa, was a mathematical understanding that had not been there before.

It had started the week we got back. The New Trails Center now had several local autism families coming every week, and I now had three horses living there full time: Clue and Hope, both quarterhorses like Betsy, who still lived with Taz and Chango at Stafford's, as she always had; and El Capitan, a grey Arabian gelding. I had given them some trick training, so that they would encourage the kids to develop social skills (I smile, the horse smiles; I shake hands with the horse; I bow, the horse bows . . .) as well as general instruction. One morning, soon after our return from Namibia, I had taken Rowan on board Clue with me and gone into the round pen. 'Let's ride all the way round,' I just casually said, and we'd cantered in a circle.

'Now let's go halfway round,' and so we cantered halfway and stopped.

'And now let's do the other half – want to do that at a walk, trot or canter?'

'Canter!'

We cantered the second half and stopped. 'That's interesting: so two halves make a whole! I wonder what half of a half is? Want to do that at the walk, trot or canter?'

'Canter!'

'Okay. Canter in an evil Godzilla voice with horns on your head, or canter in a nasty voice with tickles?'

'Evil Godzilla voice with horns!'

'Okay, then. *RIDING . . . fffprrt . . . HALF . . . splrrrt . . . OF . . . phplrrt . . . A . . . splurrrrrt . . . HALF . . . frrrppplt!*'

He giggled as Clue came to a halt. 'They call that a quarter, I'm told,' I said conversationally.

The girl we had hired both as his teacher and to start running the playdates for the families who came in the afternoon, when the 'school day' was done, picked the ball up and ran with it. Within two weeks, Rowan, having had no maths at all beyond some very basic addition, was doing simple arithmetic on paper. Within six weeks, he was doing fractions. Within twelve weeks or so, he was adding and subtracting fractions in double columns and carrying the numbers.

Was this the result of the Bushman healing? Was it because I had tapped into some basic principle of kinetic learning – the idea of having a casual conversation about a concept, like fractions, and then doing it with one's body, the horse's body, or both? More than that, the horse could carry us through these exercises . . . Kinetic learning, learning not by sitting at a desk and reading the information, but by doing it with one's actual body. *Hmmmm* . . . my little brain (slightly smaller than a squirrel's) began to tick.

Meanwhile, New Trails was really taking off. The families coming out were bringing kids aged from as young as two to teenagers. We even had one man, Howard, newly diagnosed with autism at sixty-five, who had been regarded as just plain 'odd' all his life. And we were getting results. When we laid autistic people on the horses – no saddle, just letting them relax there as if on a big old couch, like Rowan first had on Betsy – their 'stimming' would frequently just fall away. When we rode with them in front of us in the saddle, especially when we went at a canter, their brains would seem to 'switch on', frequently followed by a rush of euphoria and laughter and then, as often as not, words. When the whole family came out together, or at least one parent and a sibling or two, then real healing seemed to occur. The mother, always so stressed, could relax in a place where she and her children weren't judged. The girls could get a riding lesson. And the boys benefited too: maybe they didn't like horses but just wanted to kick a football. As chance would have it, the boyfriend of another girl I hired happened to be a pro soccer player for the local Austin team . . .

Normally, for autism siblings, having an autistic brother or sister meant that all the time, money and emotional energy of the family (or more usually, the single mother – as I was finding out, 80–90 per cent of autism marriages break up under the stress) were funnelled into the autistic child and hence their own dreams and desires were being shut out by it. Now the doors to their dreams were being thrown wide open *because of*, not in spite of, their brother or sister's condition. The family dynamic, the family's attitude to autism itself, often changed before our very eyes.

The other girl I had hired to help with Rowan's teaching was an ABA therapist. ABA, or applied behavioural analysis, is a type of therapy in which young autistic children are encouraged to mimic 'appropriate' social behaviour as a prelude for learning to cope in the wider world. It was something I wasn't altogether comfortable with: to my mind, what I had seen of it was at best Pavlovian, at worst coercive, verging on abusive. The first two ABA therapists we had tried some years before had been, in the first instance, bitchy and bossy and, in the second, sweet and engaging. But each had argued that Rowan would *have* to mimic the socially appropriate behaviour that she wanted before he could get a 'reward' (going outside to play, having a snack . . .) – no matter if he threw himself at the door, the walls, screaming in distress. He would need to 'cry it out', they said.

I wasn't interested in having my already anxiety-ridden son throw himself at walls or self-harm in any way, so after just two or three sessions of this, Kristin and I had called a halt to the whole proceedings. It had also been frighteningly expensive. But as ABA at the time was regarded at the most effective autism therapy, Kristin and I had taken a fair amount of flack from other autism parents, who believed very much in ABA, until eventually they prevailed upon us to give it another go. There was a new generation of ABA therapists, they said, whose techniques were based on intrinsic rather than extrinsic (reward-based) motivation. So we interviewed various therapists before choosing one who had assured us that, yes, if Rowan wanted to be in a tree, she would teach him in the tree. If he wanted to go on the trampoline, she would teach him on the trampoline. It sounded just what Rowan needed: being taught appropriate social skills – asking people their name, introducing himself, saying please and thank you, learning the back and forth of conversation – alongside his academic subjects. And of course other staff (local volunteers) would be available for the kids of the other families that came in during the afternoon.

It quickly became clear that Rowan didn't much want to be around when the other families came, in any case. So either Kristin or I would pick him up from the centre mid-afternoon – and usually that's when he and I would go and ride Betsy, and the other families would then come for their sessions. It seemed that here was a workable system, a really good replacement for the dysfunctional special-needs class we had pulled him out of back in 2005, and an improvement on the hippy-style schooling he had had in between. His academic teacher was alternating between following the national curriculum as best she could, and tailoring it, in consultation with us, around Rowan's love of animals and wildlife, punctuating the schoolwork, every fifteen or twenty minutes or so, with bouncing on the trampoline under the open sky. And the sky was very open at New Trails, swept by the prevailing breezes. In summer a south wind blew constantly across the blackland prairie – called 'blackland' because of the rich black clay that nourished the grass on which bison had once grazed. In winter the place was cooled by the northern fronts – or 'blue northers', as they call them in Texas, owing to the colour of the sky – bringing arctic air down from the northern plains, sometimes with ice storms in their wake.

And there were the usual Texas eccentricities. Knowing how good it had been for Rowan to have pygmy goats to interact with when he was younger (he had used to bring them into the house and tuck them up in his bed, saying, 'No baby goats in the ho-ouse . . .' to tease us when we found him snuggled up with them, having followed the little trail of telltale black droppings from the front door up the grey-carpeted stairs to his room). So we'd bought more goats for New Trails, but every so often that autumn, as the warmth gave way to the first frosts, they would break out of the pen we had built for them and go AWOL for a while before returning to the centre, occasionally with one particular neighbour screaming in their wake – waving a gun and yelling that he'd shoot them all if we couldn't keep them in. He didn't specify whether this meant goats or people. I sat up waiting for him a few times, but suspected that he only wanted to come by when the young female staff were around.

We learned to keep the goats in. And the families thrived. The only problem was New Trails was haemorrhaging money; we had bought the place, refurbished it, bought horses, hired staff . . . and I couldn't bring myself to charge the families, as I knew they were as broke as I had been in the early years of Rowan's autism – and might become again if I kept on like this, without a clear game plan. Although we were now a functioning non-profit organization, I was going to have to learn how to fund raise properly, or none of this would last.

But for the moment, Rowan – and all the other kids who attended – appeared to be doing well, riding, learning, thriving . . . Winter came and I finished *The Horse Boy*, both the book and the film. Michel and I, plus the two editors we managed to hire for what we could afford, had assembled on computer material from the 250-odd hours of footage we'd taken before, during and after Mongolia, putting together what we hoped would be a reasonable documentary. Which, seeing as we'd never made one before, was something of a tall order.

We showed it to a test audience of friends. They hated it. 'All those shamans,' said one of them sarcastically. 'It's like you're going to some spiritual Kmart or something!'

'Spiritual Kmart?' I was incredulous. 'You're going to sit there and look me in the eye and tell me that I went with my son to Mongolia the spiritual Kmart? You really think that?'

She considered. 'No, no, of course I don't. But I'm not feeling it – what can I say?'

So back to the drawing board we went, again, again and again, until, at last, people told us it was watchable.

It was torturous, watching it over and over, wondering how much screaming tantrum footage was too much and how much was just enough, reliving all that suffering. Rowan would come in and out of the room sometimes while I was watching the rushes at home, trying to make decisions about what should stay and what should go. Sometimes I'd ask his opinion and he'd say 'Keep it' or 'Take out'. And so I would, as he directed, and gradually a better film emerged. If Rowan had a sense of how he himself appeared in the movie, he didn't show it. It was more dispassionate, his reactions on the lines of 'There's Tomoo!' and 'Whack, whack, whack on the back like a shaman' or 'Crying Rowan' and 'There's Blackie'. There seemed to be no ego involved, only observation of what actually *was*.

Finally, when the film was done, we submitted it, a little cheekily, to Sundance. To our amazement, they accepted it. So we went to the Sundance Film Festival, wondering if we'd be rubbing shoulders with movie stars up there in the little ski town of Park City, Utah, where the festival takes place. We didn't: the movie stars who do attend stay off in secluded compounds surrounded by security and only show up for specific events. But although we met no celebrities, we did – to our vast surprise – sell the movie to television and cinema. We couldn't believe it.

Then, that same spring, the *Horse Boy* book was published. It was exciting – for about a minute and a half. The day the first review came out in the *New York Times*, the same paper's online threads built up an immediate and stunning mass of hate mail. Who was I to expose my child to crazy shamans? Who was I to say horses could cure autism? That shamanism could cure autism? What kind of a deluded idiot would write a book like this?

Of course, no one had actually read the book yet – it had only been out a day, so none of the haters knew that I wasn't actually saying any of those things, didn't even want a cure, but simply wanted to relate our experience. But that made little difference. In the UK, things were much the same – hoots of derision from critics and social media. Kristin and I weren't that surprised – I mean, after all, if you put your head above the parapet, people will throw mud at you, it's part of the human condition. But the ferocity of some of the reactions the book attracted was disturbing. The conservatives thought we were straying from orthodox approaches, giving false hope and leading others astray – even though we stated explicitly that we had tried and *continued* to try *all* the orthodox methods, even ABA, and had merely added a couple of unorthodox ones as well (horse riding and healers). The liberals thought we hadn't gone far enough, that we should have mounted a full-on attack on Western medicine and the orthodox approaches – which would have made us hypocrites because we used both. As one Fox News reporter who came to interview us for CBS's Katie Couric show joked: 'Wow, you've managed to piss off both the liberals and the conservatives at the same time. That's quite an achievement.'

But there was one group that did support us: parents. Much of the motivation for telling the story in the first place had been my own despair at the time of Rowan's diagnosis. If, back then, there had been some story of hope, some tale of autism as an adventure rather than as a catastrophe, I would have taken heart sooner, despaired less, made friends with the condition sooner and most likely found solutions more quickly. But the physicians, the therapists and other professionals were all united in viewing autism as, at best, a problem to fix, though they had no idea how to, and at worst a disaster from which you and your child would never recover. They wanted you to buy their therapies but hadn't actually 'fixed' anyone with them – how could they when autism is a clinical not a medical diagnosis? But it didn't stop them presenting themselves as if they could. And they scaremongered – if you didn't do ABA, you were going to lose your child; if you didn't try Ritalin (which we never did and never will), your child would spiral out of control and never learn anything. And yet, as shown by both the book and the film (which, after all, were pieces of journalism – straight-up accounts of what happened, no more, no less), the diagnosis had not stopped us as a family from having the adventure of a lifetime. Indeed, it had been the *cause* of our having the adventure of a lifetime. In fact, it was the autism, not so much the journey, that had been the adventure.

And we weren't the only ones coming to these conclusions. For every piece of hate mail or critical derision, we got three letters from parents saying either that they too had found their child's autism bringing them to a better place than they had been in before the diagnosis, or that *The Horse Boy* story had given them some hope, that maybe the professionals' presentation of their child's autism as one big disaster might not be true. Some people, of course, had even taken their child to see shamans, especially those (like a Jamaican couple who wrote from New York, and a South American couple now living in London) who had cultural ties, as I myself did, to places where shamanism existed. Word spread; the book and movie started getting translated into language after language. With the sheer numbers of kids being diagnosed with each passing year, a lot parents were finding themselves in the same boat as us, bumping their noses against the limitations of the orthodox approaches and looking for alternatives.

In France, as I found out when I went there to do a small book tour, kids with autism were still being treated by psychiatrists, institutionalized and given psychotropic drugs even stronger than the Ritalin and other mood-altering pharma-concoctions that we had so assiduously avoided (not to mention the Prozac, Xanax or other drugs we might have taken to relieve our own stress) back in the States. Worse, some French psychiatrists were still blaming what they termed 'refrigerator mothers' (lack of affection in the early years between mother and child) for their kids' autism – a fallacious theory long discredited in the rest of the world, and a wounding and insulting label for a mother only trying to help her child.

Oddly, though, we got a lot of support from, of all people, doctors. Many, like our own paediatrician, took the very honest view that orthodox medicine didn't have much to say about the current autism spike, because the growth in numbers was out-galloping the pace of scientific research into what was causing it. 'Anything that gives you a good result, as long as it doesn't hurt the child, just go for it!' our paediatrician had said. My own uncle Peter, an eminent research oncologist at University College Hospital in London and not afraid to speak out against what he regarded as any form of pseudoscience, also had an interesting response. We had just shown the *Horse Boy* movie at a small private cinema in Soho, a private screening for family and close friends so that they could have a preview before it came out on TV. When it was over, I waited for my uncle's reaction. Horses, shamanism, surely he would think it was all bullshit? As he came up to me, I mimed opening an umbrella and holding it over my head to protect myself from the inevitable deluge. 'Go ahead,' I said. 'Do your worst! I'm ready.'

But, to my surprise, what he said was, 'Actually, I think this is interesting. You're putting something out there that says autism isn't the end of the world. That alone has value. I don't know anything about horses, but I do know a lot of people are reporting good results from therapies that involve them. The shamanism is interesting, too. After all, one could say there is something perhaps not dissimilar in Western medicine – the placebo effect. Many of our current medical practices rest on it, even though it's completely irrational and we can't yet explain it. We know it works, but we don't know why. It could be that something similar is going on with the shamans.'

An intriguing thought and one I hadn't really considered until then. As my uncle and other doctors I spoke to have pointed out, when we take a prescription drug, we think of it as a highly rational, scientifically based treatment. But it's not entirely rational, in fact. Before any drug gets approved, it has to go through a drug trial. As part of the trial there is a 'blind' control group of sick people who do not get given the drug being tested – they get a placebo instead. And some of the people in that control group get better. They don't just think they get better, and then fall back into their sickness again later. They actually get better. We don't know why this happens, but no drug gets approved for sale unless it has been through such a trial. Now of course we, as drug consumers, are not present at that trial, so we don't see the people being given the placebo and getting better, we just go and get the drug. At a shaman's fire you see the whole process unfold before your eyes. But is it necessarily so different? Just as a shaman might explain an illness in terms of the sick person's connection to his or her ancestors, a doctor might talk about genetics. Both mean to a large extent the same thing: an inherited condition that needs to be treated accordingly.

I began to dig around and found that there was surprising overlap between Western doctors, often very eminent and well regarded, and shamanism/traditional healing. I met a South African-born surgeon, for instance, Dr David Cumes, now living and practising in the US, who had also become a traditional *sangoma* or witch doctor (one of the nice kind, not the sort who practise black magic). He explained that having seen the efficacy of herbal remedies for physical ailments and witnessed the healing of chronic conditions by traditional means, he – as a trained physician himself – could no longer justify not using every type of healing at his disposal. For him, he said, it was about broadening his professional competence. He also told me how doctors running hospitals in many tribal areas of the world routinely allowed a traditional healer – whether a shaman, witch doctor, *curandero*, *sangoma*, *inyanga* or whatever the term was in that country – to visit and treat patients on their wards, and that often the best policy in an unfamiliar part of the world was to ask the local doctors and nurses in tribal-area clinics to recommend someone whom they regularly called upon to conduct traditional healings, as this seemed to get people out of hospital beds (alive, not dead, of course) faster than more orthodox treatments. This could be done through the internet and email, he pointed out – a seemingly unlikely yet logical meeting of the old world and the modern, and proof positive, perhaps, that there is nothing new under the sun.

Then there was the woman whom I met at an autism conference in Orlando who told me about her own son. He had sustained a traumatic brain injury in his early teens and had had to rebuild his mind, his speech, motor skills, everything, from scratch. His injury had been so severe he'd been treated at Johns Hopkins Hospital, the premier centre in the US for treatment of neurological disorders. It was while he was on the children's ward there that he had been treated by a faith healer, a woman called Rosalyn Bruyere.

I did a double take. 'Johns Hopkins Hospital had a faith healer on the ward?'

Yes, the mother confirmed, the doctors there allowed the faith healer to work with the children on a regular basis. Hold on, I stopped her – this is *Johns Hopkins Baltimore* we're talking about here? Absolutely, she laughed, acknowledging that it seemed unlikely, but adding that this woman also visited numerous other American hospitals and institutes. Her son had made a recovery to the extent that he was now back playing basketball. How much of that did she think was attributable to this healer, I asked. Rosalyn Bruyere was not a tribal healer, it appeared, but an American woman from a more Christian-based background. The mother shrugged. 'All I know is that the doctors there fully endorsed her and the kids she worked with seemed to get better really fast.'

The book and film were going to be released in Australia late that summer, or rather winter, as it was down in the Southern Hemisphere. The publishers and distributors had invited to fly us down there to help promote both, and it occurred to me that this might, therefore, be a good place to seek Rowan's next healing. After all, Ghoste had told us in no uncertain terms that we needed to make three more journeys to three more shamans after Mongolia for the healing to be complete. Australia seemed a good choice to look for a good shaman; my understanding was that the Aboriginals still had a very strong culture of healing. But I knew no one down there.

So I started looking up tribal-area clinics in the far north and the northeast of Australia, up near Papua New Guinea, including the Torres Strait, Northern Territory and Daintree Rainforest areas – vast, logistically difficult regions to travel into, as places that have good shamans often are. As expected, it took weeks, months, for my emails to be answered; most merely disappeared into the ether, but those few replies that I received spoke, at least apocryphally, about a woman healer in the Northern Territory and a man in the Daintree Rainforest as having achieved good results with outsiders. So it seemed that it would be one of these two areas that we targeted.

Naturally, I was doing other research as well, talking with anthropologists, reading up as much as I could, trying to check my sources against one another. When going into tribal areas, no matter how much preparation you've done, there are never any guarantees, of course. Maybe the shaman will be there at the time you visit, and maybe he/she won't. Maybe the shaman will feel that, yes, this is something they can take on, and maybe they won't. Maybe the information you've got about how to reach the area will be accurate or maybe people will neglect to tell you of a seasonally dry riverbed that, when you get there, is boiling with flash-flood waters that hold you up for a week. Or maybe torrential rains, or wildfires, or something as banal as a local transport workers' strike, or some other unforeseen event, will delay you either getting in or coming out. Either way, you need to allow for some wiggle room.

I was also a little leery of the Aboriginal healing culture itself: some of the peoples of that continent are warrior tribes, and warrior tribes, unlike pacifist cultures such as those of the Bushmen and the reindeer people of Mongolia, can be prone – as old /Kunta had warned – to using shamanism for black magic. Equally, sometimes the right warrior healer can be a good person to go with. But, as I was reassured, the majority are not that way inclined, and the chances of blindly running into one of these nastier practitioners, who tend to operate as much below the radar as possible, are slim.

So now, as I searched for an Aboriginal healer from among the various names sent by doctors in tribal clinics and from other sources, one particular name kept popping up – a man called Harold, from the Daintree Rainforest, a member of the Kuku Yalanji tribe and the healer I'd heard about anecdotally. The Yalanji, it turned out, were indeed warriors, but my gut was starting to tell me that this was the man for the job. Would he be a man like some of the Mongolian shamans I had met before Ghoste – warrior tribesmen who had managed to stay untainted by the power magic so often associated with such tribes? I hoped so, because all my instincts – and since Mongolia I had learned to trust my intuition as never before – were telling me that this man Harold was the healer I had to take Rowan to see.

Meanwhile, as I began putting the logistics of the upcoming journey together, I had to admit that New Trails was not going quite as I wanted it to. I started to wonder if there was maybe an element of burnout here: admittedly, being Rowan's tutor in the morning and then running the playdates for the families, plus looking after the three horses represented a fair bit of work for his teacher. Then again, we had a quite a few volunteers who helped in the afternoons as well as others providing backup for the academic work. We tested Rowan and found that he was somewhere ahead of his grade level, despite the fact that proper back-and-forth conversation was still eluding him – though at least there was no regression so far. But he wasn't always that motivated to go to New Trails, and I noticed that the earlier, happy goofing around with the female helpers, so important to him – to all kids, really – wasn't happening any more. His teacher began to report that it was becoming harder and harder to get him to concentrate when he was trying to sit still. I pointed out that, because he was autistic, of course concentration was going to be hard. I felt it might help if he spent more time on the trampoline, or on the swing set. She was certainly a gifted teacher, but maybe we should take a different approach?

I talked this through with Kristin. It was so hard to know what was right. Clearly Rowan was a child who needed to move, move and move. Then again, as my mother pointed out, he had to learn to sit still. Right, but if he was learning to sit still, would he have any bandwidth left for learning anything else or would the stress of that be too great? Well, he still had to learn how to operate in the 'real world', others quite rightly observed. True, I'd respond, but then again, when I train a horse to be able to, say, go into town to take part in a parade, or to go a busy horse show, I don't train him in those stressful environments. If I did, there would be an accident. I train a horse in an environment specifically set up for horses and then gradually introduce, over months, even years, elements of noise and traffic and busy horse shows until he's clearly ready to handle himself in those non-horse-friendly environments. Only then do I take him there – that's just common sense.

But your son isn't a horse, people would say. True, I'd reply, but there are crossovers between all animals, especially mammals. What scares a dog – a loud noise, a perceived threat – scares a horse or a human just the same. Plus, most kids – and Rowan was no exception – spend so much time out in that 'real world' that surely we could tip the odds in their favour during their learning time when we require them to open up their brains to things like maths or reading? And, in fact, there are, it turns out, some rather interesting similarities between the autistic brain and the horse brain. Dr Temple Grandin, for example, professor of animal sciences at Colorado State University, best-selling author of such works as *Animals in Translation* and herself an adult autist, has written of the many parallels between animal and autistic brains, including an overdeveloped amygdala, which initiates the fight or flight response, and a tendency to think in pictures. Indeed, Dr Grandin had once told me how she had had her own brain scanned and found that, like those of other high-functioning autists who had been scanned, hers showed key differences when compared with the brain of a 'neurotypical' person.

For whatever reason and despite my best intentions, New Trails wasn't serving Rowan or the other kids quite as well as it should. It still felt like we were trying to impose things from the outside. Sure, it was streets ahead of the special-needs class I had taken Rowan from when he was four, but I felt we could do better. I just didn't quite know how yet; I was still a beginner at this homeschooling stuff. And it was costing a fortune employing both a teacher and therapist and paying for the general running of the place: surely we could develop something simpler, cheaper and more effective? But what?

Part of the problem was that Kristin and I were still going back and forth in our minds about whether we wanted to homeschool him at all. Part of me wondered how any kind of institution could possibly work better than what we'd been developing for Rowan – and also for the other children at New Trails. We even had an evening session each week for adolescent autistic kids to get to know each other and socialize. Despite my reservations, we were getting somewhere, after all, even if we had to go through a couple of models before we really cracked it. But I still wondered if a 'real' school still might not do it better.

Certainly Kristin still held out, though I wasn't quite sure why, for Rowan being able to attend an actual school some day. While I was open to the idea in principle, it didn't sit right in my gut somehow. I acknowledged it would be cheaper than trying to run New Trails without a proper fund-raising strategy, but the more I talked to other autism parents, the more it seemed impossible for an autistic child to avoid bullying and victimization of some sort within a school, no matter how progressive. And let's face it, not many people really knew what they were doing with autism, even the professionals. Most were more full of opinion than real knowledge and few seemed to get any real results. So why did Kristin still want to try school, I asked one warm spring evening, as we sat drinking wine on the back porch, listening to the crickets and the tree frogs singing out in the Texas night.

She sipped her wine, considering. 'You know, it's a good question. New Trails is great. But if I'm honest, maybe I still have a desire, somewhere deep inside me, for Rowan to be normalized. If I admit that . . .' she paused, her powerfully perceptive mind working almost visibly. No one I knew could self-examine more clearly and dispassionately than Kristin: it was a real skill, honed over years of meditation as well as academic study. 'Okay, maybe it's this: maybe I simply want to try and give him a shot at normality. I mean, we know socialization's no problem – he has regular playdates with other children now, not to mention the kids that come into New Trails.' She paused again, marshalling her thoughts.

'And also, I was talking to Cisco the other day when I went to pick Rowan up' – Cisco was one of the higher-functioning of the young adult autists who had started coming out for the adolescent get-togethers – 'and he told me, and I think it's true, that autistic kids, outside of Asperger's anyhow, aren't necessarily that desirous of a peer group friend base. Most of them, he said, feel safer with adults and socialize that way until their peer group comes up to their level. I believe Cisco. So you're right, why do I still want, somewhere in me, to at least *try* school for Scub?'

'Maybe it's just the desire to know we tried everything we possibly could for him?' I suggested.

'I guess so. We should at least look, right?'

'Right,' I said, pouring more wine. I wasn't at all convinced, but not to look: Kristin was right – perhaps that wasn't doing right by Rowan either.

So, if only to say we'd examined every option, we went to talk to a couple of schools. They seemed very confident – one in particular that had beautiful grounds and seemed to take a very flexible approach. But I didn't notice anyone there who was as 'spectrummy' (i.e. autistic) as Rowan. And I couldn't tell how well those spectrummy kids that I did see were or weren't doing. Then again, maybe I was just being closed-minded. Kristin and I agreed to keep the conversation open and at least re-examine the issue when, come the following spring, places would be available.

I would broach the subject occasionally with Rowan, just to try and gauge his reaction – casually throwing it in while riding, for example, as when we were cantering up the hill of the Arbuckle pastures, singing a Dr Seuss song: 'So, how d'you feel about maybe trying a school, like a real school, some time?'

Rowan just kept right on singing.

Summer came. We closed New Trails due to the hot weather, arranged horse and animal sitters, and set off to visit family in the UK for a couple of weeks before heading to Australia. Over in the UK, I worried about spending too long in the city. My parents live in the very middle of London, not close to a large park, and while their house is very tranquil, outside it is still London with all its neurosensory irritants: incessant traffic noise, thunderous, crowded tube trains, barking dogs and all the other sounds of sheer massed humanity. When Dr Johnson wrote that 'when a man is tired of London, he is tired of life', he meant adults: cities are adult playgrounds. Children tolerate them, for sure, but they don't enjoy them.

Rowan would always become more obsessive, more generally anxious, when spending more than a few days at a time in London – we all did. I never understood how my parents could live there year after year. So I wondered whether we might be able – for a week or so – to manage to emulate some kind of hybrid between the life in Texas and the Mongolian trip before we flew off to see the healer in Australia. I would go with Rowan while Kristin took the opportunity to go on a short mindfulness retreat. I spoke with a girl I knew who ran a wilderness camping company in the UK that took people on wild food and tracking weekends, and she helped me identify a campsite in south Wales, in a forest close to wild beaches, where a local pony-trekking stable would be prepared to rent us some horses to camp with. By then, I'd made contact, via the internet, with some British parents who had recently read *The Horse Boy* and told them what I was planning.

A few of them expressed an interest in coming along too, and, in next to no time, a bunch of us – none of whom really knew each other – found ourselves congregating in a temperate rainforest woodland (yes, in the UK) of quite unearthly beauty: sessile oaks, thick with moss, whose green canopies shaded wide clearings of pink mallow. Beyond that stretched grassland, dunes, where samphire and blue cornflowers grew by a small estuary haunted by otters. You could see their tracks and narrow mudslides going down into the river from green banks along whose bluffs stalked curlew and small sandpipers. Beyond the dunes, the vast and open beach – the long sweep of Cardigan Bay with the silver-grey Irish Sea rolling in from the west, seals and even dolphins playing in the endless, churning surf. Britain as the Celts knew it, as the Vikings first saw it. All the beauty of our jewel-like kingdom contained in a few square miles of magic between Bridgend and the Gower Peninsula.

There passed a few short days of miracle, more than I'd ever expected. I had anticipated something fairly easy-going, just relaxing in the woods, with a bit of splashing in the sea and exploring the dunes and horse riding – as much as Rowan felt comfortable doing. I had some rebuilding to do in that department, for not long before I had made a classic horseman's mistake that had almost cost my son his life, and had certainly dented his confidence. I was still shocked at myself for having been so stupidly inattentive.

That year, Rowan had been steadily growing in confidence and ability as a rider – routinely trotting and cantering Betsy around the front field before we took off to ride together. Betsy had had children ride her solo a fair amount – she still belonged to my neighbour Stafford (my three horses, Clue, Hope and Capitan, lived over at New Trails, some fifteen minutes' drive to the north). Stafford's grandson Blake had ridden her by himself all over the neighbourhood, as had some of his friends. Betsy was as quiet a horse as they come – but at the end of the day she was still a horse. As Rowan became more like a 'normal' kid riding her, she became more like a normal horse, testing him with questions like 'Do you really want me to move forward?' and 'Do you really mean stop?' Nothing bad, just the standard resistance that all horses give beginner riders but which helps them learn. After all, as any good horseman knows, it's the horse, not the instructor, that teaches you to ride. I could give Rowan the basic cues to move her forward, stop her, turn her and so on. And the field was small enough that she couldn't escape, so it was a good place to let them find their way together.

One late afternoon, after I had picked Rowan up from New Trails, we had gone to catch Betsy and this time he had ridden her by himself all the way along the forest trails between the barn and our house, guiding her easily through the trees along the narrow path. I could not always be next to him and sometimes the faster walking pace of the horse meant that the two of them forged ahead a little, but I wasn't concerned as he was holding the reins lightly, putting no strain on the bit. Then, before we had set off together in the same saddle, Rowan had gone a stage further – taken Betsy around our small front field for a spin, cantering her, stopping her, turning her. An amazing performance – far in advance of anything I had ever seen him do before. He was riding! Really riding! My autistic son, the one who'd been non-verbal, shut inside himself, floating away from us, who could not coordinate his hands, his body . . . it was more than I could ever have hoped for! I found myself crying as I shouted, across the field:

'Oh my God, Rowan! You're amazing! AMAZING!'

And he had turned her, easily, elegantly, and trotted her back to me. His seat was impeccable, the fruit of so many years of riding in front of me without using the reins. In the Spanish Riding School of Vienna, which produces perhaps the most pure practitioners of the art of classical dressage on the planet, the new riders spend months and months being lunged – going round and round on a horse attached to the end of a line held by an instructor standing in the middle – with no reins and no stirrups, until they are completely secure in the saddle. Then, and only then, are they allowed to touch the reins – and the result is a rider so elegant and so effective that the reins are almost superfluous for the rider can direct the horse using solely their hips and core, with none of the kicking and pulling that a horse always finds a thousand ways to resist.

Rowan came over, brought Betsy to a perfect stop. I was speechless. I thought, why break the magic? Why not let him ride her back home through the woods with me walking next to them? So I opened the gate for him to ride through, watched, amazed, as he turned her towards me while I closed the gate. As I fumbled with the latch – a little stiffer today than normal – Betsy, all of a sudden, turned away towards home of her own volition. And then, faster than I could grab her bridle, she was off into the woods and down into the dry creek between my house and the home pasture, running away. '*DADDY!*' Rowan's terrified voice rose to a shriek. '*DAAAA-DDD-YYYYY!*'

I took off, running into the trees – knowing I could never catch her on foot, as Betsy thundered out of control and out of sight – following my son's shrieks. Shrieks that were suddenly cut short.

He had fallen.

I came upon him in the sand of the dry creek-bed, a small crumpled heap. Hurt? Dead? How could I have let this happen?

Rowan raised himself on his arm, his face green-white. Christ, what a terrible father I was! 'SCUB!'

'Daddy!' His breath came in sobs. I touched him tentatively – all limbs moving, nothing broken, it seemed, thank God, thank God – and hugged him to me.

'I'm so sorry, Scub, I'm so sorry . . . I should have known better . . .'

I cursed myself, wondering what the long-term consequences would be.

A few weeks later, we found ourselves in the magical forest in south Wales. To my relief, Rowan still wanted to ride, and had ridden after his fall, but I was very careful – these being unfamiliar horses – to keep everything very cool and easy. Even so, we witnessed some things that were little short of miraculous. One child, Jack, started using words for the first time while in the saddle; another, Sam, became interactive where before he had been completely shut in. We stabled the horses in the forest in picket lines under the trees and lived as a tribe, finding mutual support as autism parents, as autism families – for the siblings were right there with us too – that all of us had never really experienced before. Swapping stories and information about therapies, war stories of public tantrums and humiliations, stories of our hopes, our fears, over wine around the camp fire at night. Passing through the dunes to the sea each day, to ride on the beach, where we chased each other in the shallows, watched by curious seals, occasionally glimpsing the flashing silver-grey of dolphins out in the breakers.

We foraged for wild foods: salty, chewy green samphire, like tiny spineless cactus, growing in the grasses cropped croquet-lawn smooth by wild greylags; wild chicory and plantain – not the tropical banana kind, but the more prosaic dock-leaf cousin that grows all over the Northern Hemisphere and makes a good salad green; linden leaves and wild violet. And we tucked into the usual camp food of chicken pieces grilled over a fire and copious amounts of tea and chocolate biscuits.

It was beautiful – not unlike Mongolia. After the first day or two of coping with change, new conditions, sleeping in tents, being out in nature all the time, the families relaxed. An easy pace set in – we would get up in the early-morning dew, make up the fire, make breakfast. I and a couple of others would go and tend to the horses. Then, as the day warmed, we'd mess around with some of the horses at the camp – maybe teaching them tricks, like how to smile and bow, or count by stamping their feet. Then we'd take a gentle trail ride in the forest for those kids that wanted to, arranging other games for those kids that didn't. After lunch we'd set off for the beach, alternating which kids sat on horses, shoulders or walked, going from forest to dunes, dunes to estuary grassland, grassland to beach, beach to sea, and back again. Kids on the autism spectrum have a notoriously difficult time coping with change, with transition. By the third day, you would never have known it. It was like Mongolia but without the stresses. Out in nature, no bad sensory triggers, operating as a tribe, taking each day at a natural pace, sleeping on the good green earth. Waking fresh.

Rowan and I shared the little two-man tent under the great moss-grown oaks, cuddling together in our sleeping bags, reading books by torchlight, going in search of frogs and other creatures in the dark, picking up eyes in the torch beam. I still cringed inwardly at the awful, near-fatal mistake I had made with him and Betsy a few weeks before, but I seemed to have been forgiven. And he was still riding. But I also knew autism well enough by now to know that sometimes traumatic events can have a delayed response. Whatever, I cherished this time, listening to his breathing as he slept next to me in the moist British summer night, realizing that childhood was not for ever, that times such as these must be cherished and not taken for granted.

Then as the first rays of sunlight penetrated the tent walls, Rowan would sit bolt upright, unzip the front flap and go trotting over to the next-door one, belonging to Khatiche – a girl who had read *The Horse Boy*, had an autistic brother and was looking to work in the field of autism. She had contacted me, and – having hit it off with her and been impressed with her knowledge of autism – I had arranged for her to come to help me with Rowan on the trip to Wales. She instinctively knew how to let Rowan lead the way, watching and observing what he did, then gradually participating in his games until he was communicating fully with her and had claimed her as his own. Which gave me time to get the horses fed and watered, have a powwow with the team of volunteers about the day's activities, and make a cup of tea while she and he played '*Hup!*' just as he had with Tayaba in Africa the summer before.

And there was another girl who showed up to volunteer in the final stages of the camp – Jenny, a recent graduate in psychology from the University of Edinburgh who was also drawn to work with autism. She and Khatiche hit it off immediately, delighting Rowan and the other kids with their knowledge of the full range of *Lion King* songs and a seemingly tireless stamina when it came to chase and tickle games. They seemed able to get a response from even the most closed in of the children on the camp. Wow, I thought – these were the kind of people I needed at New Trails. On the last day of the camp, both Khatiche and Jenny asked if I took live-in volunteers there.

'I do now,' I said. 'When do you want to come?'

So it was arranged. Jenny would come out to Texas that same autumn, when we were back from Australia, and Khatiche early the following year. It was just what we needed – more and more families were wanting to come out to New Trails: if we were going to keep growing like this, then we would need more help. So if we had live-in volunteers there that Rowan knew, was comfortable with, who could help teach him, help look after the horses and other animals, and learn to work with the families in the way we had been evolving to gain communication, surely that would spread the workload and only improve the services we offered.

In fact, we were now starting to receive lots of letters and emails asking if we took volunteers from further afield. The more I thought about it, the more sense it made. One email in particular stood out: from Susanna, an American undergraduate from a medical school on the east coast. What a team that would be: Khatiche with her lifetime of autism skills; Jen with her background in psychology research; and this third volunteer, Susanna, with her medical know-how. The only problem, as usual, was how to fund it all: I tried not to think too much about that, because it made me begin to panic. But pushing it aside wasn't going to help either. There had to be a way – I just couldn't see it yet. Still, we had achieved something rather wonderful during these few weeks in the UK – the first Horse Boy Camp. The parents and I agreed, as it drew to a close: this was something we needed to do a lot more of. More than that: it was something we needed simply to *live*.

8. The Oldest Forest in the World

Reunited as family, off we flew, away from the UK and into – for us – truly uncharted territory. In Mongolia we had had Tulga to take care of us when we landed. And Africa was my old stamping ground so I knew my way around well enough to feel confident. But Australia was something completely new – and completely intimidating.

It started well – a massively long security line, but, despite the fatigue of the long plane flight, we managed to keep Rowan's frustration levels down by reading aloud to him as we shuffled forward, and by deploying a new secret weapon I had discovered: protein. I guess it had been staring me in the face for some time: we had got across Mongolia largely on bacon, after all. But that summer, and especially during the Horse Boy Camp in Wales, I had noticed a marked correlation between Rowan's moods and his intake of animal protein. At the camp, when it had been solely me responsible for his every need, I had observed that when he was starting to get rocky emotionally, if I managed to get chicken or bacon into him right away, his mood would improve within fifteen minutes. Not so with other foods. It was as if, at a certain time in the day, his brain would start to implode, his reason and intellect become compromised, but so long as I could hustle some chicken bites or a piece of bacon into him, he would recover – his brain would appear almost literally to re-inflate, as if a bicycle pump had been attached to his head. In a matter of mere minutes, he'd be back to normal. Of course, we all know that food is mood. But this was so immediate, so extreme. And we had tried other diets before – the gluten- and casein-free thing, for example – without much discernible effect. Was I the only autism parent out there to be seeing this protein-related, gut–brain connection?

Either way, it saved us here in the immigration line. From the first whimpers to the immediate bacon injection, to his smiles and giggles with the passport control officer who wished us 'G'day' and hoped we had a fun stay – so different from the surly, uninterested British immigration officers and the American ones who treated you like a criminal for wanting to enter their country and spend your money.

And then we were there. In beautiful, bustling Sydney, our heads half underwater with the jet lag, figuring out rental cars and directions, and within a couple of days we were heading north.

Such a strange country, Australia. Something in the quality of the light that was different to any other continent I had ever visited. Warmer, and yet at the same time I could feel something alien, unsettling. There were so many half-familiar references – in some ways it looked a little like California, in others like South Africa. The great stands of eucalyptus that I was used to seeing in other countries as plantations, exotic trees, here growing wild in great forests. Wallabies skipped across the highway. The most extraordinary and beautiful birdlife I think I had ever seen. Parrots of every description: rainbow lorikeets walking through the open door of the little cottage we rented on the beach halfway up the New South Wales coast on the way north, rose-pink galahs, enormous white cockatoos, blood-red king parrots and a host of other jewel-coloured avians flitting past the windscreen as we drove along. Pelicans, kookaburras, tawny frogmouths that were half owl, half – well, one couldn't quite describe it. Nothing was quite like anything I had ever seen before anywhere in the world.

And the towns: half American suburban strip-mall schlock, half elegant colonial – it was hard to know quite where one was.

The feeling of uncertainty, of being off-balance somehow, was exacerbated by Rowan suddenly becoming rocky again. I was perplexed. Perhaps it was the jet lag that seemed to have thrown us all off.

And then my own mistake came back to haunt me. While staying in a small beach town on our way up the coast, and wanting to keep

Rowan riding, I hired a horse for me and a pony for him, with a girl from the riding stables to walk alongside him, and set off into the forest, where he wanted to go because we had heard that there were deer to be seen up in its gladed heights. At seven, Rowan – always big for his age – was starting to get larger than most saddles and horses could cope with when we rode together. Betsy was a very strong quarterhorse, and the saddle we used was an oversized Western cutting saddle with ample room for two. Not every horse and saddle could accommodate us, so by way of an experiment I thought to maybe try him on a quiet pony with someone leading – after all, he'd been riding Betsy by himself, even after his fall.

It started well enough, the horses stepping out happily on the gradually steepening trail, hooves sucking rhythmically in the red mud left by the previous night's rain – we were here in July, the Australian winter, and so it was cool and wet rather than sunny and hot. But then, perhaps half an hour into our deer-seeking adventure, Rowan began to whimper. Whimper and then cry. The crying became wailing, then sobbing. What was wrong? The horses were both behaving themselves so well.

'What is it, Scubby? What's wrong?'

He couldn't speak for tears. Perplexed, I got off my horse, led him over. Hugged my son where he sat sobbing on his pony. 'What is it, Scub? Can't you tell me? Shall we go back?'

'Go back . . .'

And that was all I could get from him. I gave my horse to the bewildered girl to ride in my place and tried leading Rowan on the pony. More tears, but no communication. So in the end I took him in my arms and led the pony – no easy task on that narrow, slippery trail, as my son clung to me, crying.

'What do you think's wrong?' the girl couldn't help but ask.

'I don't know,' I admitted. But in my gut I knew. It was a delayed reaction to the fall I had caused through my own inattention back home all those weeks before. I had seen this delayed reaction before a few times, such as when Rowan had fallen into water the previous summer one day while down by the San Marcos River. It hadn't been a bad ducking, just a momentary trip and fall, and I had grabbed him and pulled him out in a moment. And he had been happy, the following week, to go splash in Barton Springs, the cold-water natural springs that bubble out of the rock in the middle of central Austin. He still didn't swim, which worried me, as I couldn't seem to break through his resistance to wanting to learn, but he loved to paddle and splash. However, two weeks after his fall into the San Marcos, he started flat out refusing to go near any water. Even the bathtub became a place of fear for a while. It was the same delayed reaction this time, I was certain.

I felt so ashamed. I, a lifelong horseman, had let it happen through a moment's inattention. Had I now cut off his lifeline to the very thing – horses – that had opened the door to communication between us, between him and the world? We walked down the mountain, crying together, the poor girl on the horse in front of us not knowing what to make of it, and the little pony stumbling along behind us.

We would be with the shaman soon. I had hoped for real conversation to come from this year's healing. Now, as the previous year in Africa, I would be content with simply returning him to where he had been before my stupid mistake.

Cairns, the beginning of the subtropical far north (so strange to think of it getting more tropical the further north one went, rather than further south), suddenly felt much more familiar than the eucalyptus-clad south, more like the landscape I had seen on assignments to Central America, East and central Africa. I don't know why it made a difference, but it did. And the road north from Cairns to Mossman, the small town near which Harold, the Yalanji healer we were on our way to see, lived, was beautiful beyond compare. Jungle-covered mountains tumbling to the sea, narrow beaches between wooded headlands. We were at the southernmost edge of the Daintree Rainforest.

Over 135 million years old, it is the oldest rainforest in the world – as far as we know, at least. And it offers a glimpse back into how much of the world must have looked at the time of the dinosaurs: vast hardwood trees; strangler figs encasing forest giants and slowly squeezing the life out of them; trees whose bark is massed with thorns that raise rashes and welts if they scrape you; giant ferns and cycads; creepers twisting between a green cathedral of trunks. Shy but fierce cassowaries stalk the woodland edge – great flightless birds that can deliver a kick that will open a man from gizzard to groin. Huge saltwater crocodiles hunt the estuaries and sea shallows, quite happy to add human to their menu *du jour*, while smaller freshwater crocs lurk further upriver. The most poisonous snakes in the world slither through the undergrowth and giant Shelob-like spiders hang between trees in webs big enough to catch a bat or bird.

Yet as harsh, even hostile, as the forest seems, it is also a place of great healing. The Kuku Yalanji people, who have lived here for the last ten thousand years or so, have a amassed a plant pharmacology that in recent years has caught the attention of all the big pharmaceutical companies – raising issues of intellectual property and exacerbating the mistrust felt universally by native peoples towards whites. Because, as elsewhere, the indigenous inhabitants have had a raw deal.

Beginning like any other conquest of foreign parts by Europeans, the first encounters between early explorers – notably the eighteenth-century Captain James Cook – and the Aboriginals were sometimes friendly, sometimes not. It's worth noting here that many people regard the Chinese as the first 'outsiders' to discover Australia, back in the Middle Ages. The Aboriginals themselves were originally outsiders too, coming in from Africa by land and coast-hopping across the Indian Ocean. But seeing as their arrival was about forty thousand years ago, it does give them a pretty clear precedent.

Captain Cook found his first landfall challenged by the people living there, as he recorded in his account of the voyage:

> as soon as we approached the rocks, two of the men came down upon them to dispute our landing . . . Each of the two champions

> was armed with a lance about ten feet long, and a short stick which
> he seemed to handle as if it was a machine to assist him in managing
> or throwing the lance. They called to us in a very loud tone, and in
> a harsh dissonant language ... brandished their weapons, and
> seemed resolved to defend their coast to the utmost, though they
> were but two, and we were forty ...

Cook's party also had muskets and cannon, of course, not to mention syphilis. For the natives, the next two centuries were not going to be fun.

Venturing northwards, on its way to the Indies, Cook's ship foundered off the northeast coast, at a part of the Great Barrier Reef they dubbed 'Cape Tribulation'. This led to a brief foray inland, where they met the Kuku Yalanji, whom they found exotic, as indicated by Cook's description of one individual they encountered:

> [The] gentleman was distinguished by an ornament of a very striking appearance: it was the bone of a bird, nearly as thick as a man's finger and five or six inches long, which he had thrust into a hole made in the gristle that divides the nostrils.

Luckily for that generation of Yalanji, Cook and his crew passed on, but some seventy or so years later, in the mid nineteenth century, Australia became the object of mass British settlement, and the native world collapsed, along with its spiritual realm, the Dreamtime – or perhaps it's fairer to say that it went underground. The rainforest, because of its harsh conditions and remote location, escaped white settlement longer than most regions. And for the Kuku Yalanji, life between the coast and the mountains was good, with plentiful food in each season. They would hunt wallabies, catch fish in the waterfalls, mangrove creeks and tidal pools, using tree poisons to stun their prey, and they'd harpoon sea turtles out on the tidal reefs. They'd search for 'sugarbag' (wild honey), gather and crush a myriad of seasonal nuts and pick yams (which required considerable processing to be edible). For recreation they'd play spear-throwing games in which wheels, covered with bright mud and feathers to make them easier to see, were rolled down mountainsides while young and old tried to spear the moving target. They would mix love potions, keep pets (some women even suckling puppies of the tamed dingoes they kept for wallaby hunting) and heal the sick through 'smoking' ceremonies and the laying on of hands. They'd meet for trade fairs in the dry forest interior on the west side of the mountains, and they'd swim in the magical waterfalls and pools of the Daintree and other rivers that tumble down from the mountain tops . . .

And then, in the 1870s, the first white prospectors came. And found tin. And then other settlers came, and began first logging, then clearing for sugar cane, beef, tropical fruits. The native population took a nose dive: rape, venereal disease, violence from armed police units and settlers, land taken from them – 50 per cent of the Kuku Yalanji disappeared within a single generation.

Yet for us, driving the coast road north from Cairns, all we could see was beauty. Mountains falling to the sea, tropical forest fringing pristine beaches, cane fields and cattle pastures, a riot of tropical flowers and the ubiquitous multi-coloured birdlife. The sadness of the region's human history was hidden, at least to the casual observer. We drove through the town of Mossman. Somewhere off to the west – there it was on the signpost – was Mossman Gorge, where I had been told the healer Harold lived. We drove on, the forest and mountains to our left, the road passing through cane fields until the forest reached back out from the rocky hillsides once more and the tar road ended, a finality of immediate civilization, at an eco-lodge where cabins were set among the trees and a small waterfall came down the mountainside. We had arrived.

We were staying here because, during the research I had done that had led me to Harold, various leads had pointed to the owners of this lodge as people who knew him, so I had emailed them about our trip and made a booking.

Only they weren't there. We'd arrived late and they'd gone home, leaving other staff in charge. Okay, no worries: the place was beautiful – cabins on stilts because of the seasonal flooding in the rainy season, with a central lodge built around a small lake where wild duck and black-necked swans cruised. Brush turkeys strutted and pecked on the paths – delighting Rowan, who immediately set off in giggling, if futile, pursuit. Dark was about to fall and the dusk became a-dance with fireflies. Strange cries came from the crowding trees. There was magic here, one could feel it. Old earth magic – one of those occult landscapes; like the northwest Highlands of Scotland, or the forests of Table Mountain in the Cape, or the canyons of the American Southwest. Beautiful, seductive, strange. Older than we men.

And even though the lodge owners weren't there, everyone – the bar staff, the waiters – seemed to know who we were and why we had come. 'Sure, just go down to Mossman Gorge tomorrow, ask for Harold. He's a good guy, you'll see.'

It seemed so casual. So strange. So ordinary in this clearly extraordinary place.

We went to sleep in our cabin. A young moon came up, its light filtering into the room from the ancient jungle and the even more ancient sky. What would tomorrow bring? Would the healer even be there? Would he be able to handle us, our strange requests? If so, would it work for Rowan? Would we finally have conversation, some kind of normality? Was that even something to hope for? Were we wrong to hope for that? The night birds screeched, the moon poured in, laughing, silver light. I lay awake, watching its shadow patterns move on the beaded wood of the cabin ceiling.

It rained during the night. Hard tropical downpours that beat tattoos on the roof and brought the green scent of forest into the cabin. We breakfasted by the little, water lily-clustered lake, Rowan filling up on good-mood-inducing bacon, and climbed into the rental car to drive back down to Mossman.

'Time to go see the shamans!' he trilled as he got in. Well, at least he was into it.

Mossman is one of those towns that exist on the edge of colonial history, like flotsam washed up on a beach after a long storm. A main street that is part elegant colonial, part strip mall, a park with a skateboarding ramp where young white kids polish their shredding skills, and semi-destitute Aboriginal families wandering the sidewalks. A touristy edge – backpackers' lodges and coffee shops; this is close to a national park, after all. Yet for all the modernity, the feeling is of being on the fringe, of one world lapping uncomfortably against another, of wrongs compounded over time into almost a culture of wrongs, of ancient magic growing like moss on and in the industrial machine. The whispers of the ancestors perceptible amid the roar of truck engines.

We turned west at the sign for Mossman Gorge, heading for the forested mountains from which the Daintree River tumbled. Still the road led through sugar cane fields and beef cattle pasture, the rainforest rising beyond, aloof, dreaming, old. White egrets flew across the road in front of us. A horse, grazing in the field with the cows, lifted its head from the green grass and cocked its ears at us, watching as we passed.

The forest fingers reached out, as if grabbing the farmland in leafy knuckles, and pulled us in. Green light. The road suddenly winding between tree trunks once more. And then we were there, at the motley collection of clean-looking shacks and houses that made up the Kuku Yalanji settlement of Mossman Gorge. We parked, amid vibrant tropical flowers in reds, oranges, purples, and approached the main building that surely was the visitor centre. From its verandah, an overweight young man with midnight skin looked down on us, leaning on the railing and screaming, in a weird, high-pitched voice:

'Shit! Fucking fuck! Fucking fuck off! Fucking shit! Fuck *fuck* fuck!'

A strange welcome.

We mounted the stairs to the building, squeezing past the young man who continued his shower of expletives but made no move to take it beyond the merely verbal, and entered what seemed to be an art gallery. Painted wooden shields, spear-throwers decorated with intricate designs made by burning patterns into the wood, brightly coloured paintings and batiks.

The lady behind the counter looked up grumpily as we entered. 'Can I help you?'

'We've come for healing,' I said honestly. 'I'm looking for Harold.'

'He's leading a bush walk right now, so you'll have to wait.' The woman's attitude softened only slightly as she eyed Rowan, rolling on the floor, holding pebbles up to the light and squinting at them autistically.

'When will he be back?'

The woman looked at the clock on the wall behind her. 'Not long, maybe another ten minutes. Would you like to book a walk with him?'

'Thesaurus!' said Rowan suddenly, getting up from the floor. Kristin went out, and came back with Rowan's book of words.

Though proper conversation still eluded us, Rowan had recently discovered a healthily obsessive interest in the definitions of words. A reader since our return from Mongolia, he had started to ask the meaning of words now and then – increasingly so of late. So we had bought him, in Sydney, an illustrated children's thesaurus. He had been poring over it during the journey north, mouthing the syllables of the words that caught his attention. It was now his favourite book. He grabbed it happily from Kristin and, stretched out again on the floor, began to read aloud in a half-whisper: '*Por-poise – a mammal that lives in the sea and is related to dolphins and whales. Pract-ical – something that helps you do things . . .*'

Kristin and I, of course, found this fascinating. I had not been reading thesauruses at eight. When I first heard the word as a kid, I had thought it meant some kind of dinosaur. Now here was my autistic son, who not so long ago had been non-verbal, and who still couldn't properly converse, examining the meaning of the English language.

But my reverie was broken by voices from outside. First an

explosion of expletives from the young man with Tourette's before an older Aboriginal lady appeared and led him off as the group of tourists arrived back from their bush walk. I went to the window and saw their leader – a slender, dark-skinned man, perhaps in his forties, wearing khakis. This, then, must be Harold. I got only a glimpse of him, however, before he disappeared off into the trees, no doubt intent on business of his own before the next scheduled walk began.

We bought tickets for the next nature walk, which was due to start in fifteen minutes or so, and went outside. I was worried that Rowan might be disruptive, unable to not shout and run and leave the path. Formal group situations were always stressful, hard to navigate. When all were there, Harold reappeared and in a quiet voice introduced himself, said a few words of welcome in the Kuku Yalanji language and led our little troupe off into the trees.

I wish that I could remember what Harold told us in the extraordinary, ancient forest that had stood since the Cretaceous Period, when *T. rex* stalked the earth. I was too busy running after Rowan, containing him with 'We have to *whisper whisper*' when he talked loudly and stopping him from diving off into the undergrowth after the brush turkeys that occasionally ran across the path. We were getting looks, but not too bad, considering.

One thing did get Rowan's full attention, however. We stopped at a small rock overhang, where a great boulder stuck out like a moss-grown, green-knuckled fist. On the flat, sheltered side of the small cave made by the overhang were daubed rock paintings, put there by Harold's ancestors centuries before. Half animal, half human, they looked very similar to the Bushman rock paintings depicting shamans' visions during healing trances that you find all over the mountains and rocky places of southern Africa. Rowan had seen some in pictures in books about the Bushmen that we had lying around the house.

'Bushman paintings!' Rowan now said, out of the blue. Harold paused in his explanation of the ritual significance of the healing trance, and looked at him with penetrating brown eyes.

'Kind of, young feller. You could say I'm a bushman too. A bushman from the bush right here. But the real Bushmen live in Africa, don't they?'

'Yes, they do!' chirruped Rowan happily. Kristin and I looked at each other. That kind of exchange was unusual. Almost conversation. Harold turned his gaze to mine, held it a moment, then went back to his explanation, while Rowan, demanding tickles, writhed in the sand and leaf mould at my feet, giggling in *whisper whisper* voice. Had Harold clocked that Rowan was autistic? Did he know who we were? Would he be prepared to work on Rowan? I felt hopeful.

We hung back as the group dispersed at the end of the walk. Harold did not disappear into the trees this time. As the last people melted off towards their cars, the young man with Tourette's reappeared briefly from the nearby wooden houses to scream high-pitched expletives at them. Harold turned to me. 'I guess that's your boy come for the healing, then.' He nodded towards Rowan, who was running in circles, shadowed by Kristin.

'I'm Rupert' – I shook hands – 'and this is my wife, Kristin.' They shook hands too. 'And that's Rowan over there. He's autistic, yes.' My words sounded so lame there in the bright jungle sunlight. Harold was quiet.

'Yes, the blokes at the lodge told me you'd be coming. I've worked with some young men with autism before. Your boy there strikes me as a bright spark. Shouldn't be too much trouble.'

It was so strange to be talking to a shaman in plain English, even my own colonial vernacular English of 'blokes' and 'young fellers'. It seemed almost too direct, too . . . normal. Could it really be this easy, this casual?

'Let's go for some tea and damper and talk it over,' suggested Harold, and led the way to a long hut with thatched palm roofing, a little way off into the trees. Open-sided, it had benches and a long wooden table, with bread and jam and a kettle whistling on a slow fire.

Tea and damper – 'damper' being soda bread cooked in the ashes of a fire, similar to what the Scots call 'bannock' and the Bushmen call 'ash-bread'. Served with jam and a nice hot cup of tea. It felt so, well, *British*. So colonial. As I munched the bread and jam – which really was very good – Harold asked me to tell him our story so far. So I did, trying to find the right words.

'I guess what I'm looking for is healing, not a cure,' I said, watching as Rowan looked at a book in the sunlight a small distance away. 'I don't want Rowan to stop being autistic. Not at all; in fact I'm seeing so many gifts in his autism now that I honestly wouldn't exchange his autism for normality. I just want him to be as effective and happy and successful as he can be.' I paused, not enjoying the sound of my own voice. 'I guess I just want to be the best father I can be. And so often I don't even know if I'm doing the right thing. I make mistakes all the time.'

We sat in silence a while. Then Harold spoke. He told us of his grandfather, who had been a healer, himself from a long line of healers, and how when Harold had reached adolescence his grandfather had begun teaching him about the properties of plants, the geography of the spirit world. How there were sacred waterfalls, and ancestral grave sites, all over this vast, primordial forest, from which he and the Yalanji's other healers drew their power. How outsiders had started to come to him for healing. White Australians working in the area as incomers from the cities in the south, drawn by tourism and the search for a better life, and less racist than the longer-term cane and beef farmers of the area, had heard of him and begun approaching him with ailments, both physical and mental, and then word had spread.

He reached into a bag that was sitting on the wooden bench next to him, pulled out a little wallet of photographs. 'I guess because of that people started coming up to see me from Sydney and Melbourne. This young feller had problems with blood cancer. I took him on long distance, did the healings from here. That can work almost as well, you know.'

'So . . .' He glanced over at where Rowan was making letters in

the sand with Kristin: R-O-W-A-N . . . and then P-O-O!!!!
Rowan collapsed into peals of laughter. 'Let's see what we can do
for your boy over there, eh? Whyncha see if he'll come over here
and we'll smoke him.'

'Smoke him?' Kristin sounded alarmed. Harold laughed. 'Yes,
just sacred smoke, from the bark of a tree that cleanses you. It's
what we do. So I can see what's going on in there, and deflect any
bad spirits that might be operating, you know.'

'How does that work?' Kristin asked.

Harold smiled. 'Don't worry, he just sits in a chair and I wave
smoke from a particular bark around him. It's easy, nothing to
worry about. After that I'll be able to tell you a little more about
how we might go on.'

'What kind of bark? And what does the smoke do exactly?' I
asked. Harold's face closed. 'There are some things I can tell you
and some things I can't. Oh, and no pictures or filming, okay?'

I had been prepared for this. Whereas the shamans and healers
in Mongolia and Namibia has been easy-going about, even encouraging of filming and photography, I had heard that in Australia, as
in the States among the Native Americans, healers were often
actively opposed to it. No worries. I strolled over to where Rowan
had been stick-writing in the leaf mould of the forest floor, trying
to keep it casual, but – as so often before – with my heart in my
mouth. What if he didn't want to? What if we had come all this
way and he just wasn't into it? Would that matter? My gut told me
it would. But it also told me that if I showed my anxiety, it would
put too much pressure on him and he might shut down.

'Hey, Scub,' I said, my voice self-consciously light. 'Wanna
come meet Harold?'

'Time to meet the shamans!' To my intense relief he got up
without fuss, let drop his writing stick and walked with me over to
a plastic lawn chair that sat a little apart from the thatched hut, in
a small clearing of its own, where Harold now bent over a slow,
smouldering fire of palm leaves and great pieces of a kind of bark
I hadn't seen before – each section of which looked a bit like a

curved turtle shell or plate. He was blowing on the fire, getting it to flame. Cool as you like, Rowan just sat in the chair, hands on his thighs, as Harold picked up a large piece of the burning bark, waved it to and fro to stoke and then kill the bright flame, and then waved the aromatic, cedar-smelling smoke around Rowan's head. All the while he just sat there, quiet, easy; he normally never just sat still – unless, I realized, it was for a shaman.

The whole thing lasted perhaps three minutes, if that. Then as Rowan still seemed calm, Harold nodded to another, younger Kuku Yalanji man who had wandered up, seemingly randomly, but whom Harold clearly regarded as some kind of assistant. The younger man, his hair bound into a long dark ponytail, nodded good naturedly at us, 'G'day', and squatted next to Harold, holding up a small ceramic mug. Harold let the bark drop back into the slow fire and put his hands on Rowan's head. I expected Rowan to flinch, pull away, yell. He did no such thing, but merely sat there, the same strange, unusual, un-Rowan-like calm settling upon him as Harold ran his fingers lightly over his scalp, seeming to give little pulls at the air just above his cranium, not unlike the way Ghoste had done in Mongolia, then flicking his fingers into the tea mug.

Curious, Kristin and I craned our necks to look at the inside of the mug. It was empty. Then, gradually, it wasn't.

Right there in front of our eyes, as Harold flicked his fingers into it, the bottom of the mug began to fill with a strange, viscous, plasma-like fluid. I looked at Kristin, she looked at me, we looked into the cup. More mucus slowly filling. Harold seemed to be pulling it out of Rowan's head somehow and flicking it into the mug. Yet there could be no sleight of hand: his sleeves were rolled up, there was nothing in the palms of his hands that could be hidden because his hands were wide open when he flicked – you could clearly see the palms.

Yet the mucus in the mug kept filling, little by little.

And nothing physical was coming out of Rowan's head. Just Harold's hands on his scalp, then pulling lightly at the air above his head, then flicking into the cup, but nothing visible coming out of it. Just the stuff in the bottom of the cup slowly getting more and more full.

Mind-blowing. Literally.

I mean, I had seen all manner of strange and amazing things with the Bushmen and other healers over the years. But this . . . nothing like this. Ever. The mug was by now about a quarter full. Suddenly Harold's hands stopped moving, and he gave Rowan a pat on his little shoulders. Rowan sighed, deep and happy-sounding, got off the chair and came and hugged me round the middle.

'He'll be all right,' he said – showed us the contents of the mug, briefly, then tossed the mess into the fire.

'What, I mean, how . . .' Kristin was lost for words. So, for once, was I. Harold shrugged. 'It's what we do,' he repeated. 'Bring 'im back tomorrow about four and we'll have another go. We got most of it out today so it shouldn't take long. Oh, and before you come, have him take a dip in the pools below the water-falls on the Daintree River up there,' he indicated the gorge behind us. 'Sacred healing waters. You might feel a little strange as you go in. Feel something in your head, maybe. Don't worry, it's all part of it.'

I looked at him, at his assistant, who just smiled, got up and stretched.

'But how, I mean, what . . .'

'Tomorrow at four, see you then.' And with that he turned on his heel and headed off back to the village.

We wandered to the car, Kristin and I amazed.

'I've never, ever seen anything like that, ever!' I was saying it over and over, like a stuck record.

We drove out of the car park, the high-pitched obscenities of the young Tourette's man echoing around us as we drove back out towards the cane fields and the town of Mossman.

9. Theory of Mind

Kristin and I talked about it on and off all night. How could we not? Round and round we went – was there any way Harold could have tricked us? He didn't seem to be hiding anything. I had read about this kind of healing in Australia, Borneo, the South Pacific before, where stuff was removed from inside someone's body without any incision or intrusion. I had read about a famous healer in Brazil called John of God, who apparently asked people whether they wanted an internal or an external healing. People described having lumps, cataracts, even cancers removed this way; I'd even spoken to a couple of people who had come back from John of God and reported it first hand. All these stories were completely apocryphal and I had no idea if I believed or disbelieved them. But now I had seen it for myself. Or something very like it.

What was that fluid? Why was it slightly bloody? Was it brain cells? I knew, from conversations with scientists and adult autists such as Dr Temple Grandin, that in the autistic brain there was sometimes an overabundance of white matter that could inhibit connection between different parts of the mind. Was that what Harold had been taking out? Had he indeed taken anything out at all? Was it some kind of hypnosis? Was it even real? Did it matter?

And how casual Rowan had been about the whole thing. But maybe there was a wisdom in that. To just take it as it came and not over-think it. But how could you *not* over-think it?

We drifted to sleep, the sounds of the ancient rainforest, cries of night marsupials, the patter of rain, lulling us to dream.

So next morning, as directed, we drove back to Mossman Gorge, this time driving on past the Aboriginal village, and stopped at the point where the road gave out, the sound of tumbling water coming from beyond the forest fringe immediately to our right. We parked on the dirt where the gravel ended, and got out. In front of us, a series of wooden steps led up the first bit of the mountainside towards the waterfalls that we could now hear roaring from that direction. Rowan was the first to go trotting ahead towards the wooden stairway, which led up into a cool green tunnel.

We followed, the walkway taking us over great boulders of volcanic rock. And now there was the river, flowing in huge cataracts and falls, its spray misting our hair and the greenery around us, the air moist and alive, the water pure as the springs and rain from which it had been born, rushing down the mountainside and through the forest with an abandon that made us laugh aloud to see.

And then it hit. Like a strange, psychic wall, felt somewhere behind the eyes. Kristin was the first to feel it, stopping dead on the wooden walkway that led us deeper into the forest, closer to the falling water. Then I hit it too.

'Do you feel that?' Kristin asked.

'Yes.'

Rowan had momentarily stopped too.

'Like going through some kind of . . .'

'Portal?' My voice tailed off – aware of how lamely sci fi/New Agey that sounded. But it jolly well did feel like that. I backed up a pace just to be sure. Yup, the feeling receded. I then stepped forward. Yup, there it was again, right behind the eyes, palpably there, inside the skull.

'Just as Harold said,' Kristin remembered. I wondered a moment what she meant – then recalled. That's right, he'd said we might feel something as we went to the falls to bathe Rowan. 'He said not to worry,' Kristin added. And truly it didn't feel like anything alarming. It just felt *there*.

So 'through' we went, feeling that strange membrane-like sensation once more, and then there, in front of us, were the pools. Between two sets of thunderous cataracts, the river widened out into great blue freshwater lagoons of the purest, crystal water, studded with huge black boulders. Like something out of a dream. A few people were there already, wading or leisurely swimming. Had they felt the strange force thing as they came here too? Rowan went trotting down to the water's edge. We sprinted after him.

'Go for a splash!'

He was climbing out of his shirt and shorts as he ran. 'Keep your underpants on, Scub, there are people here,' I called, as I hurried to do the same and then caught my breath with the cold as I launched myself in after him.

God, but it was good. The cool water rushing by, pulling at one's legs but not so hard as to cause alarm, the cool green of the forest canopy overhead, the sun starting to break through, warming the skin that peeped above the water's surface, the fish coming to nibble at one's legs, making one jump. Rowan climbed up on to a rock to sun himself, so calm, so . . . normal-looking. Kristin, a warm-weather California girl with no intention of getting into cold water unless she absolutely had to, watched from the bank. Smiling.

'Enjoying the river?' one of the swimmers asked Rowan. Of course he ignored her.

'On the spectrum?' the woman asked me quietly.

'Yes – yes, he is.'

There was a pause. 'Yes, I am!' Rowan said suddenly out of the blue, his voice small against the thunder of the cataracts.

'Thank you for talking to me,' said the woman.

'You're welcome,' said Rowan, not looking at her, but down at the sunlight sparkling on the water.

'He's doing well then,' she said to me.

'I think so. I hope so. How did you know?'

'I am an OT – occupational therapist. There's a lot of autism about at the moment.'

'There is,' I agreed. 'There is.'

Rowan launched himself back into the water and waded – he still resisted all my efforts to teach him to swim – back to me. He jumped into my arms: '*Booooyeeee!*'

And we began singing our Scubby songs together, our private father/son hymns to happiness, as the river roared loud around us.

Harold was waiting in the palm-thatch hut when, much, much later, we came down at last from the river pools. He had the tea and damper ready, and the smoke fire smouldering.

'Nice up there, eh?' He poured the tea while Rowan rambled around the clearing.

'You were right about feeling something strange as we walked into the pools,' Kristin said. 'What was that?'

Harold just smiled but offered no explanation. We didn't push it.

He performed the smoking ritual as before, Rowan again sitting unusually still in the chair as the purifying bark smoke was wafted around him. Then we went into the hut and, as before, there was the burly, smiling, ponytailed assistant with the ceramic tea mug. As he had the day before, Harold then began gently, undramatically, massaging Rowan's scalp – and again I was amazed at how Rowan calmly allowed this – then pulling with quick finger movements at the air just above Rowan's head and the back of his neck. In fact, his finger movements were almost identical to those Ghoste had made when he had performed his final healing on Rowan up on that mountain in southern Siberia two years before. Then Harold began flicking his fingers into the tea mug.

Kristin and I looked at each other, then into the mug. Sure enough, it began to fill once more with the same slightly bloody mucus, though this time only a finger deep or so. It took just a few minutes before Harold looked in the cup, gave a snort of satisfaction, tilted it so we could see better. 'Much clearer than yesterday and much less of it. That's good. Very,' and he tossed the contents out into the bushes. Rowan, as the day before, gave a deep sigh, got up and wandered outside. It was all so matter of fact. So easy. So little fuss.

'What was that?' Kristin asked.

'Like I said,' Harold replied, 'there's some things I can tell you and some things that I can't.' He paused, watching as Rowan pottered happily in the sunlight outside. 'Come back one more time tomorrow,' he said, 'and that should about do it, I reckon.'

We spent the next morning as tourists, driving north up to Cape Tribulation, where Captain Cook's ship had foundered back in the eighteenth century, causing them to go ashore and meet the Yalanji for the first time; visiting a rescue centre for fruit bats captured in predator traps or injured by cars or cats. Rowan was charmed by them, their doey eyes and furry faces contrasted by their Dracula cape wings and vampire claws. We drove back south towards Mossman, stopping at a rainforest information centre, where we, along with dozens of other tourists, climbed a high watchtower to look out over the tumbling, frothing green canopy and beyond towards the rolling blue of the Pacific. We dropped in at a backyard zoo of Australian animals – two great, dinosaurian, saltwater crocodiles, a pile of smaller freshwater ones, some kangaroos and wallabies. 'When can I go to a zoo that has African animals?' Rowan whined, causing me to dive for the protein bag. But was it me, or was he using better, more structured language in the way he was whining?

Harold had the fire, tea and damper prepared once more – a bit, it felt to me, like we were some sort of collective Lucy from the Narnia stories coming to visit Mr Tumnus in his cave, where he had tea and crumpets ready. There was something comforting about it – the familiarity, the domesticity amid the jungle. I was grateful for it. This time, after the initial smoking ceremony, Rowan sat in the shade of the thatched hut, again unusually quiet, as Harold's fingers flickered about his head and once more flicked the invisible substance into the tea mug. Again, I looked inside as he did so. There was liquid again, but very little of it – just enough to cover the tip of your fingernail, maybe, or perhaps even less – and completely clear this time; no trace of the viscous, bloody stuff we had seen on the previous two days.

Harold gave one last flick into the mug. Looked inside, nodded in satisfaction, and shook his head and shoulders, as if to release tension. 'Done!' he said, and patted Rowan on the head. Rowan – again, as on the previous two days – gave a deep sigh of apparent satisfaction, very unlike him, and said, to no one in particular, 'I feel better in my head. I feel happy,' then jumped down off the bench and ran outside to chase a brush turkey that was pecking at the sunlit grass between the hut and forest.

He'd never said anything like that before, ever.

So that was that. The second healing done. We took our leave of Harold – 'The young feller'll be doing better now, you'll see' – and headed out once more, south, down the long coast road.

Queensland is vast, about the size of Western Europe, and the road for the most part a simple two-lane highway down which you cannot drive particularly fast. Plenty of time, then, to view the great spreads of dry grasslands, the tall eucalyptus forests, the mountains marching away to the west, the sparkling coast always there to the east. Plenty of time to try and digest what we had seen. We had given up talking about it – after all, what was there to say, other than we had witnessed perhaps the strangest, most inexplicable thing that either Kristin or I had ever seen. We had no way of explaining it, nothing to relate it to. As Kristin had said to people when we had come back from Mongolia, people who wondered how she, as a scientist, felt about the whole shaman thing and whether she believed in it: 'At a certain point' – her words were measured, to the point as always – 'at a certain point, whether as a scientist or just as a regular person, you just have to become comfortable with sometimes saying, "I don't know."'

About two days after we had left Mossman, at a little town

drunk with sunshine, just inland from the tropical beaches of the Great Barrier Reef, we stopped at a Burger King – junk food being all that was available – to get some chicken nuggets for Rowan's three-hourly protein fix. We got it to go. As we drove on southwards from the little town, Rowan munching away happily on the deep-fried, processed chicken (we'd have to try and wean him to something healthier soon, I knew), he reached forward from the back seat, proffering something in his hand.

'Daddy to share.'

Still slightly scripted speech, not real conversation; oh well. I looked around to see what he was holding out. It was his box of chicken pieces. Rowan NEVER shared his food. In fact, sometimes, just to rile him, I would pretend to steal a piece of his bacon, or other snack, and be treated to a '*No no no no no no no – my food, Daddy!*' protest, after which I would giggle – 'Just kidding' – and then return the stolen item. My attempt at beginning to teach irony and perspective through humour. I had no idea if it worked but felt I at least ought to try.

Anyway, I was touched. Rowan sharing his food: something new.

I took the box and opened it. Then recoiled with a squeal of alarm, the car swerving crazily for a second before I brought it, and myself, back under control.

Rowan let out a peal of laughter. Inside the box was a very life-like latex toy squid we had bought him a few days before at a tourist shop on the road to Cape Tribulation.

'*Hahahahahahahahahahahahahahahaha* – Daddy thought it was chicken!'

He'd totally got me.

We drove a while, laughing, wondering at it, Rowan collapsing with giggles in the back. 'It was a squid! Not chicken! A squid! Daddy thought it was chicken.'

'Oh, my God,' said Kristin in a quiet voice beside me, the countryside zooming by outside the window. 'You know what that was, don't you?'

'Um, a joke? A pretty good one too.'

'Exactly. Don't you see?'

'See what?' Rowan's giggling laughter continued to peal, like little bells, from the back of the car.

'It's a *practical* joke. That's theory of mind!' She was more excited than I'd seen her in a while.

'What's that when it's at home?'

Kristin rolled her eyes. 'The ability to see something from someone else's perspective! It's a developmental milestone – one of the most important ones!'

'Errr . . . okay . . .' Rowan's giggles continued to peal deliciously from the back seat.

Kristin took a breath and, in her Professor Kristin voice, explained: 'Playing a practical joke is one of the most surefire signs that shows a child has reached that milestone – theory of mind and false belief, I mean. Most kids develop it around the age of three. It's like . . .' she searched for inspiration, 'when a kid sees, say, a picture of an elephant on the cover of a book and she holds it up and says, "Look, Mummy! An elephant!" Before the age of two and a half to three, she holds the picture up so only she can see it, so she's looking at it herself, assuming that her mother can see what she sees.'

'Okay,' I offered, hoping I was understanding.

'But then, somewhere around the three-years-old mark, she picks up the picture of the elephant and *turns it around* so that Mummy can see what she sees – because now her brain has gone through a developmental milestone that allows her to know that Mummy sees something different to what she sees. Before that, she didn't. That's theory of mind and false belief, more or less.'

'Um, right.'

More giggles from the back. 'It was a squid . . . ! Daddy didn't know . . . !'

'What's that got to do with practical jokes, though?' I asked, feeling stupid – as I sometimes did when struck by the sheer awesomeness of Kristin's brain.

'It's is one of the most advanced forms of theory of mind. Let's say you – oh, I don't know . . . you put a bucket on top of a doorway and someone walks underneath and gets the bucket and water dumped on their head. Why is that funny?'

'Um . . . because they got a bucket of water on the head?'

'Right. But it's also the surprise factor, correct? It wouldn't really be funny if the person knew the bucket of water was there, would it?'

'I guess not.' I thought about it a moment. 'Yes, you're right. You're always right. Try to do that a bit less would you?'

'Noted,' said Kristin, smiling.

'Daddy thought it was chicken! It was a squid! He went *AAAAARRGH!*'

'I sure did, Scubby!' I said.

'Daddy didn't know!' Rowan was killing himself fit to burst. The vastness of Australia cruised slowly by the window.

The next day, on a wide, white sandy beach – we were still following the coastline south – Rowan came up with an amazing idea. He had been reading the thesaurus as usual, starting, despite his difficulties with actual back-and-forth conversation, to become obsessed with words and their meanings.

We were walking along the beach, barefoot on the cool wet sand by the surf's edge.

'Daddy, what means "endangered"?'

I stopped. This was interesting. 'It means something that is in danger. With animals it's an animal that's in danger of being wiped out completely by hunters or maybe people destroying its habitat. In danger of becoming what people call extinct.'

Was he understanding? I was never sure.

'And what means "dangerous"?'

'It means something that can hurt or kill you. Some animals are dangerous – like lions that might eat you. And some of those dangerous animals are endangered themselves – like, say, black rhinos.'

'That makes them "endangerous"!'

I stopped dead. His first proper play on words. 'That's genius! Yes, Scub, that totally makes them "endangerous" – you're dead right!'

'Can I see some endangerous animals?'

'Absolutely you can. We saw some in Africa last year – the black rhinos were both endangered and dangerous. We could take trips just to see endangerous animals, if you like. We could film them, even.'

'Yes!'

'Can I come too?'

'Yes, Daddy to come! Yes! Endangerous!' He took off running along the pounding surf, sprinting hard with all his little-boy energy. When I caught up with him, he was squatting in the sand, tracing letters with a stick. E-N-D-A-N-G-E-R-O-U-S . . .

10. From the Ashes

That autumn, we started the New Trails Center up once again, and families began to come out for the playdates once more. But I still felt we hadn't quite got it right. We were still teaching Rowan with rewards: 'Do this boring thing and you can have fifteen minutes on the trampoline' – that kind of approach. But more and more this seemed the wrong way round to me.

Why not *teach* on the trampoline? His ABA therapist had originally suggested this but had never followed through. Might that not get a better result? Now was the time to try again, perhaps, with more commitment to following what Rowan actually wanted, or rather, needed, in order to learn.

Later that evening, Kristin and I talked it over. Surely the whole point of homeschooling was to be as creative, as non-institutional as possible? In fact, shortly after returning from Australia, I had been invited to talk at a conference called 'Rethinking Everything', where the focus was on, among other things, something called 'unschooling': education by following the child's interests, and cleverly tailoring the schoolwork to those interests. Say the child was into *Dungeons & Dragons* or *Grand Theft Auto*, then you designed all schooling around that game, to which the child was intrinsically motivated to give his or her attention, slipping your academic curriculum in almost by stealth. I had never heard of unschooling before, but I was intrigued, especially as several of the other speakers were young men and women who had been educated this way and had subsequently gone on to get a degree, a master's and even a PhD. The families attending the event, which took place over several days, seemed unusually connected, unusually happy, and the kids were clearly doing well.

It did indeed make me rethink. Okay, I was sold on the home-schooling idea, at least here where I lived because the school's special-needs programme had been, well, what it had been. Kristin, I knew, still wanted to try and get Rowan to some kind of regular school, but I wasn't convinced. So often people talked about their kids being 'mainstreamed' into regular schools as if that represented a kind of victory, a certificate of normality. And I could see their point to an extent. But then, was that environment the right one for these fragile, vulnerable kids? In the long run, might it not do more harm than good?

With the arrival of our two new volunteers, Jenny and then Susanna, we suddenly had a much more creative atmosphere, not to mention double the full-time staff. Rowan, who had started to become lacklustre about going to New Trails earlier in the summer, now started getting up and saying, 'Time for New Trails' and 'Time to see my ladies!' The playdates for families in the afternoon began to look more freestyle too: children bouncing on the trampoline chanting Dr Seuss; having riding lessons in the round pen or doing tricks with the horses – getting them to lie down, smile, present their legs for salutes; families rambling in the woods towards the back of the property where the wild pigs and coyotes roamed at night.

Jenny began to babysit a little – and I noticed that her interaction with Rowan was always somehow educational. Such as when he dropped his ice cream one day, and cried and asked, 'Why did the ice cream drop?' She comforted him and explained: 'Well, I suppose it's because we live on a planet called earth, which sits in the middle of something called space, or what people call the universe, where all the stars are, and what stops us from just floating off into space is the fact that there's this thing called gravity that keeps us here. Kind of sticks us to the earth, which is good, or we'd all just float away and that would never do. But annoyingly, it also means that when things fall, like your ice cream' – she had already spooned him a replacement scoop – 'they hit the earth with a thump! Or in this case a sort of splosh. All because of gravity!'

Rowan stopped a moment, and looked at her. Then teared up again: 'When can I be a little boy who lives on a planet with no gravity?'

'Ah, precious,' she said, and hugged him.

But he had got the hang of the concept. This was what I was talking about. Education through experience, imparted by a mentor with empathy and humour. My son might not be able to carry a full conversation yet – though he seemed to be slowly getting there, and there had been no regressions since the healing with Harold – but he was learning physics. Or starting to. But what would I do when Jenny left at Christmas? And I had other worries – I still didn't know how I was going to finance New Trails in the long term. I was determined not to charge families to come – and anyway, even if I did, it wouldn't even begin to cover the expenses. And I also realized that I had to get some other riders trained. None of the volunteers rode horses well enough to ride with children in the way I rode with Rowan – at a canter, out in the open, with the child in front of you in the saddle, which was where one got the best response. Thank God, Rowan had decided he wanted to ride again upon our return from Australia. More and more, I realized his relationship was with Betsy herself, rather than with horses in general. So at some point in the day, most days, he and I still headed out into the woods and pastures surrounding our house, father and son, as one body in the saddle, singing Scubby songs together under the oaks and elms.

But at New Trails we couldn't offer this with the children unless I was there. Clue and Hope, the two quiet quarterhorses I had bought, and Capitan – the grey Arabian horse, who could bow, lie down, get up on his hind legs and walk for the kids – were really only useful if I was there to ride them, and that was seldom. And what about the kids who were too big to share the saddle? Leading them around was no use, because not only did they feel bored and disempowered by that after the first few goes, but leading a horse by its head also pulls the centre of gravity too far forward and makes the horse move unrhythmically, depriving the rider of the feel-good, oxytocin-inducing effect of moving at a steady canter. So what to do?

That November, Iliane, a young German dressage rider who lived in Texas, contacted me, saying that she was putting on a horse festival in the area and wanted a local charity to benefit. We met to talk through specifics, including how we would, in between the different horse acts – roping, jumping, mounted shooting, dressage, polo and so on – do a demo of the methods we used at New Trails. 'Horse Boy Method, I guess one could call it,' I said, for want of a better term. She asked me to describe it. So I did, explaining how we tried to set up an environment where the child could roam freely, with no negative sensory triggers to upset them, then how we calmed their sensory issues the way Rowan had done with Betsy – by lying body to body on the horse, bareback, which made all the stimming just fall away. Iliane was particularly interested, as a dressage rider, in the use of collected movements – the horse moving in a slow tempo at the canter, the reins very soft in the rider's hand – and how it helped with getting the kids to talk. The oxytocin effect, in other words.

'Collected movement is what dressage is all about – and that's my passion,' she said thoughtfully. 'I'd love to see it used for something other than just sport, to heal kids. That sounds amazing.'

So she came out to see a couple of sessions. And then to ride with me and Rowan. I saw how Iliane sat, her hands so light on the reins, then brought Betsy's field-mate Taz – a horse with no formal training – and watched how he came immediately into her hand, his neck arching softly, his jaw relaxed. Here, I realized, was a very, very good rider indeed. Could she help train the volunteers and horses to work with the kids better? I took a couple of lessons with her trainers and was convinced that her training was sound – the point being to get the horse to move its centre of gravity back under the rider and dance (easier said than done) to create balance, ensure safety and a horse that says 'yes' to the rider. I realized that I was going to have to really understand this dressage thing properly myself, because this way of training a horse was clearly the key to getting communication from the children.

I had been dabbling in dressage for a few years now, on and off, but hadn't really committed to it, being up until then much more of a jumper and trail rider and general adrenaline-seeker on horseback. But even the small amounts of dressage training I had put into Betsy were clearly the key to getting Rowan to communicate more. I would have to learn properly.

There comes a time for most riders when they realize that to go the full distance of their passion they will have to relearn from scratch. I had started this dressage adventure a few years before, back in 2007, while briefly in the UK before heading out to Mongolia. Back home in Texas, I became intrigued with how, when I reduced Betsy's canter to an almost on-the-spot softness, Rowan and the other kids would communicate so much more. And I knew, from conversations with neurologists and other scientists, that this was helping the children produce the feel-good hormone oxytocin in their bodies, which presumably was why they were so suddenly open to learning and speech and communication in general. I also knew, from having grown up cross-country riding, hunting, competing successfully over fences and training horses to do that for years, that at least a minimum of dressage was always necessary to create a horse that could balance on the turns and negotiate fences correctly, neither knocking them down nor tripping. But to really learn dressage was a big undertaking. I was going to have to go back to the beginning and develop a finer, more precise, softer way of riding. So I spoke to some professionals I knew in the field and asked them what someone would do who, as a rider later in life, wanted to learn classical dressage in the most efficient way possible. And they all said the same thing: 'Go to Portugal.'

'Why Portugal?'

Because, they explained, Portugal was the best place for it. Dressage, though a sport in its own right today and a generally very good way of training a horse, was originally used to 'dress' the horse for war – so that it could sit on its haunches, spin and dance, while warriors traded blows. The horse itself could also be used as a weapon: taught to go up on his hind legs and slash with the hooves or jump into the air and kick out – movements known as 'airs above the ground'. And Portugal, my friends went on, was the last country that still bred and trained horses specifically for war. 'For war?' I didn't understand. So they explained further: because all of the phases of the Portuguese bullfight (bar two) are done on horseback, and because the ring is small and the bull goes faster than a man and horse together (at least in a dead sprint), and because if the horse isn't totally with you, the bull *will* get you, the Portuguese bullfighting horse has to be impeccably trained. So that's the best place to go to learn, they said, because the trainers really know how to get a horse that says 'yes' in no matter what situation, and can dance around the bull like a boxer. I was intrigued – not because I like bullfighting (I don't, even though in the Portuguese bullfight, unlike the Spanish, they don't kill the bull), but because I could appreciate the horsemanship required. And I was also intrigued that a horse could be trained to harm or heal through the same system. I wanted horses that would be balanced and safe at all times. Ones that could really heal. Really offer that oxytocin effect to the kids. So off to Portugal I went.

It was a revelation, that first week, sitting on their horses – the breed is called Lusitano. So fine and light that it felt like, literally, riding the wind. I began to learn the intricacies and accuracy required. How to get the horse to relax underneath you and stretch his back and neck; how to establish a connection that allowed the horse to keep a steady head carriage; how to manage the push and thrust and power of the horse so as to move sideways, diagonally, at all speeds while still keeping that dancing rhythm and that softness underneath your seat and in your hand; how to keep the horse's shoulders in front of his quarters, controlling his hind end with your hips and his shoulders with your hand. How to sit him on his hind quarters so that he danced in place (what is known as the *piaffer*) and then came up, beautifully controlled, on his hind legs (the *levade* and the *pesade*); how to gallop him on the spot like riding a stationary, ever-rolling wave (the *terre-à-terre* and the *mezair*); how to trot the horse so that he hung in midair for a half-second like a ballet dancer in mid-leap, or a note plucked on a harp string, before coming back down to earth, then springing up once more (the *passage*).

Every chance I got, I trained. First in Portugal. Then I found trainers in the UK and finally in the States. By the time Iliane appeared at New Trails, I was almost in my third year of this quest for dressage training but finding it virtually impossible to put the requisite time into the New Trails horses. So when she appeared, with much of this knowledge already in her, and with the time and desire to train the horses to provide the soft, 'collected' rhythm so beneficial to the kids who came out to New Trails, I knew I had found the missing link.

We were starting to look like something of a team. Jenny was enjoying New Trails so much that she pledged to come back in the spring, and Iliane started work on the horses. My big worry was that, while Rowan continued to do well, apart from his time with Jenny and Susanna, he still wasn't really enjoying New Trails that much any more. The families, however, were really benefiting. I wasn't sure what to do.

That Christmas we went back to London to spend time with my parents. While in the UK, we decided to run another Horse Boy Camp, this time up in Argyll in Scotland. Argyll in the winter seemed ridiculous. But the woman who was helping to organize the Horse Boy Camps had managed to find something rather amazing: a castle, no less, right on the Mull of Kintyre. Jenny met me and Rowan at Edinburgh station and we drove out from there, taking a ferry across to the mountains of Argyll, Rowan loving the adventure of it all.

As with the first camp in Wales, magic happened. One child spoke for the first time while up on a horse. Another family had made their first foray outside the immediate home area since their son's diagnosis. Despite the initial stress of finding himself in a new place, their non-verbal autistic child, Sam, allowed himself to go riding first on my shoulders, then on the horse, away from his mother and sister, giving them a break, a chance to have fun. Yet another family, all the way from Italy, brought their autistic teenage daughter and their non-autistic son. The daughter turned out to be a natural rider, loving the lessons we gave her. As in Wales, the families, hitherto isolated, were finding community, exchanging experiences, giving support and advice about different therapies. And as previously, the non-autistic siblings weren't left out but having their needs addressed too.

More than that, Jenny and Rowan really bonded during this time. He started the week bunking in with me in my room and ended it firmly camped out with 'my Jen-Jen', as he now called her. The camp was a roaring success – children learning to ride, becoming verbal, discovering a way out of their anxiety, parents and siblings finding respite while still remaining connected to their autistic child, brother or sister.

On our return I was going over the events of the camp with Kristin, both of us packing to make ready for our flight back to the States next day, when the phone rang. An Austin, Texas, number. Who could be calling us from there? One of our employees had been looking after New Trails and the animals while we were away. But it wasn't her number. I picked it up.

'Hello?'

It was a friend of mine from Elgin – Tiger, the local blacksmith.

'Tiger!' I was surprised. 'How're you doing, man? Everything okay?'

'Ru, dude, listen, your place is burning, man.'

'Burning? What do you mean? Which place?'

'The farm where you have the kids. New Trails. I could see the smoke from Elgin, drove out to see. It's on fire, man.'

My skin went cold.

'Like, how on fire? I mean like how bad?'

Kristin was watching me, frozen.

'Like, really fucking burning, dude.' As he spoke, I heard the wail of sirens. 'We called the fire department, looks like they're here. I'm really sorry.' I could hear the roar of the flames. Jesus.

'It's okay.' I couldn't think of what else to say. It wasn't okay at all. Why do we say these things – perhaps to comfort ourselves? I put the phone down, looked over at Kristin. Rowan, luckily, was playing elsewhere in the house with my mother. 'New Trails is on fire.' All that work. All that money. All that effort and love. All destroyed, gone up in smoke.

Kristin was speechless. Shit, I thought – the horses. But there were fifteen acres of open pasture – no barn close to the house – so they must be okay, must have run over to the far fence. But there were other animals: one of our employees had a dog, a little black Labrador/German shepherd mix, along with a cat and a python in a tank. And we had rabbits, guinea pigs and a couple of small parakeets (the green one and blue one that Rowan had asked for back in Namibia the year before) that lived in a cage in the kitchen. What of them?

What were we going to do?

Then, right as we sat there, I had a brainwave. Stafford owned a little guest house that sat in the middle of his lower pasture, right by our boundary fence – the same fence Rowan had gone through years before when he made his first contact with Betsy. It had sat empty for a while. Now, as I stood in my mother and father's house in London, my dream for serving autism families through horses fast vanishing on the other side of the world, I remembered that little guest house.

I grabbed the phone, dialled Stafford's number. He answered.

'Hey Rupert, what's happenin'?'

'My place – the one I built for the kids – is burning. The fire department's there now but it sounds like it's a goner. Listen, Stafford, is your guest house still vacant?'

'It is.'

'Listen, can I rent it – to do the thing we do with the kids and such? It'll mean moving a couple of horses on to the pasture.'

'That's fine.'

'Thank you. Thank you . . .'

'You bet.'

And it was done.

I turned to Kristin, who was crying.

'You know,' I said, 'I have to admit this – I feel guilty about admitting this – but I feel kind of relieved.'

We hugged, holding each other for a long, long while.

'All that time, all that money, all that work . . .' Kristin's voice was small against my shoulder.

'I know, love, I know.'

So back we flew next day, to new beginnings.

11. New New Trails

Weirdly, Rowan had taken the news in his stride, especially when I'd told him we'd be renting the little house he knew so well but had never actually been in. 'A new New Trails,' he'd said.

'That's right – New New Trails.'

'*Noo Noo* Trails,' he'd laughed. And then: 'Will Jenny be there?'

'She will,' I confirmed, as the plane rose above the clouds and we headed west for America.

'I love Jen-Jen,' he said, looking out through the window of the plane at the great masses of cumulus.

Back on terra firma, I went with the fire marshal to inspect the old site – the charred ruin of our hopes and dollars. It had happened like this, he explained. One of our employees had gone into Austin to visit her boyfriend but – it being January – had left a space heater plugged in on maximum to try and keep the place warm while she was out. In her absence, some time in the small hours, her cat had knocked the heater over on to a pile of magazines . . .

Soon after the fire, Jenny and Khatiche, who had helped me at the first Horse Boy Camp in Wales, arrived and set to work with a will. The families immediately started coming to the new location and the girls, drawing on their Horse Boy Camp experience, began putting on playdates that were far superior to what we had been offering so far – partly because, owing to her experience with her autistic brother, Khatiche had great empathy with the children, her judgement calls always spot on, and partly because Jenny, who had ridden since she was a young girl, was able to ride with the kids on Betsy at a canter, just as I did. And Iliane began to come riding with the kids more and more too.

The various news outlets in Austin had reported on the fire and the community responded generously, donating enormous, wonderful quantities of saddlery, tack and furniture to replace what had been burned. We were up and running again almost immediately, and better than before. For the time being, my three horses still grazed the fifteen acres surrounding the blackened shell of the burned centre – we would bring them over in due course. For now we had Betsy and Taz, the two horses that Stafford had owned for years and that Rowan and I always rode together – not to mention Chango, the old black Mexican pony. And Jenny, who had spent the previous autumn with us and therefore knew what stage Rowan was at academically, stepped in to fill the teaching gap.

And that's where things started to get interesting. I had told Jenny that I always got my best results teaching Rowan when up on the horse or just running around in nature. One day, as spring began to green the buds of the woods between my house and New New Trails, she came with Rowan back to our house, grinning from ear to ear. After he had gone upstairs to play, she said, 'Something rather amazing has just happened.'

She had, until then, sat with Rowan at the kitchen table at New New Trails, trying to get him to concentrate on maths and other subjects, before rewarding him with time playing outside. He had tried, as usual, and, as usual, had soon grown restive. 'But this time it was as if he was really suffering,' Jen reported. 'He started to whimper, really, really wanting to go outside and bounce on the trampoline even though our fifteen-minute round of schoolwork wasn't yet up.' She went on: always a chair rocker, Rowan, in his desperate need to move, had started to rock with more and more agitation until, all of a sudden, he rocked so hard he brought both chair and table together down on top of him.

'I was just about to say,' Jenny recounted, 'that if he did another five minutes and concentrated well, I'd let him go out and bounce. And then when he fell right over backwards like that, I thought, wait a minute. This is totally backwards, just as I remembered you saying. He wants to be on the trampoline. Why don't I do maths on the trampoline!'

So out they went and Jenny, up on the trampoline with Rowan, started to call the times tables and then bounce him the requisite number of times. He was enchanted and lay there letting Jenny bounce him while he squealed with delight.

'Then he started calling out how many times I should bounce him, and suddenly he took over,' said Jen. 'It was amazing. We went through all the times tables up till twelve, first with me shouting them and bouncing him, which he found highly amusing. And then he just took over and did them, calling them by himself! It was incredible!'

'You must be knackered,' I said, wondering how many hundreds of bounces that must have been.

'Well, I suspect that I'm going to get into rather marvellous shape through all this. But it works. It really works. From now on I think we should completely abandon trying to do anything at the table . . .'

'Unless he parks himself there and it's his decision,' I interjected.

'Exactly!'

All right then: no more old-style ABA approach. No more rewards for compliance. No more coercion. No more 'you must'. From now on we would let Rowan lead us, and it would be up to us to accept the challenge of keeping up with his curriculum this way. Maybe this was what those folks had meant by 'unschooling'. And, honestly, at this rate we'd soon be jumping a grade or two ahead. The twelve-times table done through trampoline bounces. Extraordinary!

Then something else happened. One day soon after this, Jenny came in from her session with Rowan saying, 'I can't believe this – and I have to tell you while it's still fresh in my mind. We were on the trampoline today and Rowan was getting bored with the multiplication and he said he wanted to "ruin" it. Make it all wrong because he was sick of it. I said sure, go ahead. He said, "You ask me the numbers this time – I'll tell you what to ask. Ask me zero times two." So I did, still bouncing, and he said "zero". Then he said, "Ask me one times two." So I did, and he said "one". I thought he was getting it deliberately wrong, but I was just going with it. Then he asked me to ask him what two times two was; I did, and he said "four". Then he asked me to ask him what three times two was – and I did, and he said "nine". Then it was four times two, and he said "sixteen", and finally five times two, and he said "twenty-five".'

'I'm lost,' I admitted. 'Why is this good?'

Jenny said nothing for a moment, just looked at us, as if waiting for light to dawn. Kristin – the mathematician in the family – got it first. 'No way . . .' she said, quietly. 'No way. He was squaring the numbers! That's incredible!'

Jenny nodded. 'I know. It took me a while to work it out, but I finally clocked what he was doing! This little boy is a bit of a genius, I'm afraid.'

So from then on Jenny started deliberately encouraging Rowan to 'ruin the lesson'. Getting things deliberately wrong as a strategy for learning. He found it hilarious, and all sorts of inventive learning games were spawned as a result. The first was 'duck academics'. Rowan asked Jenny to let him bring his two ducks, Ron and Taylor, down into the woods in a cage to do lessons with him. Jenny would hang great sheets of paper from the trees and do sums there, or history timelines, or diagrams of cells. And then she'd ask the ducks to repeat back what she had written, and Rowan, answering as the ducks, would get the answers deliberately wrong. Answers like the Great Plague of London of 1665 being spread by ducks, rather than rats, or the ducks asserting that eight divided by two was five thousand. Rowan then would erupt into laughter, and insist that Jenny get 'very very cross' with Ron and Taylor. So cross that she became red in the face and her neck flushed. (Once percentages were introduced, he insisted that Jen should be cross 'exactly 75 per cent of the time'.) Then, his laughter done, he would correct the ducks by giving the right answer.

In March, Iliane also moved into New New Trails, bringing all her horse-riding skills, so we could move the other three horses over at last, and suddenly we were feeling like a proper centre, a real tribe. And when I thought about it, that was what this whole Horse Boy thing came down to – tribe, extended family living in a rural setting. Wasn't this the way human beings were supposed to live, in the countryside, surrounded by animals? They say it takes a village to raise a child, and Kristin and I, hitherto so isolated – like so many autism and other special-needs parents – were suddenly finding ourselves in the centre of that village, and Rowan was thriving.

But when I looked back, I realized that this whole tribe thing had actually started way earlier than that. It had started the first week that Kristin and I had moved into our little wooden house with the porch under the big oak tree, in October of 1999, two years before Rowan was even born. Not a fortnight after we had moved in, knowing no one, Stafford had ridden down the dry riverbed at the back of our land on Betsy, had ridden right up to our front door, dismounted and knocked. I answered to find a medium-height, good-looking man, broad set, clad in cowboy hat, boots and spurs, holding the reins of a bay mare with a high-pommelled Western saddle. A bit like having Robert Duval or John Wayne ride up to your door. It seemed I had indeed moved to Texas.

'Afternoon.' He held out a hand. 'Stafford O'Neal. I have the property backing on to yours. I've been riding this land for some years now, and I wondered if you'd have any objection if I were to keep riding it from time to time.' His accent was Deep South, the tone courtly. I introduced myself and Kristin and told him I had no objection at all.

'Do you ride yourself?' Stafford asked me. I told him I did. Would I care to go trail riding some time, he enquired. I told him that I'd love to. In return I asked if he'd like a beer, for the day was warm. He said he didn't mind if he did. I brought a couple of cold ones out to the porch. Did I like to hunt, he asked. I told him I did, but maybe not in a way he was familiar with, then described the process of hunting with horses and hounds that I'd grown up with. To my surprise, he told me that a friend of his up the way had a pack of hounds and they went after wild boar on horseback most weekends through the winter and would I like to come? I told him I absolutely would, and a friendship was born.

Stafford and I could not have been more opposite in terms of the political spectrum. I a long-haired hippy tree-hugger, he an ex-Vietnam veteran and true-blue Republican. These were the Bush years, with Obama yet to come – an era of political polarization, a sickness at the heart of America unseen since the days of the American Civil War, a hundred and fifty years before. People simply were not, are still not, friends across this polarized divide. But for Stafford and me, such distinctions didn't count. We enjoyed horses, the countryside and beer. We'd go for the odd trail ride together and even more occasional hunting foray, stopping at a local bar in Elgin afterwards to have a beer or two and swap stories: about Vietnam, his North Carolina farm boyhood, horses and dogs on his part; about Africa, my Leicestershire farm boyhood, horses and dogs on mine.

So when Rowan went through the fence that fateful day in 2004, and made his own connection with Stafford's mare Betsy, instead of Stafford saying, 'Sorry, you can't bring your autistic two-and-a-half-year-old on to my property – there might be an accident and I might get sued,' instead he gave me the key to the saddle room.

With Stafford the sense of community, family, clan, tribe, was already there long before Rowan went through the fence to Betsy. Without that, nothing, none of the miracles that followed, could have happened. It all came down to the quality of human heart that had led Stafford to ride Betsy down the dry riverbed and knock on our door in the first place.

And now here we were after the fire, renting the little house on his property, transformed into New New Trails (known, after a few months, simply as 'New Trails' again), and families were finding healing – not just us, but many others – and the tribe was growing. Moreover, it solved the financial issue: it was a fraction of the price to rent the house and the few acres that surrounded it than I had shelled out for the mortgage and rehab of old New Trails. Suddenly everything was affordable, which meant, as we gradually learned the ropes of fund raising, that I could finally see a real future to it all.

The growing tribe wasn't just local. That spring, families started coming in from far afield – Australia, Malaysia, Holland, France. And extraordinary things began to happen: over in the UK, camps started running at various locations.

In late spring there was a camp in Cornwall, in the UK, that I was able to attend. The woman who had helped us put the first Horse Boy Camp together in Wales the previous summer, as well as the one in the castle in Argyll, had organized this one too. Kristin, Rowan and I all attended on this occasion, and it was on this camp that I learned a seminal lesson in how to truly follow the child. One of our fellow attendees was a boy, Scott, whose behaviour was pretty wild. He would grab the shoes that people had left outside their tents and chuck them into the stream. He could be violent. He was just about to enter his teens and was possibly the most handsome human being I have ever seen. He had a sense of humour, he was intelligent. But he was non-verbal and he was incontinent – sometimes. In short, he was a challenge.

On the second day of the camp, things were going better; the worst of the wild behaviour had calmed somewhat after we'd had a chance to generally chill out – riding, running around barefoot (deemed calming for the sensory system) on the wet West Country grass, sitting in the sun or splashing in the beautiful, water lily-strewn river than ran down from Bodmin Moor through the yellow gorse and broom. We were all gearing up to go on a trail ride, children in the saddle in front of us, others on our shoulders, others walking or being led, with the idea of reaching an old stone cairn up at the moor's edge. Scott did not want to ride, however. All he wanted to do was splash in the water. His mother became upset: she had brought him all this way to ride horses. I thought she should let her son be: after all, this camp was all about letting a child do what he wanted, not forcing him do something he didn't; or at least starting from what he preferred doing, not from what one wanted him to do, because honestly that was only practical.

'But he always splashes in water. It's just stimming! I want him to ride!'

I looked at Scott, happily playing in the bright stream. He seemed to be doing it in very set patterns, with great concentration, and every few seconds, or sometimes longer, he would throw up his arms and throw back his head in a kind of ecstasy. Was there a pattern there?

'I dunno . . .' I was reluctant to force the kid on to a horse; I knew by now that that was very definitely not the way to go. But I didn't want to contradict his mother, either – she had come so far to be here.

Then one of the volunteers, himself a high-functioning young man on the autism spectrum, stepped in.

'I think I know what's going on,' he said. 'You guys go ride. Leave me here with my camera, and if I'm right, when you come back, I should be able to show you something.'

So off we went, the mother not pleased but not too displeased either, and explored the old turf alleyways of the gorse forest for an hour on horseback with the other families. When we came back, Scott had left the water and was quietly sunning himself on the bank, looking contented, all his mania gone.

'Here,' said the young man who had stayed with him, showing us the camera. 'I think you should see this.'

The mother and I looked. She burst into tears, as did I.

'I focused on the middle distance between us – where Scott's hands were,' said the young man by way of explanation, then added: 'I wasn't dissimilar to him when I was younger, you see. So I kind of thought this might be what was going on.'

The images showed Scott making sculptures out of water. Beautiful, intentional sculptures. 'They weren't all this good,' said the young man. 'I just saved the best.'

And the best were indeed the best. The intentionality on Scott's face and the purposeful movements of his hands were clear to see as he shaped the moving water into sculptures of a horse, a dolphin, a series of helixes. It brought to mind the work of landscape artists like Andy Goldsworthy and Richard Long who use nature, time and tide to create extraordinary art out of anything, from leaves pressed on to rock or scattered over water, to the patterns made by sticks, sand and snow when thrown up into the wind.

After a shot of one particularly beautiful water dolphin, the next picture showed Scott throwing his arms out in ecstasy at what he had created.

'Oh, my God,' said his mother. 'I had no idea.'

'We should try and get these into galleries,' I mused.

If I had tried to force Scott on to the horse, we would never have seen these amazing water sculptures. Later at the camp Scott did ride, and rides regularly to this day. But I had learned the lesson once again – always follow the child; start from where the child is, not where you want him or her to be.

It wasn't always so clear, though – and this was where the real magic came in. There was another family who came to New Trails that spring from Holland. Their little girl – eight years old, verbal but still in nappies – did not want to ride, but wanted to just hang out with me while I let Clue graze at the end of a rope, going up and down the driveway as he nibbled at the grass. She didn't want to get on the horse, and I felt, at the end of an hour or so and the family having left after a cup of tea, that I had somewhat failed them.

A few months afterwards, I received an email from the mother asking us to send her – at her little girl's request – photos of Clue, so that they could blow them up and put them on the girl's wall.

What had happened, she explained, was that a few days after they had left us, they had gone camping and the little girl had thrown her nappies into the rubbish bin and used the toilet by herself for the first time. When her mother asked her why, the girl had said, cryptically, 'Clue taught me.' And in the months since then, the mother wrote, her daughter had made all kinds of further leaps – including much more involved conversation, much less tantrumming, better social skills. And each time that her mother praised her for these, her little girl would say again, 'Clue taught me.' And now she wanted pictures of Clue for her wall.

What was going on between these children and the horses?

Reading the email, I couldn't help but feel a little jealous, though. Conversation, the mother had reported: for Rowan it still hadn't come. Sure, he expressed very articulately what he wanted. He could do his schoolwork with little or no problem. He could even now say, 'I love you, Daddy' and 'I love you, Mummy' spontaneously, which meant the world to us, of course. But if you called his name, he often still did not respond. If you asked him, 'What did you do today?' he would look blankly at you and then either run off or start talking about something else entirely. He could walk up to you and tell you very intensely, looking you right in the eye, that lobsters had a pincer claw and a crusher claw. But if you asked him how he felt about something, or to fetch you something from the fridge, or what he wanted for dinner, you got just a blank stare – or rather, a deer-in-the-headlights freeze as he clearly registered that he was supposed to respond in some way, but couldn't for the life of him figure out how. For all his amazing gains, back-and-forth conversation – the real stuff of survival in human communication – was still beyond him.

He had other strategies to cope with this, however. For example, he might not tell you what he wanted for dinner, or wanted to do that day, but he'd help you figure it out through a process of deduction. Jen or Khatiche might say, 'How about chicken strips for lunch?' And if he didn't want that, Rowan would answer, 'Or . . .' And then the girls might say, 'Or we could have bacon . . .'

'Or . . .'

'Um, okay – think, think; or we could have popcorn chicken!'

'Popcorn chicken!'

It was functional, but it wasn't exactly conversation. We were still stuck in this enigma: a beautiful one, but an enigma nevertheless. Would my son ever be truly healed? Not cured of his autism – his autism was great. I was happy with his autism; indeed there were so many gifts there: the lack of ego, never comparing himself to others, his ability to concentrate on the task at hand, his seemingly photographic memory, his sheer *Scubbiness*. But healing – getting to the point where the autism was no longer a deficit, no longer held him back . . . this was what I wanted so passionately for him, for us. We seemed to be so on the cusp of it. But not quite there yet.

We still had one healing left to do, to complete Ghoste's charge to us of making three more healing journeys after Mongolia. We had fulfilled his instructions to the letter so far, and I wasn't about to give up. I had already been planning this third, final healing journey, had it in hand. And the best thing about it was that we would not even have to leave the country to do it.

I had been in touch with an autism mother in Portland, Oregon – Martha – who had read *The Horse Boy* and because of it, and because of earlier experiences in her life, had been moved to contact a local Mexican *curandera* or shaman living in her city. The woman had worked with Martha's son, Will – non-verbal, highly neuro-sensitive and prone not just to the usual tantrums but to physically attacking his mother and sister. Martha wrote to me, after the first session with the healer, that she had noted an almost immediate reduction in his acute anxiety, and an increase in his ability to make contact and express his needs. At five, Will was much where Rowan had been at the same age. The *curandera* had said that more involved healing was beyond her, and so Martha, partly through talking with the *curandera* further and partly through her own researches, had eventually discovered a very good healer down on the Navajo reservation in Arizona. His name was Blue Horse. Would I be interested, she asked me, in making a joint trip down to see this man?

Gut feeling again. Strong as a punch to the stomach; every instinct said 'yes'. Not just because I had had dealings with the Navajo before and knew how strong the traditions still were, down in that strange red desert where they and their neighbours, the Hopi, had lived for thousands of years. More than that: the idea of two autism families going to seek healing together, of us doing it as a tribe – that word again – felt completely right. We agreed to rendezvous in Gallup, New Mexico, that June, and drive into the reservation together from there.

Martha had made contact with Blue Horse, or rather with his apprentice, a man called Charles. By strange coincidence, Charles was also British – from north London, just like me. And an ex-journalist for the *Telegraph*, just like me, too. He had felt called to work with Blue Horse after a series of incidents while travelling in the States and elsewhere had led him by degrees into the strange world of shamanism and healing – again pretty much like me. There were so many connections here. Martha and Charles (who spoke Navajo and acted as Blue Horse's interpreter) exchanged emails, going over the logistics and set a midsummer meeting date. The final healing was set. Would it work? Would Rowan become conversational at last? Or again, was I just chasing butterflies here?

The red cliffs of the canyon country began to close in soon after we left Albuquerque, travelling westwards on Interstate 40. We'd already passed through Texas Hill Country, the oaks and limestone, rivers and lakes giving way to the flat, high plains around Abilene – a name to conjure images of old Westerns, but in fact a thriving little town on whose outskirts we had stopped to feed giraffes in the small, well-run zoo. On from there we'd travelled, rising by slow degrees in altitude to the Llano Estacado – the 'Staked Plains' which had been the Comanche heartland until just a century and a half ago. The almost waterless, ocean-sized area of arid pastureland had served as the base for this horse-born nation, who had learned classical dressage from the Spaniards, made it their own and then bred their own horses, turning their warriors into some of the finest, most effective cavalry the world has ever seen and keeping the white man at bay for four hundred years until America came up with its own Final Solution: kill off the buffalo that the Indians rely on for food and force them into reservations.

Hence, as we drove, there were neither buffalo nor Comanche (the survivors of that genocide were all removed eastward to Oklahoma, where their reservation remains to this day). Instead there were miles and miles of irrigated ploughland, their monotony broken up here and there with great post-industrial forests of wind turbines, towering out of scale like science-fiction movie props across a landscape where wind and air, heat and dust rule supreme. From there onwards via Lubbock, the city that produced Buddy Holly and the Crickets, Roy Orbison and a host of other rock 'n' roll icons. You could see why: Lubbock is not a place to stay in for life; it's a town you come from and leave – sprawling, strip mall after strip mall, concrete and glass, and tumbledown neighbourhoods of plain wooden houses sweating in the heat. Then heading westwards, into the Great American Desert.

Not a desert of barren sand and rock, like the Namib or the Sahara. America's deserts for the most part are pretty well vegetated – arid grassland and dry forest not unlike, say, the Kalahari. The low rainfall and absence of groundwater gives the desert its official title. But as you drive into eastern New Mexico out of Texas, the overwhelming impression is of grass. Grassland as far as the eye can see, the road following the railway line through an immense flatness, the sky huge, a melodrama of mountain-sized cumulus depositing localized rain showers here and there across the otherwise dry infinitude. Harsh, shifting light, the occasional turkey vulture hanging in the thermals. On through Clovis, and then largely uninhabited country until gradually the flat grassland begins to be broken first by low knolls of juniper-grown, chalky rock glarily reflecting the day's heat, then by high and ever higher ridges, the juniper becoming a ubiquitous evergreen thicket. And then – 'There they are!' – the mountains, rising to the west and north. The southern end of the Great Rockies – the San Juans, snow still on their highest tops, off to the right, and then the great knuckled massif of Sandia Peak, which towers above the desert city of Albuquerque. West of there, you are in Indian country.

It was so strange to be taking this, the final healing journey Ghoste had told us to do, as an American family road trip. No planes, no border crossings, no leaving one world and entering another. But just getting in the family sedan, heading west, stopping at fast-food joints, with a night first in a Holiday Inn Express in Abilene, followed by a cheap motel in Clovis, and then back into the car, eating nuts and chips, listening to Manu Chao, Fischerspooner, Desmond Dekker and Deee-Lite.

Kristin and I sang along to 'Groove is in the Heart' as we headed west to Gallup and our meeting with Martha, who had driven down through the high West from Oregon with her friend Shari, her thirteen-year-old daughter Sarah and Will.

I say that we had not had to enter another world this time. But that isn't strictly true. Once you go west of Albuquerque, from there until I-40 spits you out two or three days later on the coast of the Pacific, you are in the land of Indian tribes that never left, were never displaced, at least never for long, and whose reservations – and traditional culture – still determine both the character of the landscape and the life that goes on there. The real America, in fact.

This Four Corners region, as it's known – where New Mexico, Arizona, Colorado and Utah all come together – is the sacred heart of the USA. Pre-Columbian American, the America that was there before the whiteys showed up. The Pueblo, who kicked the Spanish out and then resisted further incursions from their fortress-like adobe mud towns and stayed doggedly on when the Spanish reclaimed the region and when the Anglos in their turn claimed it. They are still there, still living in their pueblos, which are as old – some of them older – than any medieval village in Europe. The Zuni, secure on top of their mesas, natural fortresses set high above the desert floor, are still there too, where they always have been.

The Navajo own a stunning four million acres – about the size of Ireland – that comprise a little bit of three of the states. The Hopi, whose square-shaped territory occupies the uplands of the centre of the Navajo reservation, still live in the same clifftop dwellings they have occupied for about five thousand years. They were there when Stonehenge was built in England, and are still there to this day – no mean feat in the face of colonial incursion, climate change and tribal war. This is America as it was before it became known by that name. When it was still the Turtle Island of Iroquois and Algonquin myth, when its great interior was unknown to Europeans. Another world. Reachable now by freeway.

It was not my first time in pre-Columbian North America. Back in 1990, I'd got my first breakthrough into journalism by reporting on the Cree Indians' ultimately successful fight to prevent Hydro-Québec – the government-owned hydro-power behemoth of French-speaking Canada – from flooding an area of their territories roughly the size of France. I had spent time up on the traplines with the Cree, where they still lived under canvas in the snow, eating otter and beaver, caribou and moose, trapping for fur, fishing – and keeping the whiteys out. Then, when I moved to the States to be with Kristin in the mid 1990s, I heard about something called the Black Mountain Dispute and went to report on that. Black Mountain was in the heart of the Navajo reservation, right where it bordered the Hopi lands.

Black Mountain was interesting because, on the face of it, the dispute (for said mountain) was between the Navajo and Hopi tribes. But in fact it was a manufactured dispute, or rather an existing dispute that had been exacerbated by the power giant Peabody Coal (the red mountains and mesas of the Navajo reservation conceal vast deposits of coal, uranium and other minerals). The story went like this. Peabody wanted to mine the coal reserves of the aptly named Black Mountain, which happened to be sacred to the Navajo and on their sovereign territory but located right where it adjoins the Hopi reservation. The Hopi, for the large part no more a friend of white-owned mining companies than their Navajo neighbours, are still enemies – since hundreds, if not thousands of years – of the Navajo. Black Mountain – being Indian territory – was off limits to the coal company . . . unless one of the tribes invited them in. Black Mountain was disputed territory between the two tribes. So Peabody, over many years, managed to bribe members of the Hopi Tribal Council to lobby Washington to have the tribal boundaries redrawn to put Black Mountain inside Hopi lands, and then – in return for further remuneration and substantial other payoffs – license the mining rights to Peabody. So far, so easy – another white-man ploy to play indigenous tribes off against each other, then go in, grab the goodies and run.

Except for the fact that one very tenacious old Navajo biddy called Roberta Blackgoat refused to move off the mountain. As long as anyone still lived on it, the mountain couldn't be mined. So began a process of intimidation, Hopi police hassling the old lady, impounding her sheep (the Navajo are largely a sheep-herding people, having acquired livestock from the Spanish some five hundred or so years ago), arresting her family when they came to visit, for this vehicle violation or that aggravated trespass order, and generally making her life miserable. This of course had only made old Roberta more stubborn and eventually the story leaked out into first the regional and then the national press, as people rolled their eyes at Indians still fighting what looked to be old tribal wars, while Peabody bided its time on the sidelines, ready to come in and take the spoils. This in turn alerted environmental and then human-rights groups; and so for a while Roberta Blackgoat became something of a national heroine: the human hub of a story that went to the heart of America – a modern reliving of how the West was actually won.

I managed to get a couple of British papers and magazines interested and drove in to meet Roberta, who still lived in a hogan – the traditional round hut of the Navajo people – surrounded by her friendly goats and sheep. Surprisingly friendly, given that she was stewing one of them in an open pot – the smell pungent and gamey in the evening air – over a fire out front of the hogan, the goat's entrails heaped neatly to the side and its flayed skin stretched on a frame of sticks.

'It's not even the Hopi who are to blame,' she sighed, as we chomped on pieces of tough, recently alive goat and watched the sun set over the great emptiness around us. 'They're just pawns, bought by the white man, by Peabody. That's our Indian history – pawns for the white man. But I won't let it happen without a fight.'

It had been a privilege to spend a couple of days with Roberta, helping her herd her stock, drawing water and cutting wood for her as she told us stories of the other America, *her* America. 'Even the medicine men, the bad ones, have got involved,' she told me. 'The Navajo skin walkers trying to scare the Hopi ones and vice versa,' she chuckled. 'I've even had spirits sent against me here, trying to make me come out of the hogan at night so they can skin *me*. But no, I'm too old, too clever for that.'

'Skin walkers?' I asked. 'What are they?'

'Bad medicine men who try to harm people for money. We have good medicine men and bad, good and bad like everything else in life. At night they can take the forms of other things – coyotes, deer, mountain lions, other types of spirit – and lure you outside to do you harm.'

'How do you know when a deer or a coyote is a skin walker?'

'It's in their eyes, the way the walk, the sounds they make.' She chuckled again. 'You don't believe me, I know, but I tell you this. Life is different here from in the white man's cities.'

I'd left knowing that I'd had a glimpse of a life few in America ever get to see. Even in crisis, it was good, somehow, to know that that old life was still there, alive and strong. I filed the story as a stalemate piece, a snapshot of how colonialism was still there, still pirating the more vulnerable peoples of the world as effectively as it had back in the bad old days of the nineteenth century. A few years later, when I became involved with the Bushmen, I read that Roberta had died and that the mountain, finally, was being mined – but only on the Hopi side. The Navajo side, as if protected by Roberta's ghost, remained intact. The experience of meeting her, of seeing how much difference one person could make, following on from observing how the Cree had managed to see off a much larger white-man company than Peabody Coal, had made me realize that the Bushmen, in their own struggle to stay on lands earmarked for diamond mining, could also be successful against the odds. In short, Roberta, and the Navajo in general, had inspired me.

So when, in 2004, the year that Rowan was diagnosed, the Bushmen came to America to plead their case at the United Nations, I brought them to stay with the Navajo, so they could consult with people that had also managed to hold on, endure, despite all. Now, as Kristin, Rowan and I drove back into the red canyonlands, echoes of that previous journey came back clear as day. For it had been here, on that earlier journey, that I had been asked to make a sacrifice for Rowan. A sacrifice of something very dear to me.

The Navajo had invited the Bushmen to attend a ceremony for the return of their land, down in perhaps the remotest area of the Navajo reservation – Canyon de Chelly (pronounced 'Shay'). A ritual with some Navajo elders who wanted to bless the Bushmen, give them spiritual strength before they took up the fight in New York and Washington. Half of our party – the older folk, including the eighty-year-old Roy Sesarna, an incredibly tough old Ganakwe Bushman who had more or less single-handedly taken on the Botswana government, and therefore De Beers diamonds – went into the canyon by vehicle, a several-hour bump-bump by 4x4, while we of the younger crew, including Jumanda (who helped bring Besa to heal Rowan four years later and was Roy Sesarna's right hand), rode on horseback down the steep cliffs of the canyon itself.

The night before we set off, an old Navajo medicine man, unconnected with the group waiting for us down in the canyon, had shown up at our camp.

'I hear you're here with the Bush people from Africa to try and help them get their land back,' he said.

I confirmed that, yes, indeed we were.

'Would you guys like to sweat and pray for the return of their land?' he asked. He was referring to a sweat lodge – a sort of hand-built temporary sauna constructed over a pit of white-hot stones, where you crouch in the dark, and sweat and pray to purify yourself and send your prayers to the ears of the divine.

Roy and Jumanda thought this a fine idea. So the medicine man took us to a sweat lodge at a short distance away, and into the lodge we went, stripped off and sweated and prayed. We did one round, came out to cool down, then a hotter round, came out to cool again under the desert stars. Then a third round: much, much hotter than the previous two – what they call the 'warrior round', which really scorches the lungs – praying and singing for the return of the Bushman land. After that, in the sweaty darkness, the medicine man asked, 'Has anyone got anything else they want to pray for?'

'Yes,' I said. 'My son was just diagnosed with autism. I want to pray for him.'

So another round of prayers was sung, there in the darkness, and I had to sing a song from my culture, my country, in honour of my son. The song that came instantly to my lips was the song I always sang him, the old English folk song I used to sing to him when getting him to sleep, or when riding along on Betsy, 'Over the Hills and Far Away':

> And I would love you all the day,
> Every night would kiss and play,
> If with me you'd gladly stray
> Over the hills and far away . . .

As I sang, it felt that my son was slipping from me. '*Don't leave me, Rowan, my beautiful son,*' I whispered in the blackness. '*Take me with you. Don't leave me behind.*'

In the dark, no one can see you cry.

Later, as we sat outside, letting the sweat evaporate from our skins under the desert stars, the medicine man approached me.

'Do you hunt?' he asked.

'I do,' I said. 'But perhaps not in a way you are familiar with.' And, as I once had to Stafford, I proceeded to describe the grandly, beautifully pointless sport of riding to hounds. I haven't let on, in this book, just how much a part of me fox hunting was up until that time. I even partly made my living at it, hired by equestrian magazines to go round the UK and US to write up hunts, describing the thrill of launching oneself and one's horse cross-country, sometimes over fences too big to see to the other side, the fear and adrenaline so addictive that one never felt as alive as in that mad dash after the hounds. Back then, to a large degree, it defined me.

The medicine man was silent a moment, then said: 'Well, I don't know why. But I'm getting it loud and clear from the spirit world that you have to stop.'

'Stop?'

'Yes, and that somehow it's connected to your son's autism. That's all I can tell you, I'm afraid.' He shrugged.

My heart sank. But it made perfect sense. Hunting was something that went to the core of who I was. Giving it up would be such a loss, a sacrifice. Which meant that it made sense. It would hurt, but it made sense.

'Okay,' I said, sensing the enormity of what I was committing to. 'Okay. I'll give it up.'

And I did. Since that year, I have not hunted nor ridden to hounds. I miss it, but I have kept my vow.

As an aside, a month or two after I had taken the vow, a friend of mine, a big name in the fox-hunting world, called me. He had heard about my giving up hunting, and felt betrayed. 'You've become an anti!' he said, accusingly.

'I haven't become an anti, it's just a personal decision – listen . . .' and I recounted the story from the Navajo sweat lodge, but it was beyond him. 'I dunno,' he said. 'I gotta tell you, I feel let down.'

This was a good friend. I suspected I was losing him, which

made me sad, but my tale was too otherworldly for him. Then out of the darkness, into the glow of my porchlight, stepped a fox.

Now you have to understand that in the US, especially in Texas, seeing a fox isn't like seeing a fox in the UK where it's the top predator and now proliferates even in cities. In the western states, where coyote is king, foxes are lower down the chain, and coyotes routinely hunt and kill them. So spotting one near my house happens perhaps only once every two years or so. Now, as I spoke to my fox-hunting friend, a fox just plain old walked out of the dark, stood there in the glow of the porchlight, and – to blow my mind further – began to bark at me. Stunned for a brief moment, I let my voice tail off, then told my friend, 'You'll never believe what's just happened as I've been talking to you. But here – listen . . .' And I held the phone out towards the fox.

My friend recognized the sound. 'Unbelievable,' he said, in astonishment. 'Then I guess you'd better do what the gods are telling you to do.'

And perhaps to reward me for making the sacrifice, the gods of Navajoland gave me the ride of my life. The morning after I'd made the vow, we mounted up and rode down into the canyon. It was perhaps two thousand feet down to the bottom, along a track that was narrow in some places, slippery in others, with the cliffside always uncomfortably close. One wrong step and, well . . . it wasn't hard to imagine. Our Navajo guide, easy in his saddle, chatted amiably, pointing out where a mountain lion had its den in a further red sandstone cliff, a tree down below where he had once run into a bear, a pair of white mountain goats on a jagged peak a mile or so away. The horses, footsure and used to the terrain, picked their way without mishap down the long, long descent to the canyon floor, occasionally slipping on loose stones but always recovering. 'Yeah, we Navajo are pretty comfortable on cliffs – but not like the Hopi. They live on them like goats.' He grinned. 'We call them "cliff shitters".'

So racism was as alive and well inside Indian country as outside. Once at the bottom, the cliffs now towering above us, red against the sky, we rode along long sandy tracks, crossing and re-crossing the shallow river that wound along the canyon floor. In some overhangs, high above us, were the old cliff dwellings of the long-vanished Anasazi, ancestors of the Navajo and Hopi.

'Ghosts live up there,' said our guide. 'We leave those places alone.'

Finally we arrived at the rendezvous point – a vast natural amphitheatre by the riverside where the medicine men and women awaited us.

It wasn't so much a night of ceremony as of celebration, the Bushmen and Navajo swapping stories of survival, spirit, culture. However, when one of the Navajo jokingly asked if the Bushmen could make rain – for the summer monsoon storms had not come this year and the land was very dry – things took a more occult turn.

The Navajo elders were afraid that, unless they had some rain, wildfires would spring up and the autumn grasses wouldn't come. If the Bushmen were really powerful healers, maybe they could make it rain. 'Sure,' replied the Bushmen. 'We can do that.'

And so they danced.

I thought nothing of it. Until the first rumble of thunder, the first flash of lightning above the cliffs of the canyon wall.

There was general laughter. Coincidence? Who knew – but gradually the rumbles got louder and the flashes bigger until they began illuminating our faces in the dark. I asked Jumanda what he thought was going on. He shrugged. 'We danced. Now rain is coming.'

As the first few drops fell, we retired to our tents.

It rained. It rained so hard, so loudly, so ferociously, that we had trouble sleeping. Flash flooding? Always a risk in canyon country. Halfway through the night we got up, took down our tents in the steady downpour and moved them up to higher ground just in case. Sleep was fitful. Dawn came with yet more rain and the river rising fast. There was no time to lose, we realized. To get out of the canyon you had to cross and re-cross the winding, usually only ankle-deep river that ran along its wide floor, the banks edged by thickets of wolf willow and choke cherry. Those who had come by car must leave now. So old Roy Sesarna and the other older members of our delegation climbed into their 4x4s and set off, hoping they would not get stuck, because a flash flood like this one – brought on by steady rain rather than heavy squalls that quickly come and go – could trap them in the canyon for days. That is if they didn't drown while crossing a deep place when the real flood, now busy gathering in the high ground above the canyon wall, finally rolled down like a tsunami. It was only a matter of time.

Then there were the rest of us – Jumanda, myself, two other younger folk from the delegation and the Navajo guide – who had come on horseback. We could get out more directly, but that meant getting back to the cliffside track that had brought us down into the canyon – a good couple of hours back along the rapidly rising river before making the steep, slippery ascent of what would likely now be a waterfall to reach the top.

There was one minor problem, though. The horses were gone. Some time in the night they had broken out of the wooden corral and strayed. So, in the continuing downpour – the top of the canyon itself was now obscured by rain – we set off to find them. Thank God, Jumanda and the other Bushmen were there. The young Navajo guide turned out to be no tracker, but the Bushmen quickly made sense of the muddy mess of hoof prints around the broken corral fence, and picked the right direction. Having had no breakfast, and with fear in our guts, we went tracking. Or at least Jumanda and the others did. I simply followed, marvelling as I always did at how the Bushmen could read the ground and draw accurate conclusions from the smallest sign: a broken twig of wolf willow when the tracks gave out in a now flooded riverside thicket; dislodged rocks when we crossed a low piece of rising ground of bare shale that carried no tracks. They moved fast, not running, but their walk so rapid and fluid even over the now very slippery ground that one had to trot occasionally to catch up.

We came upon the horses after perhaps a mile – having had to cross the river several times, the level of the water, not even ankle deep the afternoon before, now up to our calves and knees and rising steadily. The reason for the breakout was clear. Several of the horses we had ridden down into the canyon were mares. They were grazing now with a large, grey stallion that must have smelled in the air that at least one of the mares was in season, wandered up the canyon from wherever he usually lived and called until the mares – eager to meet this dashing new hunk of a horse – pushed collectively against the corral fence until it gave way. In the incessant rain and thunder, no one had heard the whinnying or cracking of wood. And here we were – bridles over our shoulders, hair plastered with rain, our light summer clothing already soaked through – ready to reclaim them.

Fortunately, the passionate part of the night was clearly over for the horses; had the stallion still been getting busy, we'd have had no chance. You can't separate amorous equines any more than you can stop a truck moving towards you – you'd simply be in the way. So luckily it was easy enough to catch the mares now, bridle them and lead them, the stallion following along placidly enough, his energy clearly spent, back through the river crossings, now thigh deep in most places, so that we could recover the saddles. But would we make it out?

'Whose horse is he?' I asked the young Navajo guide, who had been silent since his initial failure to work out where the horses had gone and the Bushmen had taken over the tracking.

'No idea,' he said. 'But he's a good-looking animal, so I don't mind if he follows us out – my dad's got some more mares up on top we wouldn't mind letting him cover. Then I'll put the word out and someone will come along to collect him. That's *if* we can get out.' He looked up through the steady downpour at the low rain clouds that hid the canyon rim. 'It won't be easy.'

There was no time to dawdle, so we saddled up and set off at a steady trot, trying to gauge whether the ground was too slippery to go any faster. You don't want your horse to slip over sideways when you're riding; I've broken my leg that way before. But after finding that the first couple of river crossings now reached the horses' bellies, we put on the pace. First at a cautious canter, taking it relatively easy, then, after the next river crossing when the horses actually had to swim a couple of strides, a lot faster.

It was the ride of a lifetime. Having grown up fox hunting, I know something about the adrenaline rush when you're on horseback. Every fence, if you judge it wrong and the horse hits it and falls on top of you, can be your last. Riders get mangled, and worse, all the time. But this ride for the canyon wall – racing against the rising river, racing against time, hoping at every twist in the track that your horse would not fall as he slipped and scrabbled with his hooves for purchase – was pure, mad joy.

Finally, we just let the horses go, and they gripped their bits and ran, bodies low to the ground, hooves flying, in the full stretch of speed where the rider has only minimum control and where potential disaster lurks at every stride. Every few minutes we were forced to hurtle headlong into the flooded river, the brave horses chucking themselves in and swimming hard against the now swift current, as we grabbed their manes and hung on for grim death, laughing and whooping under the torrent from the sky, soaked to the bone, crazed grins plastered on our faces.

And to add a note of farce to all the drama: as we galloped along, two of the mares came back into season and began calling on Lover Boy to come attend to them again. Eager to oblige, the stallion – who had kept up with us from the camp – would bear down on the other horses and try to do as he was bid. I was seated on one of the mares in question and had to kick her hard to keep her moving, for her not to stop, lift her tail and wait for her lover to mount – with me as the potential crushed filling in the middle of the sandwich – while at the same time fighting off her ardent admirer first with the reins, then with a floating branch I'd snatched up from the river for the purpose. Hitting the stallion across the muzzle as he bore down on me, trying to keep my mare going, as, hampered by his large and sudden erection, the poor horse tried to obey his biological instincts at thirty miles an hour. What a ride!

We made the canyon wall. It was one solid waterfall – more than a thousand feet high. There was no way we could ride up it. So we dismounted, standing calf deep in the water pouring down the track that was now a cascade, and let nature take its course between the stallion and the two mares, as we considered what to do.

'No way can we go up that on horseback.' The young Navajo guide looked glumly up into the clouds. As he spoke, we heard a great boom, like a cannon.

'Rock fall,' he said. And sure enough, looking up in the direction of the noise, we saw a huge red boulder detach itself from the canyon wall and go tumbling, falling smack on to the waterfall track, then bounce, exploding into fragments, before disappearing over the cliff to land somewhere in the canyon below.

'It happens when there's too much rain.' The guide looked almost reproachfully at the Bushmen, presumably blaming them for having caused this deluge. 'The sandstone takes in the water, and when it gets too much, it breaks up and falls. Guys get killed by rock falls – you have to stay off the canyon wall in the rain.'

'We have to go up it, though,' I pointed out, stating the obvious. He nodded. I looked at Jumanda. This wasn't our first adventure together, after all. He grinned, and we had the same thought. Send the horses on up ahead of us, climb up the track behind them, and hope they waited for us at the top and didn't just bugger off back to their home barn, five or so miles away up in the high country where we had started from.

So we chucked stones, shouted, and the horses, getting the hint, began to climb the track ahead of us, the water flowing down past their knees and over their hooves, as we – slipping and sliding on mud and shifting sandstone – struggled up behind. And all the time during that strange ascent up into cloud there came the dull boom and crash of boulders detaching themselves from the red canyon wall and bouncing down to explode into the river below, the sound punctuating the soaked air like muffled artillery. At one point the horses stopped for more hurried lovemaking, and we had to wait till their mercifully quick business was done and we could get them moving again. But after the second round, the stallion, clearly drained after his exertions, simply followed as the mares, knowing they were heading for home, attacked the streaming slope in earnest.

It's incredible the speed and strength you can find in your body when you have to. The day before it had taken an age to make the slow descent to the canyon floor. Now, the scramble upwards took us all of twenty hard scrabbling minutes. A blur of water, rock, fingers grabbing for purchase, sometimes on hands and knees, sometimes running, with the ever-present bang and thump of boulders large and small crashing to their doom somewhere above or below. And then, seemingly without warning, we were in the cloud itself, three dimensions of moving air and water, the mist just thin enough for us to see each other and realize, as we approached the huddle of horses, panting from their effort as they waited at the top, heads bowed, sides heaving, that we had made it.

It took an hour to make our way along the sand track of the high country, back to the corral and the campsite, the sagebrush and juniper glowing purple-green around us in the steadily pouring rain, and a further twenty-four hours, after contacting the Forest Service to tell them that our companions in the 4x4 below might require assistance, before we were reunited with the rest of our party. Twenty-four hours after that – feeling surreal and not quite there somehow – we were in New York, walking into the United Nations so that the Bushmen could put the case for recovery of their government-stolen land before the world.

Deep down, having been asked to sacrifice what was so dear to me, and having been rewarded with that incredible ride of a lifetime, I knew that if I only kept the faith, then all would be well.

And now here I was, driving back into Navajo country once more, having kept that faith, and kept faith with Ghoste's directives too. Our final journey, here in the sacred heart of the continent where Rowan had been born.

12. The Snake in the Star

Gallup, New Mexico, is a strange town. On the one hand, it sits in some of the most spectacular country in the world. As you approach it from the east, as we were doing, you see the snow-caps of Mount Taylor and the other mountains, sacred to the Navajo, that mark the western edge of the vast Navajo reservation. They seem to float, disembodied, in the air – like Kilimanjaro in Africa – above the dry heat shimmer of the summer desert. A landscape straight out of a dream. Yet the town itself is a truck stop, bisected by highway and railway alike, an ugly scar of concrete, strip malls and cheap motels, Indian vagrants and drunks squatting in the shade of buildings. Not a happy place.

But we were happy to be here. Happy to meet Martha – bright, big-eyed, pretty, completely committed to finding solutions for her autistic son Will; and her daughter Sarah, not the usual sullen thirteen-year-old, but a young warrior as committed to her brother's welfare as her mother was; and their friend Shari – quiet, slender, kind, doubling as back-up nanny for the trip. We hugged, caught up, Kristin introducing herself, Rowan calling, 'Pool! Pool! Let's go for a swim!' and Will, small, wiry, angelically beautiful, jumping up and down in non-verbal screaming support.

I was happy also because there had already been one miracle on the journey in from Texas. Just the evening before, in Abilene, Rowan had suddenly, and almost spontaneously, learned – at long last – to swim.

The breakthrough had happened quite suddenly and unexpectedly at the Holiday Inn Express motel pool. Rowan had been happy enough to come and splash in the pool's shallows as usual. I had been standing out just a little deeper, as I often did, hoping to tempt him into taking a small risk and launching himself towards my open arms. He never did, of course. Until now. Suddenly, unexpectedly, he was in my arms, his eyes, looking up into mine, as surprised as my own.

'Whoa, Scub! How did you do that?' He was clinging to me tight, clearly a little freaked out at having dived towards me like that, knowing he was out of his depth. Not wanting to push things, but with my heart beating fast, I carried him back to the shallows and pretended that nothing was out of the ordinary. Then I stood back a little again in the slightly deeper water and this time launched myself at *him*, hoping to kick-start a second try. For once my strategy – so often unsuccessful – actually worked! Rowan launched himself back towards me.

'*Wahay!!!*' I chucked him back into the shallows. A great peal of laughter as he splashed and landed firmly on his feet. He got up a little shuffle in the water, then launched himself at me again, kicking his legs this time. I caught him – '*Wahay!!!!*' – and tossed him back. Giggling wildly, he came through the water again, a wriggling torpedo. I caught him, and this time – '*Wahay!!!*' – I held him around the middle so that he lay horizontally in the water as he wriggled back towards the shallows. At the last minute I let him go, and he made the final couple of feet or so by himself. He turned to me, clearly amazed at himself. I dared not say more than another '*Wahay!!!*' in case he got suddenly spooked at this new thing. For transitions – both physical and emotional – are notoriously difficult for autists and can shut them down completely. He launched himself again. And again – '*Wahay!!!!*' – I held him horizontally as he wriggled forwards, then sent him through the water like a little seal pup, and this time, in addition to kicking, he wriggled his arms. And found himself travelling through the water.

He turned. I had already stepped back one pace. He launched himself again, wriggling and kicking, and doggy paddled into my arms.

'You're swimming!' I couldn't help it, the euphoria was so great. 'You're totally swimming, Scubby! Amazing! You're amazing!'

'I'm amazing!'

'Yes, you are!

'I'm amazing!'

I caught Kristin's eye – she was watching from the poolside, open-mouthed.

All that long warm evening we swam, and swam and swam. By the time we climbed out, tired, happy, he had swum an entire length of the pool, he and I pretending to be killer whales.

'Killer whales are endangerous animals,' he said as he pulled himself out of the water.

'Indeed they are,' I agreed. Endangerous: the idea had lain fallow since the previous year. I should do something about that. 'We could go up to Seattle where Grandma lives and maybe go kayaking in the ocean to look for killer whales. I did that a few years ago. We could go together if you like . . .'

'Or . . .' said Rowan, letting me know in his non-conversational way that I had the wrong idea. Though who cared about conversation right now: he had swum!

'Or . . .' I searched for inspiration. 'We could go see them in an aquarium?'

'Go see them in an aquarium!' he confirmed. 'Maybe at Sea World!' Then he headed for the door back into the motel and the lift up to our room. 'Cartoons, cartoons, cartoons, cartoons!'

Kristin and I followed behind, quietly beaming.

So when we got to Gallup and met up with Martha, Sarah, Will and Shari at the Holiday Inn Express there, it was straight to the pool that we headed for an hour of happy splashing until it was time to retire to our rooms for cartoons once more. Still, for all the fun, I could see that life with Will was not easy. Martha and Sarah's arms and faces were covered in scratches and bite marks: when Will became frustrated, as he did out of the blue a couple of times in the pool, his angelic face would turn suddenly dark and he would attack his patient mother and sister with teeth and fingernails, often drawing blood. He was also on sleep medication as he would sleep for perhaps five nights a month, barely sleeping for the other twenty-five. Martha was deeply exhausted, I could tell. Even her attempts to engage Will in PECS (the 'picture exchange communication system' – using flash cards of images to get non-verbal children to indicate what they want) had merely resulted in him cutting up all the cards with scissors. Martha was at the end of her tether.

All this she told me as we splashed about the echoey motel pool. Holiday Inn Express, swimming pools and cartoons: a million miles from the way in which we had journeyed to see the shamans before. To the other people gathered at the pool, we were just another couple of families on an American road trip. We retired early, everyone tired, so as to get as early a start as possible.

The freeway was almost deserted except for a few eighteen-wheelers ploughing their way from coast to coast. It took forty minutes – through canyons, under rocky red mountains forested with pine that gave way on the lower slopes to the ubiquitous juniper and sage scrub – to reach the turn-off for Blue Horse's house. Rattlesnake and coyote country. Indian country too.

Before we knew it – so suddenly, in fact, that it seemed too smooth, too easy – we were at the freeway exit that Charles Langley, the healer's English, ex-journalist apprentice, had told us in an email to look for. From there we turned off on to a bad dirt road, bump-bumping along the corrugations, and there it was, on the right, set back down its own narrow track. Blue Horse's little wooden house, sitting by itself there in the Great American Desert.

We had arrived.

'Right. What now?' I said.

No one came out of the house. Instead, a large shaggy dog approached, growling. A stark place, windblown, hot, unwelcoming. Eyeing the dog nervously, I got out, leaving the others inside the safety of the cars. 'Time to get out?' Rowan's voice was querulous. Was this going to go according to plan?

'Good dog, hello,' I said, and to my relief the animal wagged its tail. That at least boded a bit better. I approached the door of the house, the desert wind hot on my face, and knocked.

No answer. I knocked again. Nothing. I turned away, the dog sniffing at my trouser leg, and the door opened. A large woman, four-square, maybe sixty or sixty-five, black hair now mostly grey-streaked, unsmiling.

'What do you want?'

'Um, er, hello. Um, my name's Rupert. I've come to see Blue Horse. I arranged it through Charles? Charles Langley? His apprentice?'

'Blue Horse's not here.'

'Ah. Well, um, do you know when he's likely to be back?'

'No. Maybe later. Maybe tonight.'

'Tonight?' I had thought it was us who were late. 'Has he been gone long?'

'Since early this morning. Had to leave to go do a healing for a sick woman with a kid who's also sick. Long way off in the rez.'

'Oh. Well, um, I think he's expecting us? I've come with my son. And another boy. They have autism?'

She looked at me blankly.

'Well, he ain't here.'

'I see that. Um. Can we stay and wait a bit?' I imagined how badly it would go down with Rowan if we simply turned around and drove back to Gallup. Things that don't go according to plan seldom do go down well with autistic people. Surprises aren't always appreciated.

'You can do what you like,' the woman told me and shut the door.

Okay. Right. I walked back to the car and gave the report. 'Time to get OOOUUUUT!' I could hear Rowan wailing already. I opened the door. 'Okay, Scub, let's go explore.'

'Explore! Yes!' and off he went into the sagebrush like a rocket, Kristin getting out of the vehicle to shadow him while I explained the situation to Martha. As I reported what the woman had said, I could see Rowan out the corner of my eye, now grubbing happily in the sand between two bushes, the dog sniffing genially at him while Kristin, his toy bag in hand, passed him a couple of lifelike plastic elephants to play with.

Martha took the information in with resignation. 'Well, I guess we'll just set up camp here and wait, then.' And she, Shari and Sarah got out – Will being happy to stay in the car with his mobile-phone app – and started unpacking the boot.

I wandered over to where Rowan was playing, watched over by Kristin. 'Elephants are endangerous too,' I said, the dryness and heat making me sweat and then feel the sweat evaporate from my skin almost in the same instant – a peculiar sensation.

'Endangerous,' Rowan intoned, as if from a script. 'Means an animal that is both endangered and dangerous.'

'That's right, Scub. Both African and Indian elephants are endangered and dangerous. We could go into the world and see them.'

'Or . . .'

'Or see them in a zoo?'

'See them in a zoo!'

'I'll go and give Martha and Sarah a hand,' said Kristin, and went to help them put up their tent in a sheltered spot out of the wind behind the house. I decided to do the same – after all, Charles Langley in his emails had told us to bring camping gear as the ceremonies might go on late into the night and possibly start very early. But were we welcome?

'Do you think they don't want us here?' Martha, echoing my thoughts, was trying to control her justifiable anxiety.

I thought back to all the times I had been with the Bushmen, or other indigenous groups, where things were often unexplained, and people seemed rude at first, and then turned out very warm and became friends for life, where one sometimes waited hours or even days for someone to show up after an appointed rendezvous.

'Yes – it's often like that,' I said, and went on to recount a few similar experiences, trying to reassure her. I took my hat off to Martha, stepping out of her comfort zone in the distant suburbs of Portland to come down here into the harsh desert with her child. Fortunately, Will seemed happy enough, now out of the car and digging in the sand with a stick.

'It'll be okay,' I reassured Martha, with more certainty than I truly felt. 'We're just on Indian time, that's all.'

We put up the tents. No one came out to tell us not to. But after a little while the door of the house opened and a teenaged girl appeared. She introduced herself as Blue Horse's grand-daughter and asked if we'd like to take a walk to go explore the canyon.

'Go explore!' confirmed Rowan when I relayed the invitation to him. And so he, Sarah, Shari and I set off to explore while Martha and Kristin stayed behind to unload food and sleeping bags and watch Will, who seemed perfectly at ease, despite the unfamiliarity and relative harshness of the environment. Nature itself, that seemed the magic ingredient, the thing that seemed to make everything okay.

Down into the steep canyon we went. It wasn't a giant affair like Canyon de Chelly, but it was still a few minutes of hopping downwards from rock to rock, being cautious and going as slow as Rowan, in full-on adventure mode, would allow.

'Gotta watch out for snakes,' warned the granddaughter. 'They haven't been out of hibernation long so they don't move out your way too good. If you step on one, it'll bite you.'

'Wait up, Scub,' I hopped down on to the last rock before hitting the canyon floor. 'We've got to be careful of snakes!'

'Snakes!' Rowan was delighted. Then – 'Watch *ou-out*. Snakes can be dangerous! Ouchy, ouchy, ouch!' He sang it, again as if from a script. So almost conversational it broke my heart.

We didn't see any snakes. Instead we did see an old car upside down on the canyon floor. 'How did that get here?' I asked. There wasn't any road that I could see – neither here nor up on top of the canyon rim.

'Young guys. Kids. They get bored. Get drunk. Do stupid stuff like that. Lots of drinking here. Even though there isn't s'posed to be. Lots of problems living on the rez.'

We walked on. Birds chased each other in and out of small rock overhangs.

'Do you get mountain lions here?' I asked – it looked like perfect mountain lion country.

'Nope. No lion, or deer, or turkey. People round here shoot it all. Only sheep and goats and horses.' She paused, thoughtfully. 'And donkeys. We have some donkeys too round here. And coyotes. There's always coyotes. They eat our dogs sometimes.'

At the end of the canyon, where it dead-ended into a U-shaped wall of rock, there was a tiny waterfall, more of a trickle really, welling out from about midway up, whose waters had spread an iridescence of green algae, ferns and small delicate flowering plants on the low cliff wall, a tiny, exquisite ecosystem all its own.

'You can drink it,' said the granddaughter. 'The water's clean.'

I tasted it – pure limestone water. Lovely.

'This is where the older people used to come to get married. They also used it for . . .' She made an obscene gesture, looking at once amused and embarrassed as she did so. 'It's a sacred spot. They say you'll have a baby for sure if you . . . you know . . . at the spring.'

Something on the rock above caught my eye. Streaks of white – bird poop from some colony of desert-nesting avians? Nope. It was writing, painted graffiti. '*Fucking place!*' it read.

The granddaughter followed my eye and blushed. 'Bad kids,' she said. 'Lots of problems here on the rez.'

We climbed back out once more, and when we got back to the house, saw that two more vehicles – big, weatherbeaten Ford trucks – were parked next to our own.

'Grandad's back!' said the girl. 'Grandad and Charles.'

'Will you take me to meet them?' I asked, passing Rowan a bottle of water from the bag where we kept his toys. God, it was dry. You could shrivel to a crisp in this place. And you'd likely freeze in winter too, for we were at seven thousand feet or higher here.

'No need,' she said happily. 'He knows you're coming. Just go on up and say hi.'

'Ah – when I asked the old woman earlier she seemed not to know . . .'

'Oh, that's just Grandma; don't mind her. She's just mad at Grandad for something or other. She'll be fine in a little bit. Just go in and say hi.'

So, after taking Rowan back to where Kristin and Martha sat chatting, Will still happily playing in the sand nearby, I did as she said.

The door opened, and this time a man answered. Tall, grey-haired, fit, white. 'Ah, you must be Rupert, and over there must be young Rowan. Sorry we're so late – we had a healing way over in another part of the rez. Blue Horse's inside. Come meet him.'

I went in as instructed and sat down at a table next to a massive man. Not massive as in tall, but wide, heavily muscled with a generous middle-aged but compact belly, a wide-cheekboned face and strong jaw. Charles introduced us and Blue Horse just nodded. 'Yes, yes,' he said in a small, slightly high voice, entirely out of keeping with his impressive solidity. 'Yes, we're glad you're here. Tonight, tonight we'll see what we can do for the boys.'

'Tea? Water?' His wife, the same woman who had barred the door so effectively just a short time before, was all sweetness. A plate of biscuits was placed on the table. 'Thank you,' I said, and took one.

'So you went to Mongolia?' Blue Horse asked. Charles must have told him. I nodded agreement. 'I did. We found a lot of healing. But the shaman of the reindeer people there told us we had to make three more journeys to three more healers for the healing to be complete. So we have. We were in Africa, with some healers there. Last year we went to Australia. And now, well, here we are.'

There was a silence. I presumed he knew all this anyway, through the emails I had had back and forth with Charles.

'It was actually Martha, the lady outside, who put us in touch with Charles, with you,' I went on. 'She was looking for healing for her son, too, and she'd heard about you, so we came together.'

More silence.

'Long way, Mongolia, huh?'

'Um yes, yes it is.'

More silence.

'We'll be out in a little while. Make a fire, see what's wrong with the boys, take it from there.'

And with that, I was dismissed.

Soon enough, though, Charles joined me outside. 'Help me get some wood to make the fire?' he asked. I readily agreed.

We bent to pick up wood. It had to be cedar, which burns hot and long. In the Navajo medicine system the cedar-wood fire is the tool a medicine man or woman uses when diagnosing what ailment a person is suffering from, and what approach he or she needs to take to heal it. I knew, from reading Charles's book, *Meeting the Medicine Men*, that the diagnostic fire was built so that the embers could be piled into a five-pointed star, with the tip of the star pointing towards the affected person. As the fire died down, a shape or shapes would appear in the ash that gave a clue as to the cause and therefore the treatment of the condition to be addressed. This was something I hadn't encountered. I had been at a Navajo sweat lodge before – all those years ago with the Bushmen. I had also seen Indian blessing ceremonies that incorporated corn pollen and 'smudging' or cleansing using small bundles of burning cedar and sweet grass. But the five-pointed diagnostic star was something new to me.

Charles built the fire and lit it, and when it was burning at its hottest, Blue Horse came out and we gathered in chairs around it, as he and Charles took short-handled shovels and arranged the embers into a very neat, very exact, five-pointed star whose tip pointed directly at Rowan – who, amazingly, sat quietly in his white plastic chair. I remembered how he had done the same for Harold in Australia the year before. Even now, twelve months on, he almost never sat still like this. Yet here he was, doing it again, as good as gold. Will was in his mother's arms, clearly tired but also quiet, also within range of the star's tip. As the glowing embers died down to greyer ash, we all waited to see what Blue Horse would make of whatever symbols emerged.

'Ah,' he said at length. 'I see it. There. Look.'

We looked where he pointed. 'That's pretty serious,' he said. 'A snake. Pretty strong medicine.'

There was, indeed, a discernible snake shape in the ash. Uncanny, unmistakable – the head of the winding serpent pointing right at my son.

Blue Horse looked at me. 'You been involved in a land dispute for them people in Africa, yes?'

'Yes, I have.'

'Someone sent a strong medicine against you. But it missed you. Hit your son. No problem: I'll take it out of him and throw it back at those that sent it. They will get it back times ten.'

Exactly the same diagnosis the Bushmen had given. Had I inadvertently harmed my son by being part of the Bushmen's struggle to get their land back and go home? I felt immediately guilty. Or was it ridiculous to think such things?

'I don't want to hurt anyone,' I said, just as I had to old /Kunta.

'It isn't a matter of whether you want to or I want to,' replied Blue Horse. 'When you lift a curse, it always goes back to the owner, magnified. That's just the law of the universe. It never pays to do black magic.' Just what /Kunta had said.

And he turned to Charles, asking for something in Navajo. Blue Horse searched inside a cloth bag and pulled out a long hollow bone – the shin bone of, say, a young goat. He then squatted down behind Rowan, put one end of the bone to the back of my son's neck, the knobbly tip resting at the top of the spine in that place the Bushmen call the *nxau* spot – where you pull sickness out of a person and where you push in good *nxum*. It was interesting how, two years on in another continent, another tradition, Blue Horse went for the exact same spot. Interesting, too, that Rowan, normally so hyperactive and resistant to new things, new people, sat still and allowed it.

Blue Horse put his mouth to the other end of the bone and sucked. 'Oooooow!' said Rowan and twisted in his chair. Blue Horse spat out a great stream of black muck. Then nodded. 'Okay, tomorrow we sweat, pray. Not him,' he pointed at Rowan. 'He's too young. You must sweat on his behalf.'

Rowan was still in the chair. I was amazed. He rubbed at the back of his neck and then – in an echo of the previous year's healing in the Daintree Rainforest – said, 'Ah, that's better,' got off his chair and went off to play with his toy elephants. The diagnostic part of the healing, and perhaps the removal of the thing that Blue Horse wanted to take out, was, it seemed, done. Had Blue Horse primed the bone with some kind of black gunk before the ceremony? Had Rowan really felt as though something was being pulled out of him? Was whatever Blue Horse had sucked and spat out really . . . I gave an internal shrug. It was pointless asking these questions. We were here, we were doing this. We would see. As always, we would see.

Will, more severely autistic, more locked in than Rowan, had already had a ritual performed for him. Back in January, when Martha had first made contact with Blue Horse via Charles, the healer had asked her to send some of Will's clothes and pairs of shoes, and had conducted something of a cleansing ritual using these personal items. Martha had told us about it in the motel the night before. 'The same time the ceremony was being held, I happened to be at the beach with Will and for the first time it was no longer too loud for him. Usually he couldn't take the noise of the breakers, the wind in his ears. He'd just curl up in a ball, cover his ears and scream. Not this time – he went running into the surf to splash like any normal kid. That was a pretty big change already.'

But Will was also getting sick. Where earlier he had been happily grubbing in the sand, now, with evening, he was becoming listless, feverish, drawn. 'This is the bad energy already starting to come out,' said Blue Horse, taking Martha's hand in his big paw. 'What do you want for your son?'

'I don't want him to stop being autistic: I just . . .' Martha searched for the right words. 'I just want to turn the intensity down on everything, if that makes sense.' Martha indicated the scratches, the bruises, on her and Sarah's arms. 'I mean, obviously

I'd love him to start using the toilet, become verbal, all that. But for now, just to turn the knob down a little, that would be so nice.'

The cedar ashes, shaped into a star, began to separate into different colours. 'This shows that the troubles are in the body,' said Blue Horse. 'Will's trouble spots are his head and stomach. Rowan's are just his head. This we can deal with.'

Blue Horse then took the same hollow bone he had used with Rowan and laid it across Will's bare stomach. He sucked, then spat out on to paper towel a mess of black gunk that had, inside it, a little white stone.

'That's the problem, right there,' said Blue Horse, pointing out the little stone, like a tiny piece of chalk.

'That's insane,' Martha gasped. Later she told me why. 'I hadn't told Blue Horse that in utero Will had a calcification that showed up on his intestine when we monitored weekly but didn't show up after birth. It was a major worry all through my pregnancy.'

'This is just the beginning,' said Blue Horse, as the embers died down. 'Tomorrow we will sweat, pray.'

We rose as the morning warmth turned to heat inside the tents. All night Rowan had snored gently between Kristin and me, his breathing deep and measured. I had woken, once, to the howl of coyotes – a sound I have always loved – then fallen back to dreaming, though when I awoke I knew not what of.

A slow start, firing up the camping stove and cooking Rowan's inevitable bacon – doing several rounds of it to be sure of having enough to last through the day. How to divvy up the day was the issue. I had done Navajo sweats before, of course – I wondered what I would be made to give up *this* time – and as Blue Horse had pointed out, knew it would be too hot, way, way too hot, for the children. So the question was, which of us should sweat on their behalf.

'I kind of feel it has to be me,' I said to Kristin. 'Because Ghoste did tell me specifically to make these three further healing journeys on Scub's behalf. But I'll feel bad if you have to spend the day watching him.'

'I don't mind,' Kristin said. But I could tell she was disappointed at the prospect of missing the chance to be a part of the healing, and I couldn't blame her. It didn't feel right either way.

'Why don't I take Rowan for the day for you guys?' Martha, brewing coffee, suggested. I looked over to where Rowan and Will were both taking it in turns to hug Sarah.

'Are you sure?'

But it made sense. Martha could not take Will into the sweat lodge, either, not just because he was too young – he was also clearly quite poorly still, listless and low in energy. Her friend Shari, Martha said, had elected to sweat on her and Will's behalf, so Martha and Sarah had already arranged to drive back to Gallup, where we still had our rooms at the motel, and swim in the pool, watch cartoons, relax – whatever the boys wanted. But that would mean Martha and Sarah would have both Rowan and Will to look after. Two autistic kids for most of the day: it seemed unfair.

'What if we drive out to join you as soon as the sweat is done?' I suggested. 'It probably won't be more than a few hours. I feel bad, though.'

'Don't,' said Martha. 'Question is, do you trust me with Scub for so long?'

I looked at her, this brave, warrior mother and her equally brave daughter doing everything they could for their son and brother. 'Yes,' I said from the heart. 'I absolutely do.'

'Best check in with Scubber first, though,' pointed out Kristin.

'Scub,' I asked, 'do you want to stay here and have either Mummy or me watch you? Or do you want to go swim with Martha and Sarah and we come pick you up a bit later?'

'Go swim with Martha and Sarah and come pick me up a bit later!'

Well, that was pretty darned clear. It still sounded so scripted, though. I sighed inwardly. This was the last of the three journeys. Would conversation finally, at last, happen for him, for us? Perhaps it was too much to hope for.

'I hope one day my brother will talk to me like Rowan does,' sighed Sarah. And I blushed inwardly. Rowan had come so far – so very far – and here I was, the pushy parent, always wanting more. And yet here was Sarah, unable to talk to Will at all, seeing me and Rowan communicate directly, so often so well . . . How hard it must be for her, for Martha.

'One day I have a feeling he will,' I said. Will seemed so present, so loving, so fun, so clear in his likes and dislikes. He was already communicating. 'I remember a time when I didn't think Rowan would ever . . .' I trailed off, aware that I was talking about Rowan as if he wasn't there. A terrible trait of autism parents.

'I hope so,' she said wistfully, hugging my son and her brother and then tickling both of them, making them fall about, basking in her attention. 'I sure hope so.'

It was settled, then.

Charles, along with another medicine man in training, had risen early to prepare the sweat lodge. Navajo sweat lodges are not for the claustrophobic. Or heat or dark phobic, come to that. A small 'bender' of woven willow branches overlaid with buffalo hides, canvas sheets and tarpaulins sits over the top of a pit dug into the ground. This pit is then filled with white-hot stones, cooked over hours in a cedar fire and then transferred when ready, on the blade of a shovel, and piled into the pit in the centre of the lodge. The resulting heat is fierce, aggressive, intimidating, transformative. Your body, crouched in the utter pitch-blackness, immediately begins to sweat like a demon. You feel you can't breathe. If you panic – and people do – you can shout 'Door!' and someone will lift a flap in the tent covering and you can scramble out. But if you manage to stay and sweat the full four rounds or so – each one gradually increasing in heat – you have to chant and pray, regulating your breathing, keeping your head low between your knees, sweating, surviving.

In between rounds, the healer allows you out to cool off, recharge a little, take a breather. It had been during one such cool-down, six years before, that I had been told to give up fox hunting, which I had, though I still missed it. Was another sacrifice coming?

Was this, the final ritual Ghoste had prescribed for us on that mountain top three years before, going to work?

Into the lodge we went. It was hot, dark. We entered in just our underwear and right away the sweat began to leap from our skin, pour from our foreheads into our eyes. Blue Horse began to chant. In Diné, the language of his people, a language similar in metre and construction to the language of the reindeer herders, where all of this had started for us.

Blue Horse chanted, and Charles and the other apprentice made the responses. Kristin, Shari and I, not knowing the replies, sat and sweated and tried to keep our breathing rhythmic. Strange how everything was coming full circle. From the mountains of south Siberia where Ghoste had launched us on this quest, via the Bushmen, whom I had brought here to this same sacred red earth in the heart of Navajoland. And now here I was, at the end of this quest, back in Navajo country, the disparate threads of my life seeming to come together in this sweating darkness.

Blue Horse switched to English. 'Oh, Great Spirit. Protect our brother Rupert and our sister Kristin and our son Rowan. Protect our sister Martha and her sister Shari, here with us today on her behalf, and our son and daughter Will and Sarah. Grant them healing. Free them from the suffering they endure. Great Spirit, we ask this of you. Keep their hearts pure. See what good pilgrims they are, searching for healing here at the sacred heart of Turtle Island. Grant them this healing. Grant them healing in the white-man world and the Indian world. Free them from suffering. Keep them from harm. Show them the way into a new world. Reward their faith with kindness. Smile on them. My heart is heavy when I see the suffering that our brother Rupert and our sister Kristin have undergone because of trying to do the right thing for our brothers and sisters in Africa. My heart is on the ground when I see the silence that our son Will is caught in because of the sickness of his ancestors. My heart cries when I see the suffering that our sister Martha and our daughter Sarah bear for our son Will. Grant them all healing, Great Spirit. Take our sweat, our prayers, our breath.

Accept our offering, Great Spirit. Smile on us, Great Spirit. Grant us love, Great Spirit. Grant us happiness, Great Spirit. Grant us healing. Ho!'

'Ho!' answered Charles and his co-apprentice, from the darkness. 'Ho!' Kristin, Shari and I responded with all the ardour of our hearts and minds. 'Grant us healing.'

And with that Charles opened a flap in the tent, daylight poured in and we went outside to cool.

'Pretty hot, huh?' said the Navajo apprentice, offering us water from a large plastic bottle. We felt light, both in head and body. Perhaps, too, in heart. Blue Horse sat quietly with his thoughts, his great bare chest rising and falling, eyes closed. 'All good so far?' Charles wanted to know. 'Not too hot? It will get hotter, I'm afraid.'

'It's okay,' we said. 'We're ready.'

And back into the cramped, sweating darkness we went. More white-hot stones were piled into in the pit. The temperature rose palpably. The chanting begain anew, the calls and responses in the ancient tongue, and once again, we three white people kept our heads low, our breathing rhythmic, until once again, without warning, his voice deep and disembodied in the darkness, Blue Horse began again in English. 'Great Spirit, we call on you, hear us . . .' Until at last, the prayer was done, our commitment to that prayer confirmed with a barely breathed 'Ho!' so hot was it in the lodge, and again the flap opened up and the daylight claimed us.

We did not talk while cooling this time, conserving our energy for what was yet to come. A third round, the heat now so intense that once or twice my sweat almost choked me. I put my head low, waiting for Blue Horse to begin the final prayer round in English, desperate for him to conclude, trying to keep the rhythm to my breath, wondering whether Kristin and Shari were finding it as hard as I. When at last we gasped 'Ho!' and staggered out into the light once more, our bodies ethereal-feeling, almost disembodied, the moisture rising from us in steam, I could think only of water. Would I survive the final, warrior round? I had to. No, if I needed to, I would call for the flap. No, I would grit it out. I would take it one minute at a time.

So into the final round we went. At first, it did not feel so different from the previous one, but then, as yet more stones were piled on – and more on top of those – I suddenly could not breathe for the heat. My lungs were burning. It was too much. I opened my mouth, wanting to call for the flap, suddenly desperate, claustrophobic, suffocating. In the dark, a hand felt for mine – Kristin's. Her fingers clasped my own. In that one gesture, she – another warrior mother – had rescued me. Calm returned. Not comfort, but calm. 'Are you okay?' I heard her whisper. 'I am now,' I whispered back. 'I love you,' I whispered. 'I love you too,' she whispered back, as Blue Horse chanted in Diné and the two apprentices gave the responses. Then the prayers began in English once more. Almost done, almost done, I told myself, waiting for the final 'Ho!' to be done. I can make it. Just till then. Just till then . . .

But when the 'Ho!' – croaked this time rather than gasped – had been given, Blue Horse surprised us. 'Sing, Rupert, our brother. A song from your land. A song that means something to you. To our son Rowan. A song that tells us of your love for him. A song for the Great Spirit's ears, to tell him how much you love your son. Sing, Rupert.'

I almost panicked. I had made it through and now this! How? I had no voice left. The panic rose in me. I grasped Kristin's hand tighter in the dark and then, of a sudden, I heard my own voice singing, and it seemed to me that it had never been truer. The same song I had sung in the sweat lodge with the Bushmen years before, when Rowan had just been diagnosed. Our song. The song that expressed, somehow, more than any direct words of love that I could think of, how much I loved him. The song that had taken us through the cattle pastures and woods of Texas on Betsy, across Mongolia, across worlds together.

> Oh, Tommy was a piper's son,
> He learned to play when he was young,
> But the only tune that he would play

> Was over the hills and far away.
> O'er the hills and o'er the main,
> Through Flanders, Portugal and Spain,
> King George commands and we obey,
> Over the hills and far away . . .

The song I always sang Rowan to get him to sleep, the song I had always sung in the saddle with him on Betsy when he had first begun to come out of his silence and speak to us. The song that reminded me of how he had seemed once to be slipping away from me – 'Over the Hills and Far Away' – and how I had gone over the hills and far away to find him and bring him back.

> There's forty shillings on the drum
> For those who volunteer to come
> To 'list and fight the foe today
> Over the hills and far away.
> O'er the hills and o'er the main,
> Through Flanders, Portugal and Spain,
> King George commands and we obey,
> Over the hills and far away . . .

And I had followed him over the hills and far away. I would always follow him. I loved him so much.

> And I would love you all the day,
> Every night would kiss and play
> If with me you'd gladly stray
> Over the hills and far away,
> Over the hills and far away . . .

I was crying now. Voice choking. In the dark, Kristin's hand clasped mine tight. The heat scorched my skin, my lungs, my heart. I loved him so much.

We emerged into the sunlight. It felt cool, despite the heat of the dry, mid-June, desert day. Hearts light. Bodies purified. There was no need to speak. We rested, drinking water from time to time.

And then it was time to go.

'Come back at dawn,' said Blue Horse. 'We will do a blessing with corn pollen, and the healing will be complete.'

The final part of the final healing. Would it really be so?

So strange it was, after the sweat, the prayers, the suffering and purifying in the dark, to get back into our car and drive the forty freeway minutes through red rock and purple sage back to the Gallup motel, where Rowan, Martha, Sarah and Will were at the pool.

'How was it?' Martha asked ingenuously. It was hard to find words. 'Amazing . . . good . . . hot . . .' No words could do it justice. 'How was Rowan?'

'Oh, he was a doll — told me to take him to KFC, so we went, and we've been here ever since. He's been so sweet with Will, and Sarah loves him.'

I changed into swimming trunks and joined them in the water. 'Shall I give you a throw and a splash?' I asked Rowan, happy to be reunited with him. 'Throw and a splash!' he confirmed.

I had him stand on my hands and then, on a one, two and a three, launched him into the air, shouting as I threw him — his laughter echoing around the pool.

Rowan bobbed up, delighted with his new skills in the water, and swam back to me. 'Again!'

'By the way, Scub,' I asked, as he clambered back into the 'throw' position. 'What did you do with Martha today?'

Blank silence.

'Okay then, up on my hands again, Scubber. Did Martha take you to KFC today?'

Blank silence again.

I threw him; he splashed, laughing. When he came back I asked him, 'Did you play with Sarah today?'

Blank silence once more.

And so the afternoon passed, the game going on and on until eventually I ran out of strength, I trying to engage Rowan in ordinary conversational questions and he steadfastly refusing to engage.

That evening, Will began to truly sicken.

By bedtime he was projectile vomiting and crying. Then he fell asleep, hard – out like a light, but his body hot.

'He never sleeps this early or this easily,' said Martha worriedly. 'And he's barely eaten.'

We were all worried. We would keep an eye on him till dawn. Or rather, till just before dawn, for Charles had told us to gather back at Blue Horse's at 5 a.m., before dawn broke. It was important, he'd said, that the ceremony took place exactly as the first rays of the sun came over the horizon, no later.

So we roused ourselves at 4.30, all of us grumbly and a little whiney. Martha and co. met us in the motel foyer, eyes puffy, faces drawn. It had been a bad night: Will up for much of it, being sick; Martha and Sarah trying to keep him hydrated. But he was there, wrapped in a blanket in Martha's arms. He smiled – the only one of us smiling – and suddenly it seemed as if dawn was breaking, so bright, so warming, was that smile. But we had to hurry. So out to the vehicles we went.

It was cold this early in the high desert. We were wrapped in jackets and blankets as we gathered back at Blue Horse's – he and Charles waiting for us in the cold darkness, torches in hand, stamping their booted feet to stay warm.

In silence, they led us to the canyon's edge. We stood in a line, shoulder to shoulder in the dark. And then, suddenly without warning, like Will's smile, the first rays of the orange sun came peeking above the eastern hills. Blue Horse began to chant, in Diné, saying prayers over us, blessing us. He began with Martha and Will, taking white corn pollen from a little pouch around his neck and, singing as he did so, sprinkling the soft white powder over each of Martha's crew in turn. I held Rowan in front of me, dancing him a little with my thighs to help against the chill. As Blue Horse approached us, my son suddenly wailed.

'Back! Back to the car! Go back home!' And he twisted away.

The final ceremony of the final healing, and he wanted to leave.

'Okay,' I said. I never wanted to force him. My heart was in my mouth, but I wasn't going to force him. We walked away up the now dimly illuminated track, back towards the cars, the first orange sunlight at our backs. He had refused the healing. What did this mean?

'It's okay, Scub,' I said as we walked. 'You don't have to do this, you know that. We'll go back to the car. No problem.'

And then, all of a sudden, he stopped.

'Back,' he said, in a different, surer voice. 'Go back to the shamans.'

And, his hand in mine, our eyes blinking against the now sharp rays of the sun, we turned and rejoined the group, where Blue Horse, still chanting, in his shaman's trance, dancing slightly as he sang his prayers, was blessing Kristin, sprinkling the white corn pollen on to her head, blessing her with the prayers of his people, his spirits, of the desert, of the sacred heart of the continent on which we lived, where Rowan had been born.

And then he blessed us. The pollen, weightless, flecking Rowan and my heads and chests, the prayers alive around us like winged things in the rapidly dawning day.

And then, as the great orb of the sun rose at last in splendour over the eastern horizon, the final part of the final healing, the end of the quest of three long years – four, if you counted Mongolia – was done. We had carried out Ghoste's directives, or rather the directives given him by the ancestors, the Lords of the Mountain, the Lords of the Forest, to the very letter. Diligent pilgrims, we had done as we were bid. And now the quest was done.

13. Miracle at McDonald's

We made our goodbyes. 'Come back any time,' said Blue Horse simply. 'He'll be a shaman one day, that boy.' He looked at Rowan, sitting in the car, quiet, waiting for me. Unusually quiet. 'He already is,' the old healer added cryptically. 'You'll see.'

The healers in Mongolia, Ghoste among them, had said the same thing. So had the Bushmen, so had Harold.

'Thank you for everything,' I said, though, in truth, I had no idea what the outcome of all this would be.

Blue Horse moved to Martha, Will and Sarah. His words for them were private but I saw Martha's face light up and saw Sarah smile. Blue Horse reached out, put a hand on Will's head. He smiled too.

And then it was time to go. Martha back to the Pacific coast. We by slow roads east and south, back to Texas.

We drove in silence, hungry. As we drew under Mount Taylor, the eastern boundary of the great Navajo reservation, its snow-capped peak hanging like a glimpse of heaven above the desert's shimmering brown, we knew we were leaving Blue Horse's domain. And of course, because this was America, the occult beauty of this place was marked by a casino and a McDonald's.

We were hungry, and it was the best place we'd find for miles. So we stopped, not pleased with the prospect of junk food. It was a worry – Rowan's love of Burger King, McDonald's and KFC. A year before, we'd counted ourselves lucky just to get calories into him at all, and then protein on top of that. Now we had created something of a monster. Rowan also wanted the high-fructose corn syrup-sweetened drinks, complete with weird-colour dyes, that, we realized, more and more made him hyperactive.

As we stopped, the peace of the dawn ceremony, of the previous day's sweat and prayers still resonating inside us, Rowan asked, 'Fruity flavoured?' It was his code word for one of the bad drinks.

'I can get you orange juice,' I offered lamely. It was a dance we often did. Him demanding 'Fruity flavoured!', me trying to resist – sometimes succeeding and sometimes giving way, depending on my energy and resolve in that particular moment.

As we queued up to buy bad coffee and artery-clogging McMuffins and juice, Rowan began to whine louder: 'Fruity flavoured!'

The truckers and half-asleep casino goers, bleary from doing the one-armed bandits till dawn, looked around at us.

'FRUITY FLAVOURED!!!!'

Yes, I looked around at them, addressing them in my head. 'That's right. I'm the one with the badly behaved child. I'm the bad parent.'

'FRUITYYYY FLAAAAAAVOURED!!!!'

His piercing yell made everyone wince. We paid and got out of there. Rowan threw himself on the asphalt of the car park.

'FRUUUUUUUITYYYYY FLAVOOOOOOOURED!!!!!!'

I got him into the car. Started the engine. His screams filling the inside of the vehicle with pain, with distress. I felt panic rise. This was regression. This was not healing. This was worse than he'd been for about a year. Kristin was feeling it too. I could see the panic in her eyes.

'Okay, Scub!' I had to raise my voice over the screaming. Something inside me was giving up, folding, imploding, dying. Okay. So the healing hadn't worked. Not only hadn't worked. He was back to where he'd been two years before.

'FRUUUUUUUITYYYY FLAAAAAAAAVOOOOOOO UREDDDDD!!!!'

'Okay, Scub,' I couldn't help myself. 'Tantrum, then ruin the day. Don't drink the damned juice! Just be grumpy all day. Go on! No problem. Just do it!'

There was a sudden silence. The desert slipped by. We had just rejoined the freeway but had it, at this early hour, almost to ourselves.

Then Rowan's voice came, calm and steady, from the back seat.

'Dad!' he said. 'I'm not being grumpy. I'm just telling you what kind of drink I want.'

I looked at Kristin. She looked at me. I pulled over on to the hard shoulder, heart beating hard. Who was this child?

'Scub,' I said, 'thanks so much for calming down like that. And I apologize for getting mad. I just couldn't bear the yelling. I'm sorry about the drink – it's just that they're so bad for you and it makes me and Mummy worry when you drink them that they will one day make you really sick.'

'That's okay, Dad. I was overreacting.'

I looked at Kristin again. She looked at me, hands spread, as if to say, 'Who is this child?'

'Well, we all overreact sometimes, Scubby. Me too. But it doesn't help when we do, it only makes things worse.'

'I know, Dad. I won't overreact any more. Can we go to the zoo today?'

'Um, yes. We're going to be in Albuquerque in a couple of hours. We can go to the big zoo there and stay the night.'

'Cool!'

I could barely breathe.

'Thanks for telling me so directly what you want, Scubber.'

'That's okay, Dad. Okay, we can drive now.'

And so I did, Kristin and I speechless. Rowan and I had conversed. Actually, properly conversed!

Outside the car window, the desert passed slowly by.

And it kept on like that. That afternoon, at the zoo – brief snatches of real conversation blossomed like flowers. On the little zoo train, the temperature somewhere up around 110 degrees, he commented, 'Whoa! It's hot, Dad. I think we need to go soon.'

21. Horse Boy Method in action at New Trails, Texas, 2010: riding with the families in the forest, learning natural sciences as we go.

22. Rowan riding with Iliane, Jenny by the horse's head. Iliane and Jenny join the team full-time in 2010.

23. Mara lying on her horse's neck. Sensory work – using the horse like a big old sofa – calms both children and adults so much it changes the emotional state completely.

24. On the way through the Painted Desert to see Blue Horse,
Navajo reservation, Arizona.

25. Ancient Anasazi ruins on the cliffs in Canyon de Chelly. The Navajo believe ghosts
live up there.

26. Black Mountain as protected by Roberta Blackgoat – here in front of her traditional hogan.

27. Vernon Benonie, a senior medicine man, Canyon de Chelly. The medicine tradition is still very strong among the Navajo.

28. Monument Valley,
one of the many sacred
sites on the Navajo
reservation.

29. Me somewhere
in Arizona, on the
way to see Roberta
Blackgoat, 1997.

30. Navajo family. The importance of family, of tribe, was something I learned from my time with other cultures.

31. Kristin with Will in the tent at Blue Horse's house, Navajo reservation, 2010.

32. Back in Texas. Maria, her brother Juan-Diego, my niece Zoe and Laurence, teaching language through '*Lion King* bounces' on the trampoline.

33. Jousting helps the brain develop – cause-and-effect games build perspective. Brother and sister joust; Izzy and Josh make it happen. New Trails, 2013.

34. Rowan and me in the bear hide, Romania – our first Endangerous trip, 2012.

35. Rowan is growing up fast. He, Jenny and volunteer Bessie at New Trails, 2013.

36. Iliane and Lance on Bucephalus. He is performing an elevated trot (*passage*). The rocking effect is euphoric, and as the horse moves, Lance sings and talks.

37. Dressage with my Lusitan stallion Zag. Here he perform a stand at 70 degrees (*pesade* The dressage training allows th horses to move at a rhythm th produces oxytocin, the 'feel-goo hormone, in the child's body an opens the mind to learnin

And back in the motel he said, 'I can drink a more healthy juice if you want. But can I have an ice cream with it, please?'

Who was this kid?

That night, weirdly, he was violently ill – projectile vomiting, up half the night. But by morning he was quiet, the fit having left him. At breakfast, in the hotel dining room, as I sat, needing caffeine after the sleepless night, the intensity of the past few days, Rowan got up from the table, went to the coffee maker, took a cup and saucer, poured coffee, added a dash of milk, brought it back to me and said, politely, 'For you.'

Kristin and I had finally found our child.

Like sunshine bursting through cloud, leaving Kristin and me dazzled, basking.

On the third day we reached the Texas Hill Country, within spitting distance of home, and made camp by the Little Llano River. Fast-flowing, pure, cool on the skin after the heat of a humid June day. I played water games with Rowan once more. On one throw, my sunglasses came flying off my face and disappeared with a small splash into the current. When Rowan resurfaced, grinning, he saw I was looking down into the water.

'What are you looking for, Dad?'

'My sunglasses, they came off – I'm trying to see if they're down there or got washed away.' I still couldn't quite believe he was even asking me.

'I'll help you,' said my son, and dived for them.

We never found the sunglasses. The river had taken them. It could take them and welcome, and a lot else besides. My son, my beautiful son, was conversing with me! I had entered paradise. I was complete.

When we got back home, Martha had left us a message. Will, like Rowan, had been violently sick after they left Blue Horse. Sick for the entire three-day drive back. But then, arriving home, he had started to use some words. And his sleep patterns changed – he began to sleep through the night, without the meds that Martha had had to rely on to get him down. As she put it in an email later: 'Will had lost a tremendous amount of weight by this point, but once we got home he finally turned the corner. I think he lost about ten pounds and was just skin and bones and extremely lethargic. As he started to eat and drink again, he also slept. And he was completely off the sleep medicine. I had been unable to give it to him due to vomiting and just never gave it to him again. He went from sleeping for five nights and being restless/up for twenty-five nights each month, to the exact reverse. He was sleeping really well and deeply most of the time. I didn't tell his school about our journey, because I thought it would be best to wait and see if any unbiased changes could be detected. And surprise! I got word from the teacher that Will was finally starting to understand the daily schedule and responding to PECS for the first time – no longer just cutting them up with scissors! He also stopped attacking me and Sarah. Radical changes had occurred.'

Will had also become better with transitions from one thing to another. There was a long way to go, but these were palpable, clear changes for the better. Yet perhaps more importantly, Martha, as a mum, had changed her attitude to Will's autism. She had started to see it as an adventure, an experience that could open doors, new relationships, new opportunities. The journey had exposed Sarah, her daughter, to Native America – an experience few Americans ever have the chance to explore. Sarah, a budding writer, had made a photographic journal and diary of the journey. They had road-tripped together as mother and daughter. Gone out across the High West on a shared quest for healing. Their relationship had deepened. They had made a journey to the heart. Life would be different now.

14. Prophecy Unfulfilled

For Kristin and me, in fact for all of us – Jenny and Iliane too (Khatiche and Susanna having left by now), for we were becoming a full-on tribe – the changes of the year that followed were so intense that it sometimes felt as if we had been tied to the tail of a rocket that lurched us out of normality, whatever that was, and accelerated time itself. New Trails grew exponentially – more families, more volunteers, more horses. But we soon realized that even if we served five hundred children a week, we wouldn't scratch the surface of the need even just here in Austin. And with autism you don't *want* to serve five hundred kids a week: you cannot and should not institutionalize this kind of work. It requires too much one-on-one attention. So what to do?

Around this time, a fellow autism parent who knew me well suggested, 'You should teach others to do what you guys do at New Trails.'

'Good idea,' I replied, 'but I wouldn't know where to start: the work's too intuitive, too specialized.'

'That's bullshit, Ru. You're just a lazy bastard, and don't want to write it down.'

She was right. So that autumn, after we got back from Blue Horse, with this new, fully conversational Rowan, Jenny, Iliane and I began to think. What *was* the method we used exactly? How did it work, week on week, month on month? How was it that so frequently, on the Horse Boy Camps, which were now running every few weeks or so, kids started communicating? Was there a teachable method here – something that could be systemized? We realized that there was.

It came down to a six-stage process – a pretty simple one, at that. First and most important: set up the right environment. No bad sensory triggers – no fluorescent lighting, for instance, no loud refrigerators or other machinery, no cigarette smoke, no perfume. The work with the kids should be done outside as much as possible, in nature, letting the children run and play. We had swing sets, a trampoline, a slide; woods to explore; dogs, goats, chickens, ducks – all this before the horses even came into the picture. But you needed to consider the environment in other ways, too. Rowan, back in his early days, had wanted to put things in his mouth, and I knew that with the best will in the world I couldn't always stop him. So I had learned which plants that grew around our house were fit for human consumption and we used goats to eat up any that weren't.

So much was good to eat: wood violet, evening primrose, hackberry, dandelion and chicory, mesquite beans, greenbriar tips, cucumber plant, pine needles, juniper berries, pecan nuts . . . Rowan and I even gathered acorns, boiling them until all the toxic tannins had leached out of them, and made a polenta from them. In those early days, I'd been over the moon, because I'd found it impossible until then to get healthy food, greens into Rowan. But he'd forage for any amount of wild food and, more importantly, it had helped open his world. We found this sensory-based approach to ordering the environment – through exploration and fun – translated to non-natural places like a house, school or airport. If children could first learn to make sense of the natural environment through what they could touch, smell, feel, taste – from the soil itself through the small stuff that grew as ground cover, right up to the canopy trees – then it seemed to help them understand the man-made, non-natural environment a little better. So one had to think about the edible environment too.

The family was also key. Siblings needed to be there: they knew their autistic brother or sister better than anyone, and could act as consultants for us, telling us what certain signals might mean, what their brother or sister's strongest interests were, helping us shape the playdate to really suit that child. And at the same time we could address the non-autistic siblings' needs: give the sisters riding lessons; play football or do martial arts with the brothers. As we'd found, siblings were so often sidelined because of all time and attention being lavished on the autistic child, and that often caused resentment. Now, at New Trails, the siblings found their own wishes being fulfilled precisely because of, rather than in spite of, their brother or sister's autism. The family dynamic changed, their relationship to the autism itself changed. And the parents could finally relax, be in a place where everyone understood, no one judged. And for their kids there was no whiff of therapy, just fun – but fun with a structure, a purpose. So that was the human environment.

The right environment, and everything that contributed to it, was therefore the most important factor: the foundation upon which everything else sat. Set that up right and you were already halfway there.

'Ah, but,' people sometimes said, 'does such a specialized environment help an autistic child to cope with the real world?' The question always astonished me: 99 per cent of the time that's *exactly* where the poor kid was – out there coping with all the bad sensory triggers, all the things that set him or her back. Could we not, even for just one per cent of the time, set up an environment where the odds were in the kid's favour? A good analogy was horses: Clue, Hope and the rest of our horses were trained not just to be super quiet with the kids, but also to go into the city, even into buildings, when we did fund-raising events. But the horses were trained in an environment that's set up for them and then gradually introduced to elements of the urban environment until they're ready for the real thing. That's just common sense. Why not the same for a group of kids as skittish as unbroken colts? Why not for all kids?

The second stage of what, for want of a better title, we were starting to call Horse Boy Method, was to address the sensory issues of the child by letting them use the horse like a big old couch, just as Rowan had first done with Betsy. You needed rock-steady, quiet horses for this, with one person at the horse's head and another one or two stabilizing the child. As with Rowan, stimming would just stop; sometimes the child even fell asleep up there. On one camp, a child who had never slept more than three hours at a time in his life fell asleep during this sensory work. The volunteers managed to transfer him to a bed without waking him, and he slept for fourteen hours, changing his long-term sleep patterns for good. But for the most part, the effect was that all the sensory misinformation, all the physical and emotional discomfort, would fall away. And the intellect, at last, could come to the fore.

Then came the third stage – riding with the child, or 'back-riding' as we called it. We knew that the rhythmic rocking of the hips – especially when the horse was in a slow, collected canter – produced a generally positive effect. But there was more to it. Autistic children are locked within themselves; the difficulty is relating to the exterior world. But the horse *carries* them into the exterior world. And when you sit behind the child, you are a voice in their ear. You insinuate yourself into their thought processes. You give them deep pressure, which many autists actively seek out, just by holding them steady as you ride. And – this is important – you point at and identify things. Pointing is a key stage of brain development. So with the child in the saddle with you, you point – hand over hand, if necessary – to objects, people, animals. Spell them too: 'There's Mummy: M-U-M-M-Y; Mummy! Let's ride to her!' Through all this, the child, hitherto shut in, begins to actively engage with the world around them.

After that, the fourth, fifth and sixth stages came more rapidly. Rule-based games and perspective taking (seeing things from another person's point of view) to help re-pattern the brain and instil theory of mind and false belief, as Kristin had taught me back in Australia. For this we tried tag, hide and seek, jousting, playing with swords – every kind of rule-based game that 'normal' kids engaged in automatically in the playground. The autistic child wasn't required to understand the rules of the game; instead we gave a running commentary – 'Oh no, Iliane's it. Quick, we'd better run away' – while the horse played it for them. And then, after a month or two, something magic would happen: the child would take control of the game, and say, 'Jenny should tag Rupert' or 'Iliane should tag Mummy'. Once they did that – showing that theory of mind was confirmed – we could begin the fifth stage, academic work. We'd introduce maths, science, reading and other subjects up there in the saddle, just as I had first done with Rowan on Clue in the round pen when we had introduced fractions ('Let's go all the way round . . . Now let's go halfway round'), and which Jenny had pioneered even further with her kinetic learning techniques both on the horse and using outdoor play equipment. And when the child became too big for us to share the saddle with them, we moved to the sixth and final stage, self-advocacy. Here the now older, often adult-sized child would be alone on the horse, which we would direct from behind using long-line reins, as if driving a carriage, in order to regulate the pace, make sure the oxytocin effect was still there. The point of this last stage was to get the kids to start teaching *us*, about what interested them.

We had some extraordinary sessions using this technique. One adolescent with Asperger's was brought to us because his mother was concerned that he was playing too many violent video games. As we long-lined him, we found out that his obsession was really for history since the Second World War, and the playdate ended up with him taking us through the Battle of the Bulge, the fall of Berlin, the dropping of the atomic bomb on Hiroshima, the Cold War, to the Velvet Revolution, the creation of the European Union and the introduction of the euro. We went from letter to letter around the dressage arena in the long lines, all at his volition, choosing the letters (used as markers in all dressage arenas) that began each of these historical events.

'I had no idea he knew all that!' said his mother, astonished by what she'd seen.

Another young man – brought to us after his fourth suicide attempt – came out of a taciturn, almost terminal silence to give us, while in the long lines, a lecture on Buddhism and the importance of non-attachment, completely blowing us away. A third adolescent, a girl this time, taught us – after we began chatting with her about her obsession, the *Twilight* series – how vampire stories had come to America with immigrants from the Carpathian mountains of Eastern Europe during the nineteenth century.

Self-advocacy is the ability to make a case for yourself, the most important psychological tool of survival that anyone can have. To ask for anything (food, shelter, a job, mortgage), to get someone to see things from your point of view, you need to know that another person has a different point of view, a different perspective, from your own; which means you need to understand what a point of view is in the first place. If, at the end of several years with us, a child – or by then a young adult – had acquired that understanding, then our work would pretty much be done, and that young person would now be ready to come into the programme as a volunteer, if they wished, to give a hand up to some of the younger children still battling their way through the fog of autism.

I saw an example of this one day from Cisco, one of the young adults who had come out to the old centre before it burned down. An autistic man in his early twenties, he had now begun to help out on the playdates at New Trails.

When he had visited the old centre, brought to us by his mother, he had been very much a 'client', veering between being hyper-lexic and very, very vocal to super-withdrawn with clear sensory issues and a fair degree of stimming. His mother worried about his prospects of getting, let alone keeping, a job, despite the fact that he was something of a mathematical genius. Obsessively inter-ested in the Middle Ages, he spent most of his time at the centre making chainmail – complete coifs and hauberks would emerge before our very eyes.

He'd made such strides at New Trails, however, that now he was no longer a client but a volunteer. I watched him in the fading afternoon light as he explained autism 'from the inside' to a mum whose child was busy riding. As Cisco chatted with her, his hands were constantly busy with pliers and wire, making chainmail.

'It's my stim,' he explained. 'When I was a kid I used to stim so badly, flapping, rocking, making weird noises – all of it. Somewhere around twelve or thirteen – everything before that is frankly a bit of a blur – I realized that people were going to be mean to me if I kept stimming so openly. So I found a way I could do it not only without them noticing but that also tied in with my interest in the Middle Ages: hey presto – chainmail!'

Cisco didn't just make the mail from rings: he made the rings themselves from steel wire.

The mum was intrigued. 'You say everything was a blur before twelve or so. What do you remember from that?'

'Mainly just feelings – confusion, distress. Round about twelve, my mother tried the gluten-/casein-free diet and it was kind of like a fog clearing. Apparently before that I had all kinds of toilet troubles, gut issues, as well as tantrumming. What I do remember is that once the fog cleared, as it were, I used tantrums to get what I wanted. Kind of like a delayed three-year-old. But that didn't last because I soon found out that people wouldn't tolerate it, not from an adolescent at any rate. I'd moved on, but there were times when I still needed to really stim or really tantrum, so I did that in private.'

'And now?' she asked.

'Now – yes, the same. I go shut the door and freak out as loudly as I want to with no one around to hear me and I stim as crazily as I need to. It's much easier in your own house.'

For in the last couple of years, Cisco had come a long way. He had managed to get work as a tech consultant and had, with his mother's help, bought a house and car and now lived in Elgin, the same little town as New Trails, and drove himself out to volunteer. Having him talk to parents like this about the experience of being autistic, for them to hear him say 'Oh yes, when I was five I was kind of like that . . . and then when I was twelve I was like that . . .' was invaluable. He was invaluable, too, as an 'interpreter', helping us work out what might be going on with a more locked-in child.

'We autists have to learn to fake it,' he went on, the mum drinking in this information, more useful by far than anything a professional could offer her. 'For example, I still don't make great eye contact unless it's with someone I know very well.'

'But you make great eye contact!' the mother said.

'You *think* I do!' Cisco smiled. 'But I'm fooling you! In fact I'm looking at a spot just to the right of your eyes. It works well for me, and for you, because it makes it appear as though I'm neuro-typical. But in reality I'm not.'

And with that one of the little autistic girls – completely non-verbal – came running over and, as she always did when Cisco was on a playdate, began helping him pull the wire, clip it, make the rings and join them. An older autist giving a younger one a hand up.

Would Rowan be able to 'fake it' one day too? Learn to navigate the shark-infested waters of neurotypical humanity as Cisco was learning to do? To be able to drive, have a job, stand on his own two feet? I was beginning to feel that yes, one day, he really would. For now, I was just over the moon that, since returning from Blue Horse, Rowan was ever more conversational.

'Hey, Dad, let's have a little chat,' he'd sometimes say as we walked or drove or rode together. And we would chat about the things that interested him. Animals, the rivers of Texas (he was particularly obsessed with the Brazos, the longest river in the state, and often asked Jenny, me or the other girls to drive him there); the singers on the pop station he loved to listen to ('This song is by a singer called Beyoncé, featuring Jay-Z. It's called "Crazy in Love"!' – 'Come on, Dad, let's rock out!'); or which road went where ('This road is Interstate 35. Go in the left lane, Dad, then you can overtake!'). With Kristin he developed a whole new set of games, including 'Evil Mummy', in which she had to cuddle him, tell him how much she loved him, then sud-denly erupt into cackles and chase him around the house with 'fingers like talons from a vulture'.

She might start in a soft, loving voice: 'Hey, Rowan, darling?'

'Yes . . .' he'd reply, already giggling.

'I have something I want to tell you, from my heart . . .'

'Yes . . .' The giggles would grow louder.

'*SHUT UP!*' she'd then shout, in Evil Mummy mode. And Rowan would fall about, clasping his sides.

From the latter part of 2010, Iliane, Jenny and I began offering the first trainings in Horse Boy Method to equine therapists, teachers and parents. Because the local families still came out for free, the fees paid for these workshops would be invaluable for helping meet the day-to-day running costs of New Trails. But perhaps more importantly, each person who learned the six-stage process could in turn help families in their home town. Finally, it felt, we were giving back.

Still one thing niggled at me, however. We had made the three healing journeys, as Ghoste had instructed. And the results – looking at Rowan now – were amazing. But there was something else that Ghoste had said: that after those healing journeys had been made, when Rowan turned nine – and his ninth birthday was fast approaching – Betsy would hand her guardianship of Rowan over to me. I still had no idea what he had meant – had not understood it at the time, and did not understand it now.

What *did* it mean? I got the fact that the first contact between Rowan and her – so direct, so pure – had launched us on the road to everything good that had happened since: speech, connection, communication, even his early schooling. He still rode her to school – New Trails – every morning, calling her the 'School Bus', still engaged with her daily. Up on the mountain in Siberia, and in the shamans' worlds we had entered since then, it was easier to think of Betsy, though a horse, being Rowan's guardian. But back here in the world of the mundane – even the rather magically mundane of New Trails – it was harder to keep such concepts alive.

What I did know was that Betsy was getting old – by horse standards she was pretty ancient, in her mid-twenties already. Some horses never make it that far. But she was still well muscled and in work – those old Leicestershire farmers in their flat caps and tweed jackets had taught me how to keep a horse going. But did this transference of guardianship mean that Betsy was going to die sometime this coming year? Seemingly healthy but very old horses sometimes did – munching their hay one minute, dead on the floor the next. I shuddered at the thought. And whether she did or didn't die, it still didn't explain what 'handing over the guardian-ship' really meant. I mean, as a father I had done all I could, still did all I could – didn't I?

Or did I? The little nagging voice inside me said that some-where, somehow I was still holding back. That despite my outward efforts a part of me still resisted the responsibilities, the challenges not just of being Rowan's father, but of the whole New Trails/Horse Boy Method thing, important work that held the key to Rowan's future as well as helping autism families in general. A part of me baulked at the task, just wanted to retreat back into my own world – write books, ride horses, drink too much, read historical novels – and, well, keep part of myself back, not fully commit. Turning my back on all this seemed, on some level, like a form of self-immolation, the death of an earlier, immature self.

What Ghoste had meant, my gut told me, was that I would indeed need to sacrifice myself in some way to get over the last vestiges of adolescence, of ego, that still prevented me from fully rising to the challenges – and opportunities – that life had put before me. Did I need to go see a shaman myself? I had heard that down in Amazonia, in Peru and Brazil, were shamans who specialized in a ceremony using a herbal concoction called ayahuasca, or 'vine of the soul' – a powerful but very scary hallucinogen that, it said, destroyed the ego. Did I need to do this? I was afraid of the idea, resistant to it: which meant, as I strongly suspected, that, yes, I probably did have to do it. Or something like it. Maybe as part of Rowan's first Endangerous trip? But Rowan had done his time with shamans, at least for now. Although all of them had said he'd become one himself one day, that was up to him. He certainly wouldn't want to watch me go through a ritual where I took hallucinogens and got the bejeebers scared out of me in order to tame, if not completely destroy, my ego. So no, maybe not an Endangerous trip. But what, then? And when?

For the past four years everything had been very clear: follow the quest to Mongolia, follow Ghoste's instructions for three further healings. Now I no longer had a direct, easy-to-follow set of instructions: I had fulfilled Ghoste's tasks. But intuition whispered – no, shouted – that some kind of radical change was now needed. Something that would prepare me for the role Ghoste had said was coming: this guardianship, this parenting of Rowan through the rest of his life as he became older, more complex; this doing of the greater work with the families and kids that seemed to have fallen to me, to us, our tribe. It was necessary to fulfil that prophecy, frustratingly vague as it was. Because despite all I had done, I still sensed weakness at my core.

And like all people not wanting to face their weaknesses, I thrust the thought aside for now. Rowan was doing so well. Iliane and I began to travel a lot for the Horse Boy Method workshops, and more and more people were coming to New Trails, too, to train there. Kristin was also travelling increasingly for her self-compassion workshops, which would take off even more in the wake of her book, *Self-Compassion*. When she was away, it was largely down to me to look after Rowan, and vice versa when I was out on the road. Then there was the day-to-day running of New Trails, not to mention my work as a writer. So it was easy to push the thought to the back of my mind. But while it stayed in the background, it wouldn't leave me in peace, eating away at me like some sharp-toothed rodent gnawing at the roots of a tree.

I confided my worries to Kristin, and she just laughed – with sympathy. 'Ru! We've done so much! It's okay to not know your next move, to have questions and doubts, to be anxious. Maybe you – we – should just rest up a little and take some time to savour how well Rowan's doing and not try to over-think things.'

Sage advice; and indeed, since Blue Horse's healing and the dawn of real conversation, there was much to savour.

Not a week afterwards, in fact. Kristin decided to try some of her self-compassion techniques on Rowan, now that he was so conversational, so 'present'. Rowan, for all the advances he had made, was still very, very obsessive, and the mindfulness techniques that underpinned Kristin's self-compassion practice were deliberately designed to help people overcome obsession.

She picked her moment well: one of the really hot days of early September. Rowan, not unnaturally, wanted an ice cream. He got one. Perhaps an hour thereafter, he wanted another. Kristin resisted. Rowan began to obsess – his voice quickly becoming querulous.

'Now,' she told him, 'put a hand over your heart, take a deep breath and give yourself some comfort. Tell yourself: everyone goes through this, there's nothing to judge yourself for.'

I expected her to be instantly shrivelled by a blast of princely wrath, but Rowan, to my amazement, began to try and breathe deeply, his tears slowing, his hand on his violently beating heart – which I knew, from having felt it, accelerated rapidly when he was obsessed or distressed about anything. So much so that it sometimes felt it was going to jump out of his body.

'And then,' Kristin went on, 'you become aware that your obsession is nothing to take seriously. It's just a thought, just something in your head, nothing more. You can let it go. When you let it go, that's when you can be happy again.'

'I want an ice cream!'

'Just breathe, Scub. Imagine you're sitting at a window and there's a crow flying past – that's like a thought passing across your mental vision.'

'What species of crow?'

'Er . . .' she looked at me a little desperately.

'An African hooded crow?' I suggested.

'African hooded crows have black heads and white bodies. We saw them in Namibia!'

'Yes that's right, Scubby,' Kristin went on. 'Imagine you're sitting at a window and you see a . . . what kind of crow was it again?'

'African hooded!'

'An African hooded crow flying past the window. You watch it fly. You watch it go. You don't have to follow it. That's what thoughts are. We can't control how they come up, but we can simply observe them as we would a bird flying past the window. And then let them go.'

'Ice cream!'

'Just breathe, Scubby. Put your hand on your heart, give yourself some comfort.'

He tried and – to my real surprise – after a few breaths managed to get his breathing under control. The tears stopped.

I was stunned. Kristin too – I don't think she'd really expected it to work.

Rowan suddenly smiled, looked over at me: '"He was a Whiney Complainy Boy" . . . Sing it, Dad!'

The song from when we had been in Namibia two years before – when he had been tantrumming and had started refusing to go to the toilet again. The mention of the hooded crow must have jogged his memory. So I sang the song for him, a song that had also been born out of his trying to cope with suffering, with regression. A song whose raw humour had helped him see the situation from the outside and heal himself from the trauma, the shame, the powerlessness of regression.

The song ended to peals of laughter. He grabbed my head, brought my face close to his: 'Let me squint at the eyes of that!'

Whenever Rowan was happy he'd squint sideways at whatever it was that had brought him joy, but during Scubby songs he'd actually ask for it. 'Cartoon eyes!' he demanded. I opened my eyes wide and sang the song again, his laughter a balm for the heart.

I had to admit it: Kristin's technique had worked. The toilet humour didn't hurt either. But he had changed his mood through Kristin's skills, not mine.

It came back to haunt her, though. Maybe three weeks later she was getting ready to go out to dinner with some friends and trying to decide what to wear. From where I was sitting in the kitchen, doing emails, I could hear her in the walk-in closet of the bedroom, trying different clothes on, changing her mind, tearing them off and chucking them on the floor of the closet with an irritated 'tssk'.

'Jesus! Why can't I find anything to wear!'

I called into the other room. 'You know you look good in every-thing. Just pick anything – it all looks great!'

A series of expletives greeted this typically useless husbandly offering. The sound of annoyed foot thumping and discontented sighs from the closet grew louder, bringing Rowan down from his upstairs room, where he had been happily watching videos of the San Antonio Zoo train (his favourite) on YouTube (his recent dis-covery of how to use the internet both pleased and scared us). 'What's that noise?'

He went into the bedroom. 'Mum, you're obsessing!'

'I know, I know . . . I just can't figure out what to wear tonight and I'm already running late and . . .'

'Just put your hand over your heart, Mum, take a deep breath and say: "It's okay, everyone obsesses."'

There was a silence. I could feel – even through the wall – Kristin fighting down her desire to snap.

'Just try it, Mum! Put your hand on your heart and breathe deeply and say: "It's okay, everyone obsesses."'

A little more silence, then, in a low voice: 'It's okay, everyone obsesses.'

'Well done, Mummy!' and off he went, skipping back upstairs with a happy chirrup.

Kristin came out of the bedroom, all dressed and ready to go. 'You look fantastic,' I said, truthfully.

Her eyes twinkled, her mouth twitched with a suppressed laugh. 'Thank you . . . And not a word, you hear!'

'Not a word,' I agreed, laughing.

Of course, it was my turn next. I was getting ready to go the airport to do a Horse Boy Method workshop up in Toronto and suddenly realized, on my way out the door, that this involved crossing an international border and that I would need a passport. But I couldn't remember where I'd put it. Of course I was running late, too, and so went rushing round the house searching every-where I could, swearing and cursing and beating myself up. 'God,

I'm such an idiot! Why do I always do this? Why am I so hopeless? Why do I do this to myself every time. Arrrrrrrgh!'

Scub came out from his room. 'What's the matter, Dad?'

'Oh, it's just Daddy being an idiot as usual. I can't find my passport and I'm running late and . . .'

'Here, Dad. Don't worry. Let me give you some *nxum*.'

It was something he'd been doing from time to time over the past two years since Namibia (had that been two years already?): giving us *nxum* when he saw that one of us was a bit tired, sick or frustrated – which involved rubbing one's head vigorously, shouting '*Ha-Kow!*' and pretending (or perhaps not pretending – who knew?) to pull one's pain from out the top of one's spine, just as /Kunta and Gwi and Besa had done back in Namibia. And sometimes he would ask one of us to do it to him.

'I haven't got time, Scubby. I have to find my passport and I'm running late and . . .'

'Dad, the *nxum* will make you feel better.'

He was right – it would. Besides, I was going out of town and wouldn't see him for a few days. Why would I turn down his offer of affection? So I took a breath, sat down in the nearest chair, lowered my head and submitted to a brisk, brief rub and a '*Ha-Kow!*'

'There,' he said, 'you're healed now, Daddy.'

I had also just remembered that my passport was in the inside pocket of the black leather jacket I hadn't worn for two months, since the weather had warmed up.

'Thank you, Scub,' I told him truthfully. 'I am indeed.'

That spring and summer had been the hottest on record – so hot that Rowan decided there'd be no more school for him at New Trails. 'I want to have a fish school!' he announced. So we moved the school day to Barton Springs, the clear, blessedly cold, freshwater pool in the very middle of the city. Suddenly Rowan was learning while swimming. One of the first subjects to come up was body temperature and therefore blood, how it flowed around the body, and the human heart.

One evening, after swimming all day, Jenny took Rowan out on Betsy – she and Iliane rode with him as often as I did now. When she'd brought him back, and Rowan had disappeared off upstairs to check out zoo trains on YouTube as usual, she said: 'You have to hear this: when we were in the pool today, we'd been talking about what happens to the human body when you exercise and just now when we were cantering Betsy around the big pasture he said, "Right now Betsy's heart is pumping fast so her body can get enough oxygen," then he talked about how she was also breathing faster in order to get more oxygen into her lungs.'

Later that evening, as Rowan was cuddling with Kristin after his goodnight story, she gave him a kiss and said: 'You're adorable.'

'I know,' he agreed solemnly. 'I'm adorable because I have a heart. And it's a good heart. And it pumps the blood from my head to my toes and back again in sixty seconds.'

Mixing the emotional with the academic; this indeed was learning.

Autumn finally cooled, turning to winter. Christmas and Rowan's birthday – his ninth – came and went. Spring arrived. The niggling voice began to get louder. Again, I thrust it away – though it was getting harder to do so – and concerned myself with just the day to day of Rowan and New Trails. To begin with, as I had feared she would, Kristin brought up the subject of school once more. The spring intake of the best of the progressive hippyish schools we had visited the previous year was soon upon us. They were ready to receive Rowan, they said, if we were ready to send him.

'I just feel we have to try,' said Kristin. 'Listen, if it really doesn't work, we can go back to the homeschooling idea. But I do feel we have to give it a go.'

She was right, I guessed, although I didn't like it. But we gave it a go. Located in the north of the city, the school we'd selected – the one whose approach seemed the most sympathetic of all the places we'd looked at – had several acres of very beautiful grounds. At least the environment was right, more or less. But my gut still wasn't altogether happy about it. Shortly before going to see Blue Horse, we had taken Rowan into the school for a trial day. Uneasy as he was, he had tried to please: looking at the wildlife books and trying to join in with some rule-based games that he couldn't really follow. It broke my heart to see – he was trying so hard.

So now, the next intake having come around, Kristin asked Jenny if, as a way of easing Rowan in, she could take him for his first day at the school, so he felt supported – wouldn't feel abandoned by Kristin and me. Rowan was so happy, and doing so well academically at New Trails, that I couldn't imagine the school offering anything that we weren't providing already. But there are times to argue, and times not to.

He came back sobbing, Jenny, white-faced and clearly traumatized herself. After only half an hour Rowan had regressed to an almost two-year-old state, she said. He refused to speak, cried incessantly and finally, after three hours, had taken off all his clothes and lost it completely, right there in front of everyone, so in the end she had thought it best to just bundle him into the car and bring him home.

Kristin was upset. But I could tell that Rowan was mortified, embarrassed at himself; he had wanted so badly to please us. My heart broke to see it.

'Was it really that bad, Scub?' I asked, hugging him. 'I mean, you had Jenny there with you.'

'Poor Scubby – but most kids go to school,' Kristin tried. 'And eventually they like it. I did – I liked it.'

He collapsed into tears. 'Why can't I just go to a countryside school!' he wailed.

That was it.

'Listen, Scub,' I said. 'Listen to me very carefully. Are you listening to me?'

'Y-yes . . .' he sobbed.

'I want you to hear me and to remember what I say. I will

NEVER, EVER make you go to a normal school if you don't want to. If you want to stay here and have Jenny and the girls and me and Mummy teach you, then that is what we will do. Unless one day you tell me you want to go to school, you will never have to go. Do you understand me? Your happiness is too important to me. You will never go to school unless you tell me you want to. Are you hearing me?'

'Yes.' The tears kept coming.

I looked at Kristin. She nodded. We were in full agreement at last.

Soon after this, perhaps because he now really did have faith that when he talked, we would listen, Rowan's powers of self-advocacy began to truly blossom. The most telling example, perhaps, was also the funniest.

In the summer of 2011, to combine work with visiting family, we did a series of Horse Boy Method trainings in Wales. Jenny, Iliane and some volunteers were busy preparing horses and I had taken Rowan for a walk up the mountain nearby while Kristin took some much-needed time to work in the caravan we'd rented. We were even travelling as a tribe these days, and it really did make everything easier – I couldn't believe we had persisted for so long in doing things separately.

Rowan and I had come back down the mountain, dark green with pine, purple with heather, and were now in the car, on our way to pick up the girls and go to the beach, when all of a sudden Rowan did a fart of uncanny, almost otherworldly stench. Part of me was impressed, part just struggled to breathe.

'Whoa, Scub!' I said, coughing and gasping. 'If that's what's going on with you, we're going to have to go back home before we pick up the girls so that you can have a poo. We can't have people with us in the car if you're going to do that.'

Rowan began to whine. The days of the big tantrums were, thank God, a distant memory now, as was the incontinence that had so blighted our lives. For since coming back from Blue Horse (I barely allowed myself even to think this, let alone say it out loud) there had been no regression. Even if there was still one part of Ghoste's prophecy yet to be fulfilled, even if that annoying voice still told me I was going to have to do something radical and probably uncomfortable to become the father Rowan really needed me to be, the healings seemed to have worked. Rowan was nine and – just as Ghoste had promised – had become progressively less and less autistic over the past four years since Mongolia. Granted, there had been some regression before each subsequent healing journey, yet the healings had, it seemed, not only set that straight, but had each time boosted him forward in unexpected but very tangible ways: the sudden explosion of maths after visiting the Bushmen; the equally sudden emergence of theory of mind after seeing Harold in Australia; and the emergence of conversation – real conversation at last – when we drove away from Blue Horse and the Navajo reservation.

Now, here in the car, the Welsh summer hedgerows flashing greenly past the window, Rowan fixed me with a stern eye and said: 'Dad! When I need to fart, I'm going to wind the window down and the smell will go out of the window. And then at six o'clock, when it's my time to poo, I'll go back to the house and I'll poo! Okay?'

I stopped the car. 'Shake my hand,' I said. 'You've just talked me out of my plan for you. That's amazing! You've successfully negotiated your position! We're going to the sweet shop right now and you're going to pick out whatever you want. And from now on, whenever I have an agenda for you, I absolutely invite you to try and talk me out of it. I can't always guarantee you'll be successful, but I absolutely invite you to try. Because negotiation is a skill everyone needs, and the earlier you learn it, the better.'

But from there, the year suddenly turned dark. The woman who had been organizing the Horse Boy Camps in the UK backed out, leaving us to try and run them long distance from Texas. We soon found out why. She had gone rogue, taking deposits from autism families, then cancelling their bookings and pocketing the money. It was shocking, and the fallout agonizing as I scrambled to reimburse from my own pocket the families she had defrauded. But we lurched into the autumn determined to find new partners and keep the work going.

And then our neighbour Terry, Stafford's brother-in-law, came down with cancer. It was Terry who had looked after Stafford's ranch, the horses, ever since Rowan and I had been riding Betsy together, and had become a sort of an unofficial uncle to us all. He had had a bout with cancer a year or two before, and had gone through chemo and radiotherapy which had left him feeling so sick he'd vowed, 'I ain't never doin' that agin. If it comes back for me a second time, I ain't afraid of dying.'

It came back again.

I was down in the woods, fixing a fence, when I ran into Stafford. He was crying. He loved his hard-living, warm-hearted brother-in-law. 'The cancer's back,' he said. 'And Terry says he ain't gonna do the chemo.'

I looked at Stafford, taking in what that meant for Terry, the courage of it. And so that autumn we had a lesson in dying, the way it should be done. All of Terry's family came: his ex-wives – there were a few – the numerous kids and cousins. And all his old friends: his hard-drinking, pool-playing and, in some cases, ex-con buddies and hunting companions – prematurely aged but still tough-looking men with names like 'Rattlesnake Daddy', 'Big Country' and 'Crazy Steve'. They all came and camped out up at Stafford's house, as gradually, day by day, Terry grew thinner, weaker, though still smoking weed and tobacco, still making his mustang grape wine. He met his death with dignity, with choice. I was struck yet again, as I so often was, that this was what life was about: family, friends – tribe. Not dying alone and isolated in a hospital bed, sick and scared. But dying celebrated, loved, supported. Life and death as it should be.

'I always said that ol' horse there would outlive me,' Terry had joked. 'Yep, he's gonna outlast me and it ain't fair.' Chango, the ancient black Mexican pony in question, grazed outside the window, the picture of equine decrepitude. But he hung on. Terry said he would, too – just as long as it took for the last batch of his mustang grape wine to be ready.

He'd died two days after the demi-john was emptied into the bottles and labelled – 'Grampa Bones's [his nickname because he was so lean and skinny] Mustang Grape Wine'. I still have the rose-coloured bottle in my fridge.

Rowan came to the funeral. 'He was my friend,' he said simply, addressing the usher who showed us to our pew in the chapel. Halfway through the service he grew restless and we went outside to pick up fallen acorns in the funeral home garden. 'Death isn't the end,' said Rowan suddenly, to nobody in particular. 'Uncle Terry's an ancestor now. Shamans talk to the ancestors.'

'Yes, they do,' I agreed, marvelling at how far he had come. 'Yes, indeed, they do.'

Through his lesson in how to die, Terry had given us a lesson in how to live. I did not yet know it, but soon I would learn that lesson a second time. And much more directly.

It had been strange, that year, not to be going to see shamans, not to be undertaking some sort of epic quest. It was also restful in some ways, if it weren't for that damned voice whispering that something remained unfulfilled, that there was still something left to be done. Rowan was heading rapidly for his tenth birthday, but Ghoste's assertion that after Rowan had turned nine his guardianship would pass from Betsy to me seemed as murky as ever. Added to this was the feeling that I should do something about Rowan's Endangerous idea, but exactly what I wasn't sure. Sometimes he seemed to want to go back out into the wild to do it, at other times just to a zoo. He started taking the camcorder with him on zoo trips, talking to camera about the animals we were viewing. But strange, obsessive elements still accompanied this: he would not allow Jenny to do any filming, for example. It was okay if one of the working students went with them to help with the filming, but we couldn't always spare one, because of the ever-rising number of families coming out to New Trails. Gradually a bank of zoo footage began to accrue, but what exactly I should do with it still eluded me. I felt – those damned gut feelings again – that I was somehow failing Rowan, and the quest in general. But I could not quite put my finger on why.

What was the missing link here? And if I didn't find it, would my son slip back down the rabbit hole into which we'd gone to try to pull him out, or join him in, or . . . or what? I felt I was being pulled in different directions too. New Trails had become a full-on concern: Iliane, Jenny and I were running things to the best of our ability, learning what to do as we went along, but it had started to take all hours of the day. At the same time, I was fretting about my responsibility towards Rowan. Would all that previous effort and journeying be for nothing if I couldn't find the link? There were no more easy instructions to follow – do this journey, then that journey. That was now done. This last piece of the puzzle, the answer to Ghoste's enigmatic statement – as enigmatic as autism itself – I would have to find within myself.

'I worry about you,' Kristin admitted a couple of times that year – more than a couple of times, in fact. And she was right. I worried about me, too, whether I'd be able to keep the whole thing going. And I also worried about us, as I knew Kristin did as well. Despite our best efforts, we seemed to be drifting apart. It was as if, the massive tasks of the past four years now accomplished, we were left standing in the rubble – or rather in the wonderful new garden of Rowan's rapid development – looking at each other and thinking: *What now?* Almost twenty years we had been together, but increasingly, with Kristin's self-compassion workshops and my involvement with Horse Boy and New Trails, we seemed to be moving apart. This happens to couples. It had happened to us before, but this time it felt different.

'You know,' Kristin said, as we talked it over one night, 'it's weird. I still love you; you're my best friend. But yes, it's changing.' Never one to shy away from the difficult stuff – it was part of what I loved about her. I felt the same, though. We both felt guilty about it, sad, but there it was. We didn't do anything radical, didn't force a change that would disrupt life, break hearts: on the surface at least, life went on as normal. Anyway, we still enjoyed each other's company so much. But the deeper currents were shifting – we could both feel it.

Rowan continued to thrive: but as winter came on, I became more and more stressed. The defrauding of the families at the Horse Boy Camps still rankled: I'd retrieved the situation, ensuring the families got their money back, and I'd kept the camps going, but it still hurt. Should I have done more? And now we were training more and more people in Horse Boy Method, and New Trails was growing all the time, with students coming in every three months to help and learn – all of which was a good thing, but exhausting. Despite my resolve to keep to a minimum the number of families being served at New Trails itself, the centre still kept expanding at a pace we could barely keep up with. The work was so rewarding – the healing for the children and families so obvious. But I was no longer writing. All my energies were devoted either to New Trails – training people, training horses, trying to think up fund-raising strategies to keep the whole thing going – or to help raise money for legal fees in support of the Bushmen's continuing fight, in this case winning back their rights to water, to grazing and hunting.

Yet part of me was holding back – for all this I still couldn't throw myself entirely into making Horse Boy Method and New Trails really work. Perhaps I was intimidated by the enormity of it all? If so it was not surprising, because the responsibility was enormous, the sums of money needed to keep everything afloat over the next few years daunting.

I reacted badly, like an adolescent. I began drinking heavily, losing sleep, getting short with people, mishandling situations. Twice I ended up in nasty brawls. The first was in Austin; the police were called after I ended up under four Mexicans. Fortunately for me, I came away without a scratch (and, fortunately, without a record), but forty-plus-year-old guys can't go round brawling like teenagers. Not if they want to stay alive. Then one evening in London, while over there fund raising for the British camps (I seemed to be on planes all the time now, which only added to the stress), I had a street altercation after too much wine. A fist was swung, connecting with my mouth. Drunk, clumsy, I lunged at the guy, who set off running. I caught up with him and tackled him. I don't even know why we were fighting. Stooping to hit the man, I saw him lunge, felt a strange flicker at my neck, and then he was up and running again. I lost him in Soho Square.

It was as well that I did. It was only when I gave up the chase and hailed a taxi and got in that I realized blood was coming from my neck. It had been a glancing blow from the man's blade, but who knows what he would have done with it if I had cornered him again. What was I doing?

Clearly I was the one who needed healing now.

And then Kristin too careered off the rails, but through no fault of her own. One evening, while we were at the cinema, she gripped my arm. 'I'm having a dream déjà vu,' she said. 'A bad one.'

Kristin's 'dream déjà vus', as she called them, had been a feature of our life for some years now. They had started – strange turns, or fits – before we had made the trip out to Mongolia and had recurred a few times a year ever since. She would have a strong sense of déjà vu, and then start to feel a tingling in her extremities. 'It's like a kind of seduction,' she would sometimes say. 'Like it wants you to just give in.'

I kind of knew what she meant. I had suffered from panic attacks from my teens until my mid-thirties. One night, after years of this, I grew sick of it. 'All right, then,' I had told my body as my heart rate accelerated, as if threatening to leap out of my body. 'Do your worst. Kill me, if that's what you want.'

It did. Or at least I thought it did. My heart rate sped up, unthinkably fast. I couldn't breathe. I blacked out.

And came to, eight hours later, after the deepest, most dreamless sleep; and never had another panic attack again.

So when Kristin reported her 'dream déjà vus' – which could strike at the weirdest times – I put them into the same category as my previous panic attacks: real enough but ultimately perhaps psychosomatic. Certainly not life-threatening.

Except when we came out of the cinema after this latest one, Kristin looked unfocused, woozy. 'Did we just see a movie?' she asked.

Not only could she not remember having seen the film, she could not remember the events of the previous week nor chunks of her life before that.

So we went to a doctor. Tests were done. Kristin was diagnosed with temporal lobe epilepsy. Drugs were needed to control it: if she let it go on unmedicated, it could eventually escalate into a grand mal seizure. Kristin never recovered her memory of that week, and although the missing chunks of what had gone before came gradually back, it was clear that we were now living with a very real condition alongside Rowan's autism. It was time I grew up, then, so that I could take care of my family properly.

Except I didn't know if I was up to the task.

That summer in Texas was even hotter than the previous one. Autumn came and still it wouldn't let up. The rains didn't come. Instead, scorching wildfires went searing through the county – destroying over a thousand houses. Every night we stayed up, taking it in turns to keep watch, the glow of the hundred-foot flames lighting the southern horizon. We'd try to judge the direction of the wind, planning how we would evacuate people, horses, animals, if the fires came our way. In the daytime, in the teeth of that fierce heat, we – Iliane, Jenny, myself and the working students at New Trails – drove into the burning zone to help evacuate livestock. We donated hay, labour, feed. Rescuers began to shoot horses and cattle as they caught fire in the fields and ran into the brushland, setting yet more thousands of acres ablaze. We were declared a disaster area by the Federal Emergency Management Agency. Thousands had been made homeless. The forests were dying around us. At any moment the woods around our house and New Trails might be the next to go up. Tension mounted.

Then one day I came back from a journey to find something truly shocking. In Stafford's arena, a woman was riding Betsy.

Betsy, the horse who had started it all; Betsy to whom we owed everything. But it didn't look like Betsy. It looked like the ghost of Betsy.

We had been away for a few weeks doing Horse Boy training. When we'd left, Betsy had been the picture of health. Still working with the kids, albeit less than the younger horses, she was still bright-eyed, well muscled and with a shine on her coat. But she was an old horse, even so, and the health of old horses is always fragile. I came home to a different horse. She had lost perhaps 400 pounds and was all bones. What had happened? A sudden liver or kidney failure such as old horses are prone to? The heat, massive dehydration . . . what? I stood, mouth open in shock. And how could someone be *riding* her in that condition? And who? I had never seen this woman before. Was she a friend of Stafford's? From the way she sat, she clearly was a beginner, and perhaps for that reason had not realized that the horse she was on, emaciated almost to the point of being skeletal, was unfit to ride.

And still the poor horse was trying to perform: good, calm, kind Betsy, a virtual skeleton with a saddle on, trying to go through the figures and patterns of the arena with a dropping head, no light in the eye, the worst picture of ridden abuse.

I was through the fence and into the arena before I could think.

'Excuse me,' I said to the middle-aged lady on top of Betsy, amazed at the calm in my voice, 'I am going to have to ask you to step down from that horse. You can see she's skin and bone.'

The woman – clearly an innocent who didn't know better – stopped Betsy and climbed off.

'Thank you,' I said, taking the reins.

White-faced, she began to walk away, then turned. 'Stafford asked me to come in to keep the horses ridden while he was away . . .' she began.

'Stafford is a nice guy. But I bet he has no idea what state Betsy's in. When he sees her, I think you know what he'll say!'

Betsy looked as close to death as I have ever seen a horse. The poor woman was already at her car.

I turned to Betsy. 'I will never, ever let this happen to you again.'

I had seen old horses suddenly drop off like this before. Usually they died soon after. Had I allowed this to happen by not being around to watch out for her? Was this what Ghoste had meant when he had said that, after the three healing journeys were done, Betsy would pass the guardianship of Rowan from herself to me? Did this mean we were losing her?

It was unthinkable.

When Stafford came back from his trip away, he was as shocked as I'd been by Betsy's sudden, calamitous loss of condition. In the meantime, Iliane and I had been pouring electrolytes into her in an effort to boost her health. We put oil in her feed, bought alfalfa. That year, because of the wildfires and drought, there was no hay in Texas. Rigs full of hay bales for Betsy and the other horses were being brought in from as far afield as Florida and South Dakota, 1,500 miles away. Prices had rocketed: to keep New Trails going for the families, we were going broke.

In November the rain finally came, and the fires were quenched – our corner of the county thankfully being the only one that had escaped immolation. The forests and pastures were dead. Betsy, though now on the road to recovery, had been at death's door. But still New Trails continued to grow. I was starting to learn the ropes of effective administration – how to deal with insurance, apply for grants, fund raise properly – but knowing how good I needed to be was truly daunting. It seemed terrifying, what we had taken on. There was a sense of real obligation now; I needed to grow up, and fast.

There came a point that winter, when, in the pursuit of the funds needed to put the Horse Boy Foundation (the charity I had established when setting up the old New Trails) on a more sustainable footing, I was getting on a plane up to twice a week. It had to be done, but the pace was starting to tell. 'You're going to burn out,' warned Kristin. 'I'm worried about you.' She was right, I knew it. Christmas came and went; Rowan turned ten. And still the pace did not slacken.

And then came the heaviest blow, albeit one that I'd been half expecting. Our charity went bust. Over the past few years we had run both the Horse Boy Foundation and the Indigenous Land Rights Fund – the organization I'd set up for helping the Bushmen – using a fiscal sponsor. It's a good option when you need to set up a charity in a hurry: just six weeks and you're up and running, rather than the two years it takes to become a stand-alone body. The fiscal sponsor takes a small commission and in return handles all the bookkeeping and legal matters. So yes, a good option – unless someone embezzles.

Someone embezzled. In one fell swoop, all the funds we had so painstakingly raised – all the money to serve the children for free, to pay for the upkeep of New Trails, to feed the horses and other animals, to pay the rent on the property, to cover the utility bills, to run the camps for the families – all gone in a puff of smoke. Just like the fire that had destroyed old New Trails. A straight punch to the gut – and to the heart. Even the way the news came was shocking. The FBI, no less, rang me up: 'Good morning, sir, this is the Federal Bureau of Investigation calling . . .' And just as I was recovering from the heart attack such words are bound to induce, they informed me that I was the victim of a crime and they were there to help.

Would it never end? Okay, so we would have to replace what had been lost. I felt dizzy at the prospect. Okay, okay – we would do it, we could do this.

But how? We had completed the tasks Ghoste had given us, but now everything seemed to be going wrong, even with Rowan doing so brilliantly. And the pressures only kept mounting. So where to go from here? Should I seek a healing? Go down to the Amazon and try to find a shaman and do this ego-exploding ceremony that I suspected I needed to do to get to the next phase, to fulfil Ghoste's prophecy. But how? When? Money needed to be replaced, families served. Something had to give.

And then fate lent a hand. Instead of having to go down to the

Amazon, I found a shaman right there in my own backyard. Right in the very spot where Rowan had first met Betsy, in fact. The greatest, most powerful shaman of them all.

15. The Tunnel and the Light

One morning early in the New Year, Iliane and I were due to get on a plane to New York to speak to some potential sponsors. After that I was to fly on solo to London for more of the same. I really, really did not want to get on that plane. I got up early so I could at least go out for a ride before embarking on yet another round of plane journeys.

I was riding one of our newer donated horses (our herd having grown along with the number of families), a big black Dutch horse called Marvel, one of the best we had for riding with the children. We were teaching him what are known as 'flying changes', in which the horse, in the middle of cantering or galloping, changes the leading foot in midair so that he can make a sudden turn in a new direction without losing balance – useful when playing rule-based games with a kid in the saddle in front of you. It takes months to train and more months to consolidate. He'd done incredibly well in that morning's session, really trying. So to reward him, I took him jumping. Marvel adored to jump – to hurl his thousand pounds of muscle into the air. So off we went cross-country, jumping the fences between our pastures like I used to do back when I still fox hunted, thrilling with the adrenaline, the power, the sheer joy of it.

We had recently built a new jump in one of the fence lines – a big solid thing surmounted by a thick log of pine rescued from one of the scorched forests destroyed in the previous summer's wildfires. It was straight upright, quite intimidating for horse and rider. Having only just been constructed, it was surrounded by all sorts of debris, so wasn't yet ready to be jumped – the approach was almost blocked. But, I thought, if one did a sort of pirouette with the horse on its hind legs, one could perhaps make it, provided one got the angle just right, and Marvel was a gifted jumper. I set him into a canter almost on the spot.

Don't do it, said my gut.

Ah, sod it, said my head.

I turned into the big solid jump, too slowly, at too sharp an angle. Just two strides off and I knew it was wrong.

Marvel tried, like the good, honest horse that he was, but I'd planted him too close to the jump to make the take-off properly, and hadn't allowed him enough momentum to launch himself.

He caught his front legs on the log and tipped a somersault in midair.

Marvel, all one thousand pounds of him, landed right on top of me – the shock of it was stunning, shocking – right across my legs. Then he rolled up my back. Oh my God, would he break it? He rolled back again and struggled to his feet, thankfully unhurt.

What a bad horseman I was to have ridden him for a fall like that, to have endangered such a sweet, giving horse. I tried to rise, too. I couldn't.

I looked down at my legs. One was splayed at a strange angle. No pain – maybe a dislocation? I tried to rise again. No way. Marvel began to graze beside me, unruffled by his upset. I heard footsteps: Iliane, Jenny and one of the working students, a girl from England, were running over. They had seen the whole thing from the front porch.

'Are you okay?'

'I don't think so. I think I might have dislocated my ankle or something. I don't think I'm going to be getting on that plane today.'

Kristin was called, painkillers dispensed. I was aware that, for the time being, adrenaline was blocking the real pain of what might have happened to me. Kristin arrived, Iliane helped me sit up. The ambulance, surprisingly quick, appeared at the front gate and came bumping down the field of new-sown grass, green as Ireland with the belated rains, to disgorge the paramedics.

'I think I might have dislocated it,' I told them.

The lead paramedic laughed. 'You've broken your leg, dude. Like, really broken it. What painkillers have you taken?'

We told him. He laughed. 'You're going to need something stronger than that – hold on.'

He came back with some different pills. 'This should get you to the emergency room at least.' Grateful, I took them.

The painkillers wore off as I, Kristin beside me, was taken to the hospital, thirty miles away in Austin. When they transferred me from the stretcher to the bed, the bones in my leg ground against each other. I heard a voice screaming – it was mine.

I had broken my left leg in six places; shattered it. They would need to operate, put in a titanium rod. By now I was flying on opiates. 'Yes, yes, fine,' I said. 'Sounds great.' They would operate the following day.

Kristin watched me the first night, but halfway through called in the nurses to report that I was having a slight psychotic episode, trying to get out of bed and babbling gibberish: 'Cabbage, beetroot, Charles the Second . . .'

'Maybe he's hyper-sensitive to opiates,' the nurse told her. 'We won't give him any more. I'll make a note that he should get non-opiate painkillers after the surgery.'

In the morning, they operated. Iliane offered to watch me that night.

I was hooked up to a morphine machine. Every now and then, when I felt I needed it, I could press the little button and get a shot. All well and good. In due course I started to feel sleepy – very, very sleepy.

It was so pleasant.

The next thing I knew, I was in a dark, dark tunnel, heading towards a bright, beautiful light.

The most beautiful light I had ever seen. I felt the best I had ever felt. In the tunnel, as I approached it, I was vaguely aware of other beings passing me – female-looking, beautiful – as if intent on business of their own. I was consumed by happiness, bliss. I knew what the Light was. The Light was Home.

And then the Light spoke.

It wasn't so much a voice you heard with your ears, but one you heard in your heart. And it told me this:

The world, the universe, life as you know it, is all just a big experiment in love. Like a beehive. You humans are like worker drones. Your job is simply to make the hive get bigger. For this to happen, all you are required to do is to love actively. And, if possible, help to build collective dreams of love. If you do that, you are fulfilling my purpose. That is all I ask. All you need for your happiness. All you are here to achieve. Whatever else you do is up to you. All I require of you is to love. It is that simple.

A feeling of great peace. Of coming Home. A realization – as if the knowledge had been placed inside me by some invisible hand – that, as some of the Bushmen and other healers had told me over the years, there is no heaven, no hell, that these are human things, created by the human mind, and therefore exist right here within the human experience, but are irrelevant to the divine. Whether we turn out to be the Dalai Lama or Adolf Hitler, we are loved and are put here only to love. If we stay with love, we will be happy and fulfilled because we are fulfilling the divine purpose. If we stray to hatred and to harming others, we will destroy our own happiness. But either way we are loved, and when we die, we simply return to the source, to the same place we came from when we were born. Birth and death are the same – an entrance and an exit from the source and back again. From love and back again. Everything is okay; all we need to do is love each other and the world around us. The point of existence really is that simple.

There was no sense of time passing. Only this beautiful Light, the beautiful words, this beautiful lesson. Then I turned around, or *was* turned around in the tunnel, looking back the way I had come. There I was: my body – me – lying on the hospital bed, surrounded by nurses, medical staff, the people clustered around me, clearly concerned. Iliane was with them, holding her arms as if hugging herself – worried. It seemed very remote, another time, another place, no real concern of mine.

And then I thought: *Scub! I have to go back!* And back I went.

Or perhaps more accurately: back I was allowed to go. It was like wading through some kind of thick, clear, viscous substance – slow-going, not easy, as if someone were reluctant to let one pass in that direction.

And then – *boom!* – I was back in my body. Looking out through my own eyes into those of an emergency services worker as he pulled an oxygen mask off my face. I looked around: faces everywhere, worry and concern on all of them. Iliane was there, her face drawn.

'Am I okay?' I asked, or tried to. My mouth did not follow what my brain wanted it to do. Was I brain damaged? What had happened? I tried again.

'Am I okay?' I managed to get it out this time – kind of.

Iliane shook her head.

Christ. This was serious, whatever it was. People were rushing all around me. I was being wheeled out into the corridor, taken to another place. Iliane walked next to me, holding my hand. What was going on? I tried to speak again, but the words wouldn't form.

As I was wheeled into another room, Iliane said: 'Can you hear me?'

I nodded.

'The machine giving you morphine malfunctioned. You got an overdose.' She paused. 'You were gone. I tried to wake you. You stopped breathing. I called the nurses. They freaked, and got the emergency people. You were blue by then. Gone.'

I took this in. Could I speak? Perhaps I wasn't brain damaged, then. Perhaps it was just the morphine. A surge of relief went through me. At the same time, all I really wanted was to go back to that beautiful Light, to bathe in its glow, and hear the Voice once more.

'You were gone,' Iliane repeated, crying. 'The emergency people said . . .'

I had died. That's what the emergency people had said. Heart stopped, breathing stopped, gone – for perhaps three minutes.

Earlier, I had talked one of the nurses into removing the vital-signs clip from my finger because it was irritating me. God alone knows why a professional nurse would allow a morphine-addled patient to talk her into something so counter to all her training, but she had taken the thing off. So when I flatlined, nothing showed up on the monitor to alert the nurses on duty. If Iliane had not noticed that I had stopped breathing and had turned blue, I would have died. Or rather, would not have come back from death. The moral of the story: if you're going to stay overnight in hospital, take a friend. Without a doubt she had saved my life.

They put me into an intensive-care room, started filling me with whatever they fill you with to counteract the effects of a morphine overdose. But Iliane called Kristin and she rushed to the hospital, intent on getting to the bottom of what had happened. Kristin was furious: having been with me the previous night when I'd already had one strange reaction to an opiate, she assumed it had been noted that I was probably hyper-sensitive to opiates. And then the staff had promptly overdosed me on another.

As for me, all I could think of was how blissful it had been in that tunnel; how it had simply felt like going Home; how blessed I was that the Light had spoken to me; how wonderful was the message I had been given. I knew, without a doubt, that this was the most beautiful experience of my life.

A few days later, when I was released from hospital and back at home, people asked me if I was going to sue. No way, I replied. No way was I going to do that – although I did refuse to pay for the intensive-care room when, after all, it was the hospital's negligence that had put me there. But to have sued, to try and make money from it, would have felt obscene somehow; it would have sullied an experience that I felt supremely privileged to have had. The memory of standing before that Light, of hearing the Voice inside me, was physical, corporeal; I could still feel that bliss, that utter peace, utter joy – to know that death holds no nasty surprises, to know that all death is simply a return Home. To know that it is even possible, if the Light allows it, to return from the other side. To know, to be told, what I think every human being knows deep in their heart: that the secret of life, of happiness, is only this – we are here simply to love and be loved, and, if possible, to help to build collective dreams of love. That love is all that matters.

16. Endangerous

There's nothing like dying to give you perspective. And there's nothing like being parked on the couch with a shattered leg to force you to slow down. What became clear, as the first weeks of 2012 went by, was that New Trails could operate without me. The team – Iliane, Jenny, the working students – had the horses, the programme, the families, even Rowan's education, well in hand. I could relax. For the first time since I had become a father, I could actually – albeit forcibly – relax. And heal.

Rowan was sweetness itself. I'd been afraid that he might be freaked out by my injury, or – perhaps worse – insist on jumping on me in the mornings for Scubby *geemz*, as he usually did. I didn't want to deny him that affection, but I knew my broken limb would never stand the punishment.

But no. 'Daddy's got a very, very ouchy leg,' he informed Jenny gravely when I got back from the hospital, 'So you have to be very, very careful. Don't touch his leg – okay?'

'Okay, Scub,' she laughed. 'I'll be careful.'

Rowan looked at me. 'Don't worry, Dad, it'll be okay. Here, let me show you how we're going to do Scubby *geemz* while you're hurt. We'll do it like this . . .'

And very carefully, making sure to avoid my broken left leg, which anyway was raised up high on cushions, he snuggled in next to me, and, hugging me around the middle as usual, gave me the cue: 'Mr Boy is a . . .'

'Boy!' I said, giving him the requisite squeeze and snuffling the rest of the song – with squeezes – into his hair. When the song was done, he said. 'Now sing all Scubby songs!' So we did; there were almost a dozen of them by now, all very silly, all mostly involving the central lyric of 'Boy!' All involving raspberries, squeezes, hugs, tickles and pokes: deep pressure, in other words. A question suddenly came to me as we performed this sweet, soul-nourishing but very normal ritual that he was now so considerately modifying in order to spare my broken limb: were these father–son rituals, in their own way, shamanic? Did they heal on some level? Rowan craved deep pressure. These rituals gave him that, but did the deep happiness engendered by the silly lyrics, the physical closeness required by the squeezes, tickles and pokes that accompanied them, work somehow on body and mind together?

Kristin, when I raised the question later that evening, looked thoughtful. 'Well, there's been a ton of research done on the mammalian caregiving system. The most famous study was the one they did on rhesus monkeys, where there was one baby who had a mother and another – this is pretty horrible – whose mother was taken away, and who suffered, got sick, did not thrive. And then, if I remember rightly, there was a third who got a surrogate mother – a towel over a monkey-shaped wire frame with a bottle where the nipple would be, and that baby monkey thrived but not as well as the first. So I guess there could be . . .'

A week of so after that, Jen reported that Rowan had told her: 'I love Scubby songs with Daddy. They make me feel secure, and safe and happy.'

'Yup, he said it totally out of the blue – just like that,' she said.

Was this, in a small way – and, in a larger way, New Trails – what Ghoste had meant when he said that Betsy would pass his guardianship on to me? To provide both the immediate, deeply personal caregiving through our silly songs and games (Kristin did it too – they had their own games like 'Evil Mummy' – but in this particular sphere I was his primary person), and then through the creating and running of New Trails, which in turn had brought in the important people in his life there, like Jenny and Iliane? Was this what Betsy had given him in the early years? The warmth and security of her broad back when he just used to lie on her and hug her and all his agitation would fall away. The exploration of the exterior world when we began to ride her together, offering the physical structure of her body, her self, to make it safe for him to explore. Was this what New Trails now was for him – the wider structure through which he could explore and thrive? By running New Trails, by securing its future and the livelihoods of those who worked there, was I now therefore the guardian of that structure – and by extension *his* guardian now? Was that what it all meant?

If so, then all I needed to do was keep on keeping on.

My leg slowly healed. Being a prisoner of the couch gave ample time to look more seriously into fund raising, to get to grips with social media, get the Horse Boy Foundation established as an independent, stand-alone charity, set up a sister charity of the same name in the UK, put together a strategy that would see the work become self-sustaining. The resistance, the feeling of holding something back, of not committing – the fear, in other words – had gone. After all, having died, what was there to possibly be afraid of? It had been such a gift, such a release.

The niggling little voice was suddenly quiet. It had been right – there *had* been a need for some rite of passage, some extreme experience to kick me through the hesitation and fear into commitment and action. But it should be happiness that guided you, not that constant sense of anxiety that had beset me to date, the constant sense of not being up to the task in front of me that – I now realized – had defined my whole life. It wasn't that the anxiety, the neurosis, had completely gone. But I knew, now, that I could view it, as Kristin would say, as 'just a crow (an African hooded one) flying past the window'. Could I, in time, learn not to follow it? It was a relief to think that was possible, that one didn't have to stand rooted in fear one's whole life. That it was actually okay to be afraid, to feel weak, and that one could sometimes, when the stars aligned right, get past it. And that perhaps the more one did that, the less the fear would dominate, and the more the habit of simply observing it could take over.

No need, now, to go down to the Amazon, to find an *ayahuascuero* to explode my ego and make me meet God. I had met God, who was lovely. And my ego was, well, what it was: human. There was no need to explode it. One day I would still go down to the Amazon and seek that healing, because, as the Bushman woman, the one who had been healed in front of my eyes from rheumatoid arthritis, had told me: 'You need a top-up from time to time.' But I would not be going down from desperation, at least not in this current chapter of my life. And now, I knew, Ghoste's prophecy, the final part of it, could at last be fulfilled. And no, despite the scare we had had the previous autumn, it did not mean losing Betsy. It just meant me stepping up to the task of Rowan, New Trails, the whole Horse Boy thing, with a whole and happy heart.

Working with autistic kids and horses had never been my dream. Nor had doing human-rights work. They were simply the adventures that had sprung up in front of me, work that had to be done. But weirdly, I realized, now that there was suddenly the time to reflect, by throwing myself into these things that *weren't* my dreams, by being in service to the dreams of others – others more vulnerable than myself – my own dreams were starting to come true.

What I mean by that is this. I had always wanted to be a writer. The story that the Bushmen had given me, by my taking part in their struggle to return to their ancestral lands, had provided me with my first real book: *The Healing Land*. (I had written travel guides before that but they didn't really count.) In return for that gift, the Bushmen had asked me to bring them to America, help them with their land-rights struggle. I had, and they had then worked on Rowan, and this – in combination with Rowan's incredible response to Betsy – had resulted in *The Horse Boy*, another book. And I'd always wanted to make films. The home-made documentary we had cobbled together of *The Horse Boy* had ended up appearing in the cinema and on TV – which had surprised us all. Because of this, I had been asked by another film producer, Mark Ordesky, who subsequently became a friend, what other ideas I had going on in my head. I had confessed to a couple of ideas that had been with me since adolescence, one spent listening to too much heavy metal, smoking too much weed and playing too many fantasy role-playing games – which is what teenage boys who can't get laid do. That or join a rock 'n' roll band – but I lacked the musical talent.

Mark, who had been the main producer for the *Lord of the Rings* series, told me to write the two ideas down. One was for a film called *The Goth Lords*: the fall of Rome told from the point of view of the Goths, the horse tribes who sacked it, but with a speed-metal and electronic soundtrack – history disguised as fantasy, with lots of horses and cool, tattooed people fighting and fucking. Kind of *Lord of the Rings* with sex, violence and rock 'n' roll. The other idea was to take a group of people, men and women, off the street and immerse them in the medieval world, where they had to go on a quest . . .

Mark read the synopses and, to my astonishment, hired me to write them. That had been back in 2009. Since then, one of the big stresses of the past few years had been to knock these scripts into shape while getting New Trails up and running and fulfilling the tasks that Ghoste had charged us with. Now, at last, both projects were in pre-production. Throwing myself into Rowan's autism had led first to *The Horse Boy* and now *The Goth Lords* and *The Quest*. When Rowan was diagnosed, I thought I would no longer be able to write, travel, let alone break into making films and writing for the screen. By giving these dreams up for the autism, the autism had given me those dreams back. In spades.

The same thing had happened with riding. I'd given up horses – my first and deepest love – thinking Rowan wouldn't be safe around them. He had brought me back to horses, and in a much richer way than before. I'd been required to give up fox hunting, which I had loved for all its mad barbarity, but had been rewarded for that sacrifice by learning classical dressage, which I'd always secretly wanted to learn but had always thought I wasn't good enough to do. I had learned it so as to help give kids that feel-good oxytocin effect and help them learn maths and reading, and in doing so had become a better rider and horse trainer than I had dreamed possible – or rather *was becoming* the rider and horse trainer I had always dreamed of being, for in riding, as in any art, one is always a student. The point, though, is that by first giving up my dreams, and then putting them into the service of the dreams of those more vulnerable than myself, they had started to come true.

So why had I hesitated, held back so much? Because happiness, real happiness, is a scary prospect. As Kristin would say in her self-compassion workshops: 'We tend to stick with the devil we know, because it's comfortable, familiar. It usually takes some outside force to kick us into finally choosing happiness. Plus, let's face it, it's more work to get out of your comfort zone, even though that comfort zone may be actively harming you, than it is to climb out of that hole to a better place. No wonder we resist for a time. It's all just part of being human.'

By April, when I could walk again, we had raised enough funds to be able to start developing New Trails properly: put in a covered arena with its sides open to the forest so that we could ride in the shade with the kids even on the hottest day, safe from the burning sun, and still access nature whenever the children wanted. We built proper animal pens, planted proper pasture, began to harvest the hundreds of trees that the drought and the fires had destroyed, and redid all the temporary wire fencing with wood. Then, one day in May, Rowan dropped a bombshell.

'No more school,' he said to me and Jenny over breakfast one hot morning. 'No more learning. No more school of any kind.'

My heart went into my mouth. What were we going to do now? Jenny and I went into a little huddle in the corner. Could we do this? Were we up for the challenge? We agreed that we were.

'Okay, Scub,' we said. 'No more boring old lessons. From now on, only fun. That's official!'

'Right!' he said.

'Right,' we agreed, eyeing each other a little nervously.

And kept on going in exactly the same way, except that we now did it all by stealth.

And so Horse Boy Learning was born. We'd already been fielding questions – and fairly justifiable criticisms – from autism families living in, say, London or Brooklyn, along the lines of: 'Well, it's all very well for you guys. You live in Texas. But how is this nature/horse stuff relevant to our life in the city?'

Fair comment. So now, with Rowan saying 'no' to any more schooling of any kind, we wondered: what if we could reproduce all the good stuff we got on the horse with regular play equipment, like you'd find in any city playground or park, or even in a backyard or living room? What if any mum or dad could do what we did anywhere – what if it could help free them from dependence on expensive therapists? So that *they* could decide, not feel bullied into deciding, whose services they would use. So that a professional therapist would have to be at least as good as the parent was already, to qualify for employment. So that families could engage his or her services as a choice, an option, rather than a dire necessity. And that if they ran out of money, they could offer their child the same, if not better service as any special-needs professional.

Jenny, in particular, had already been putting a lot of thought into this. These past two years, she had – in addition to teaching Rowan and helping Iliane run New Trails and the playdates – been studying for a master's at the University of Texas, researching the outcomes for families who attended Horse Boy Camps. The research was still in progress, but there was a lot of data to draw from. So, between us all, we now came up with a second six-stage process – Horse Boy Learning. It was in effect Horse Boy without horses, with an emphasis on perspective taking, or brain re-patterning, and academic subjects.

Once again, you started by creating the right environment: avoiding bad sensory triggers and doing most teaching outside in a park, or garden, away from industrial machine noise. If you had to be indoors, you ensured the teaching took place in natural light, with plants and small animals, such as a dog, around, and with no disturbing noises in the background, such as the hum from a refrigerator or air conditioner. To address the child's sensory issues, you made sure there were natural materials to play with, natural objects to explore, and – depending on the tolerance level – you hugged, rocked the child as you taught them, giving deep pressure to release oxytocin. And then: movement, movement, movement. If you couldn't go to the park that day, or the pool, you used a small indoor trampoline or created fun obstacle courses out of the furniture, and introduced rule-based games, perspective taking and academics that way. Most kids on the spectrum are kinetic, rather than visual or auditory, learners. Once the child has physically done something – 'added' or 'subtracted' themselves from their sister, for instance, in maths masquerading as a chase game – they can usually move the concept (in this case adding and subtraction) to paper after a couple of weeks.

We started to really have fun with this at New Trails, mixing the work with the horses with playground games (theory of mind) played with the children on our shoulders, in wheelbarrows, in the new pool we'd raised money to install. Rowan and the other kids started learning basic physics – force, acceleration, depth, mass, pressure – through games in perspective taking in the pool, splashing and laughing madly all the while. And poo, of course – always our best ally: when the food goes in, down and out, that's physics; what happens in the gut is chemistry; and the nutritional aspect of why we eat what we eat biology. Then you do the whole thing over again in French . . . And finally, once again, self-advocacy: getting the children to teach *us* about what interests *them*. If a kid was into *Grand Theft Auto*, we got into *Grand Theft Auto*, started learning about the programming, the graphics, the storylines, the history of organized crime, so we could carry on a conversation with that child about their obsession, show that we were interested, nurtured their interest. Because one person's obsession is another person's livelihood, who was to say that kid might not go on to write the next big computer game?

And the world is changing: there are software companies in Silicon Valley, for instance, whose human resources departments are now actively looking for people with functional autism diagnoses. So we no longer have to prepare kids for the industrial machine: technology has changed all that. The future and the economy are wide open now, in a way they never have been before, for every kind of mind. Kids no longer have to be 'normal'. They just have to be good at what they do.

Jenny and her ever-growing team began to school Rowan according to the national curriculum without him even knowing, doing it completely through kinaesthetics – movement – and even began to train others in how to do it too. Parents and schools began to contact her for seminars and workshops. Horse Boy Learning, like Horse Boy Method, started to take off.

Meanwhile, the more we started looking at education, and the brain, the more we became concerned to try and wean Rowan off junk food. We knew the connection between his mood and protein, but the more we looked into it, the more it seemed that food and brain development went hand in hand, to the extent that we could no longer let Burger King, KFC and McDonald's direct his diet. Moreover, despite the insane amount of trampoline bouncing and general exercise, he was starting to get pudgy. Were we being bad parents by letting him eat that stuff? And it was the drinks too – Gatorade and Sprite as treats when he went out on field trips, which was most days. We had to do something – but how?

We consulted a nutritionist, who had some experience with special needs. 'Don't try doing it all at once,' she advised. 'Take one thing at a time – and start with the worst, which isn't actually the fast food, it's the fizzy drinks.' She recommended a brand of electrolytes that would provide some of the taste of the drinks he liked, and added fizz, but weren't full of chemicals and – worse – the high-fructose corn syrup that sweetens most mass-produced food in America and increasingly seems to be linked to almost every disease, from diabetes and cancer to Parkinson's. I started drinking it myself, putting it in the kitchen cupboard and saying, 'No one touch my special fizzy drink stuff – okay?'

Naturally Rowan filched it and pretty soon, after we had explained about high-fructose corn syrup, he was drinking the electrolytes instead of standard fizzy drinks. One down. Then, on the nutritionist's recommendation, we tried various kinds of probiotics, from kefir-based smoothies to actual probiotics in capsule form. He took to both with no hassle and there was no question that his general mood improved as a result. Two down. But it was when we decided to try and change to organic equivalents of junk foods, of which it turned out (following up some brands recommended by the nutritionist) there were many, that we ran into trouble.

Kristin went to Whole Foods one day and came back with a super-healthy organic pizza, not the brand he usually ate at home. Rowan saw her bring it in with the shopping and was immediately suspicious.

'What's that?' he demanded distrustfully as she emptied the shopping bags on the kitchen table.

'Just a new kind of pizza,' she said airily, keeping her tone light.

'Not for me!' he replied emphatically.

She changed to subject. 'Should we go to the San Antonio zoo one day next week?'

He was undeterred. 'When can I have a regular pizza?' He knew change was upon him. And change always came with anxiety, fear. Tears began to flow, he started hyperventilating. I felt myself tense up, the old feeling of dread seeping back. Why were the simplest things always so impossible?

'If you don't like it, you don't have to eat it,' I put in. 'I'll eat it if you don't like it – it looks yummy. In fact, I think I'll cook it now.'

Rowan was crying properly by now – not tantrumming, just distressed: the normal autism reaction to the prospect of altering any established pattern, no matter how banal.

'You're fired!' he suddenly yelled at Kristin.

'What?' she couldn't help but laugh. 'Where did you learn that?'

He must have found it somewhere on the internet or in one of his cartoons. He was furious now.

'You're fired!' he repeated. Then: 'I want a new mummy! When can I have a coupon for a new mummy?'

And with that he ran upstairs.

Kristin and I ate the pizza. It was delicious. We looked at each other as we munched it – though we left a piece for Rowan just in case. Should we laugh or cry?

We poured wine, retired to the living room. 'What are we going to do about his eating?' I said lamely. 'Do you think we'll ever get him to change?'

Kristin was opening her mouth to reply when we heard a foot on the stair. Rowan was standing there, lip trembling. 'I don't want a coupon for a new mummy!' he blurted out suddenly, then ran to Kristin, threw his arms around her and stared earnestly into her eyes.

'I don't want a coupon for a new mummy! You're beautiful! I love you!'

In that moment I saw Kristin's heart go *pop!* As did mine.

'I love *you* so much, Scubby!' she said, tears starting from her eyes. 'And it's okay; you don't have to eat that pizza you don't want to eat. Thank you for not firing me.'

Next week he ate the pizza. 'I only eat organic pizza now!' he pronounced solemnly, as he munched away. 'Pizza Hut pizza is not healthy. But McDonald's and Burger King are very healthy. Say it, Dad!'

'I don't think I *can* say that, Scub.'

'Say, "I was wrong", Dad! Say, "Burger King and McDonald's are very healthy"!'

'I can't say I'm wrong about that, Scub . . .' I looked helplessly at Kristin, silently giggling at my discomfiture. 'Tell you what, Scub,' I had a sudden inspiration. 'I can tell you lots of other things I'm wrong about.'

'Yes, Daddy's wrong a lot!' Kristin confirmed. 'It's what he's best at!'

'I certainly am!'

'What is Daddy wrong about?' Rowan asked darkly.

'Well . . . a lot really.' I fished for a way to bring some toilet humour – always our best ally – into this. 'Did you know, for example, that I used to think that when Mummy went to the loo, and spent a long time in there, that she was doing a poo. But then I found out I was totally wrong! Girls don't poo! They just have rose petals and choirs of angels coming out of there. Not like stinky old daddies. So I was totally wrong about that!'

'Daddy was wrong!' Rowan thundered happily upstairs once more.

I didn't bring the junk food up again for a while. But perhaps a fortnight or so later, I was taking him out for the day and offered to stop at a Burger King, as was his wont. 'No, Dad! I only do that on special zoo days. On regular days I only eat healthy snacks!'

I tried to hide my astonishment. 'Oh, okay, Scub – that's good, right?'

'You were wrong, Daddy!'

'I was, Scub. I totally was. Silly of me.'

'Say. "I was wrong!"'

'I was wrong!'

'Say, "It was just a suggestion."'

'It was just a suggestion.'

'Say, "I won't make you eat that unhealthy food."'

'I won't make you eat that horrible, unhealthy food ever again, Scub. I promise!'

'Except on special zoo days.'

'Except on special zoo days.'

'*Except on special zoo days,*' Rowan whispered to himself, as if to confirm it in his mind.

And after that, the whole thing changed. Jenny and he started to do the science of food, of nutrition, as part of their school day, and to learn to cook and bake – a great way to stealth-teach maths and physics through the weights, measures, temperature, electricity and so on. In the process, he began to learn which ingredients were good for the human body and which were bad and, to our amazement, began of his own volition to ditch most of the old brands he'd been attached to and started to eat healthy alternatives: organic rice noodles and chicken strips, even pinches of spinach and other greens. Admittedly, it had to be served to him as a 'Happy Meal' in an old McDonald's 'Happy Meal' box. '*With a toy!*' Rowan would insist sternly. And then Kristin and I would package it all up, including a little toy grabbed from his toy box, and present it to him *as if* it was junk food.

And as simple as that, despite our worst fears, he was weaned off it.

Jenny and Iliane were intrigued. 'It's like if you drop something into the conversation, casually, but without pressure, you pique the kids' interest,' Jenny said thoughtfully. 'And then if you can find a way to *do* the thing physically, like with the cooking, then they make it their own thing, which kind of confirms it. If you do anything that way, in fact – drop it into the conversation to get them interested but don't really explain, then somehow get them to do it themselves, with their actual body – then the knowledge gets taken in and confirmed. It's amazing.'

'*Drop It, Do It, Confirm It,*' said Iliane. 'You could use that for everything: drop, say, the word 'geometry', 'angle' and such into the conversation, then maybe while in the pool or on the horse talk about what angle we're swimming at or riding – make some kind of game of it . . .'

We were getting excited now. 'You could have a protractor in your pocket,' I put in, 'even in the pocket of your swimming trunks, and just, kind of casually check the angle and explain what you're doing quickly, but without asking the kid to do it . . .'

Jenny picked up the thread: 'And then maybe when the child is used to the whole idea and has played with the protractor a bit himself, you could have, say, a treasure hunt in the woods. If the kid was into Thomas the Tank Engine, for instance, he'd find a clue with a protractor lying next to it that read something like: *Go*

to the oak tree thirty degrees to your left and you'll find a really cool Thomas
toy that's yours when you find it.'

We started field-testing the idea, not just with Rowan, but with
the other kids that came out to the playdates. And so was born the
main ethic of Horse Boy Learning: 'Drop It, Do It, Confirm It' –
not just a new phrase, a whole new approach. First introduce the
idea, allow for a gradual shift by inventing games in which the
child could learn by actually doing the thing themselves, then wait
for them to confirm it by making the idea their own – again
through a pre-arranged set of games, all tailored to the child's
interests, rather than through tests, which generally just caused the
over-anxious kids to shut down, even if they knew the answer.
From now on, we would do everything this way.

That summer, the leg now pretty much healed, we finally began
Rowan's Endangerous Project in earnest. His games with 'Evil
Mummy' had turned to 'Vampire Mummy' (Kristin's face as she
chased him round the house screaming 'Blood! Blood!' as priceless
as Rowan's delighted squeals). Because of this, he finally made a
choice for the location of his first Endangerous trip: Transylvania,
in Romania, to film European brown bears – which are indeed
both endangered and dangerous, and so fitted the bill perfectly. It
felt like getting back into the old routine of the summer healing
journeys.

The same but different, for this time it was Rowan's trip: *his*
idea; his project; his choice of country and animal; his rules. We
did it, as usual, family-style – Kristin and I on camera and sound,
Rowan with a GoPro head camera – and off we went, by plane
from London to Bucharest, then catching a train that wound across
the wide Wallachian Plain, through vast fields of sunflowers,
before climbing slowly into the deep forests and jagged mountains
that separate Transylvania (which means, literally, 'land beyond
the forest') from the rest of the country. Our Romanian friend
Alexandra met us in a hire car at Braşov and drove us out of the
beautiful medieval city, hemmed in by steep, pine-clad mountain-

sides, and out through Bran, where Dracula is supposed to have lived, to a bed and breakfast in a little village strung out along a narrow valley where pastureland merged with the uplands of the utter wild.

And then it started to go wrong. The woman running the guest house took one look at Rowan – running in circles in the yard, working off steam after the long train ride and car journey – and her face hardened. I had been a little afraid of this. Ever since Rowan had expressed interest in Eastern Europe's bear, wolf and lynx – endangerous animals all – I had felt a slight disquiet. Romania, after all, was a country where they still locked up autistic and mentally different children in orphanages, where disability of any kind was still stigmatized. And there was Rowan, running around, taking in the scene, the guard dog at the end of its chain barking maniacally at him. He then rushed up to our landlady, smiled and said, in his most charming Scubby voice, 'Hello! My name's Rowan!' Only she wasn't charmed, but recoiled as if struck.

Later that evening, as Kristin and Rowan read a story together, I went with Alexandra to the local town to buy some supplies, specifically bacon. She seemed agitated.

'They don't want us here, do they?' I said.

'I'm so embarrassed, Rupert. It's what I hate about Romania. So many amazing things, but if something, someone, is different . . .'

My heart sank. 'The annoying thing is that he's not even behaving that autistically,' I replied. 'A little running-about-y, sure. But it's not like he's taking his clothes off or shitting himself or anything. I'll go talk to the woman.'

Alexandra looked sceptical. 'I don't know . . .'

'Hell,' I could feel sadness turning to anger, 'the worst thing that could happen is they kick us out. And then we just drive back into Brașov and get a hotel – any hotel – there.'

Alexandra looked concerned but said nothing.

So back to the guest house we went, supplies in tow, and a rising ire bubbling up from the pit of my stomach. Up in our room, Rowan was watching cartoons on his laptop. In low tones, I filled

Kristin in on the situation. Her face went dark. 'I'll go talk to the lady, get her to cool out,' I promised, and went back downstairs with the very worried-looking Alexandra.

We went into the kitchen where the lady, an attractive blonde in her mid-thirties, was talking with her father, a heavy-set country-man with a kind, weather-beaten face. They flinched guiltily when we walked in: clearly they had been talking about us.

'I hear there's a problem?' I asked as innocently as I could, Alexandra translating. 'I understand you have some concerns about my son.'

The woman looked desperately at her father, whose face had immediately gone into a blank, 'you're on your own with this one' stare. She took a breath, and it all came out in a rush.

It wasn't her, she protested – she was sure my little boy was fine. It was her husband, who was away, but she had called him because she was concerned. 'Maybe it's best if the little boy stays some-where else, somewhere better for him; this little boy who is so wild. Maybe the dog will bite him. Maybe he jumps off a balcony.' She was just concerned that maybe he would get hurt. 'Maybe he marks the walls, which we have just painted. Maybe he won't take his shoes off and will trail mud through the house. Maybe he wakes up all the other guests. Maybe . . .'

'Is there mud in your house?' I asked her.

'No, but . . .'

'We've been here a couple of hours now – is my son running around making noise and upsetting anyone?'

'Well, no, but . . .'

'Has my son marked the walls?'

'No.'

'So has my son caused any problems at all for either you or the other guests?'

'No, it's not me, it's my husband, you see, he . . .'

'So it seems the only person with a problem here – is you.'

'I . . . er . . .'

I could feel the anger rising. Years of this. And Rowan doing so well, working so hard to swim in the neurotypical world. Having come so far, been so brave; only to meet this. Again and again. People telling me in supermarkets what a terrible parent I was when he did something strange. People looking at my child as if he was an alien, no matter how hard he tried, how far he'd come. I went on, impressed that Alexandra was translating all this even though it must have been desperately uncomfortable for her.

'And if you are running a guest house, why do you keep a dog that might bite your guests chained up in your garden?'

'For the thieves, the wolves . . .'

'And this dog will protect you from thieves and wolves tied up on a chain? Where I come from we have wolves – coyotes. They *eat* dogs tied to chains. Is it professional to have this kind of dog chained up where it might bite your guests, when you are running a family guest house?'

'I . . . um . . .'

'Am I your client? Yes, I think I am. Have I paid for our rooms here? Yes, I think I have. Have we caused you any kind of problem? No, I don't think we have. Are you causing a problem for us? Yes, I think you and your husband are. Are you treating us professionally? No, I don't think you are. Now, madam, have you heard of something called autism?'

She had, kind of, well, not exactly . . . I opened my mouth to elucidate, but at that moment Kristin appeared in the doorway, face like thunder.

'You!'

The landlady froze. Her father put up his hands in a placatory gesture. It did no good.

'*YOU!*'

Kristin – a tall woman at five feet and ten inches – bore down on the father and daughter both, her long arm and finger pointing right at the woman's eye.

'How COULD you? You . . . you . . .' I could feel the force of the word brewing in Kristin's throat. 'You FUCKING *BITCH*!'

There was no need to translate. The woman burst into tears.

The father tried to lay a hand on Kristin's arm. She shook him off so violently he actually cowered.

'I wouldn't stay another night in your fucking guest house if you fucking paid me! Do you hear?' Kristin was right in the woman's face now. Another moment and I could tell she might take an actual swing. I got up. 'We should go up now,' I said. 'Rowan will be missing us.'

We left the woman crying and next day found a hotel in Braşov. Thankfully, Rowan had no idea about what had happened.

But from then on things went swimmingly. At Castle Bran, Rowan insisted on going into the haunted house that was set up as part of the tourist craft market outside the castle gates. Having never had much of a stomach for this sort of thing myself – I can't even watch horror movies – I wasn't sure, with Rowan's anxiety, that it was a good idea. But Rowan was adamant, so in we went. Damned scary it was, too; this being Romania, there were no holds barred. We passed an impaled boy, cleverly done as half latex, half a living actor, so that it truly looked like a boy dying slowly on a spike. Horrible. Then we found ourselves in room with a coffin where the doors suddenly slammed hard shut, the coffin lid was flung open and a vampire started to emerge, leering nastily as he came towards us. I saw the sudden fear on Rowan's face, hoped this wasn't going to turn into a disaster, when:

'You're fired!' Rowan shouted at the vampire, who recoiled in surprise at his pointed finger, looking suddenly sheepish and all too human. The door opened and we continued through the various rooms. When, at the end, a werewolf tried to pursue us up the final staircase, Rowan wagged his finger as if it was one of our dogs at New Trails: 'Bad dog! Kennel up!'

We couldn't believe it – no sensory overload, no fear. Back in the craft market, Rowan bought a fake dismembered hand – lots of such things were on sale – and, having climbed to the gates of the castle itself, turned to Kristin: 'Be Vampire Mummy!' Kristin bared her teeth, making talons from her hands. 'Welcome to the House of Bloooooooood!' Rowan giggled delightedly. 'Shake my hand!' he told Alexandra. She did, and the hand with its faux bloody stump came away in her grasp. 'Oh no!' Rowan screamed in mock horror: 'Oh no! My hand! I've lost my hand!'

Tourists filed past us, amused.

Next morning we met Marius, the researcher into large predators who was to guide us into the forest. A big, gap-toothed, bear-like man himself, with a bald patch and hair bushing out over his shirt collar, he was charmed by Rowan, as Rowan was by him: 'You're called Marius! There was a Roman general called Marius. The Romans used to use communal toilets, you know. You're the man who's going to take us to see the bears!'

'Yes, I am!' he laughed – a loud, comfortable-with-the-world laugh. 'And how do you know Roman history? Did you know our Romanian language comes from the Romans? I'm going to take you to see Europe as it looked when the Romans were here.'

And take us he did. Piling into his Toyota 4x4, we drove, by winding dirt roads, up through high foothills, the forest pressing closer and closer until there was no more pasture, only trees, with great rock faces towering above – a return to the ancient, pre-medieval Europe. We swerved aside to let a man with a horse-drawn cart piled high with logs go by, the great patient beast clopping along in its harness as its driver, wearing waistcoat and a tall felt hat set with a sprig of pine – a man from a bygone age – smoked a pipe on the running board. Further up the track, we passed a group of women and brown-faced children, who were collecting berries into baskets. It was like taking a trip into fairy tale.

'They'll want to be out of the forest by dark,' said Marius. 'This road is crazy for bears at night.'

We stopped in the hushed, pre-dusk forest and got quietly out of the vehicle. 'We have to whisper from now on, and make as little sound as possible. The bears will be coming out to forage soon: any sound can spook them. The hide is about three hundred metres that way. Stay close and don't fall behind.'

And into the woods we went, Rowan with his GoPro strapped

to his head, filming as we filed through the crowded tree trunks behind Marius, while the professional forester who had ridden in the back of the vehicle with us brought up the rear, holding a heavy-calibre rifle ready in his hands, just in case. Suddenly the idea of bears was no longer just an idea: the rifle, the hush of the woods brought home the reality of large creatures that could eat you. It was uncanny: we could have been in any English wood-land – granted a very big one. Everything was so familiar – oak, ash, hornbeam, thorn, bracken and bramble. But these were the first woods, the original woods, the old woods – such as we have not seen in England for almost a thousand years.

It was hard, as the gloaming thickened, not to imagine one was being watched – and, from what I had learned about large preda-tors in Africa, we probably were. Predators tend to do that: stay hidden while observing, tracking any unknown creature or thing – person, vehicle, cart, boat – that enters its territory. Almost certainly, eyes were following us, soft feet padding in our wake or parallel with us as we walked, silently and in single file, down the narrow track between the trees and over a little log bridge that spanned a fast-flowing stream, like so many Little Red Riding Hoods on their way to Grandmother's house in the forest tales of our forefathers – forests that people feared for the beasts that lurked therein. We came at last to a little clearing in which stood a wooden house with a pitched roof and shingles that did indeed look like something straight out of a fairy tale. Inside we went.

And waited.

It had been four years since Rowan had learned to *whisper whis-per* in Namibia, waiting for the black rhinos to come out into the glow of the floodlit waterhole. What a long, long way he had trav-elled since then. Now, four years on, and back in a game-viewing hide once more, where the slightest noise might scare the skittish creatures away, Rowan was patience itself, despite severe provoca-tion from his parents – me tickling him and Kristin whispering, 'Welcome to the House of Blood . . .' as scary Vampire Mummy. If Marius and the forester were anything but charmed by Rowan, they didn't show it. The pain of the first evening with the woman at the guest house was steadily receding – just a memory.

From time to time, Rowan would look through the window of the hide towards the clearing where, if we were lucky, the bears would come out as dusk was fading. There was more daylight left than I had thought, this late summer evening, though gradually it grew dimmer and dimmer, and bats began to flit and flicker across the clearing beyond the windowpane. A full hour and a half we waited, Rowan, although boiling over with energy, managing to contain himself in a way that impressed me hugely: how many other ten-year-olds could wait so patiently and for so long for an animal that might never appear? The games and play were continuous in the cramped but cushioned confines of the hide; yet he kept it all to a whisper, every now and then returning to the window to look out once more. I marvelled at his self-control.

'This thing is uncomfortable,' he whispered, finally taking the GoPro camera from his head. 'But keep your camera ready, Dad.'

'I'm on it, Scubber,' I whispered back.

And then there it was. Suddenly, massively, *there*: a young male bear, wandering casually out of the tree line and into the clearing before us.

A shock, in this familiar, yet at the same time so unfamiliar, landscape, to see the big predator loom suddenly out of the half-lit trees. As if one had gone for a walk on, say, Hampstead Heath and all of a sudden found oneself back in the Stone Age when large beasts still roamed the British Isles. A reminder that for all the trappings of millennia of civilization, in Europe, as everywhere else on the planet, the wild is still there, waiting to reclaim the concrete and asphalt, the glass and brick, the high-tech skyscrapers and airports and motorways and railways – waiting till the engines powering the whole thing at last chug out of fuel and the grass can begin poking its way back up between the cracks, tendrils of vine creeping up the sides of the buildings, leaves beginning to drift and cover the tarmac. One day, for sure, bears will once again walk on Hampstead Heath and Hyde Park, and snuff for roots in the ruins of the Millennium Dome. Will we humans still be there, though?

The young bear before us was intent on digging up something. 'Ants,' whispered Marius. 'There's a nest of wood ants there – he's after the larvae.' It was the bear's place, his world – it felt almost indecent to be spying on him like this. But he was beautiful, his form partly man-like, partly animal, as he grubbed and nosed in the dirt, the shaggy brown coat a little muddy as if he had just come from a wallow somewhere.

Rowan picked up Kristin's camera, focused the lens and began to snap away. 'Wow,' he whispered. 'Look at him, he's so awesome! He's *endangerous*!'

We stayed an hour filming until the young bear suddenly sat up, froze, then bounded off, startled by the approach of a more massive elder male who – coming to investigate the younger one's find, and take it from him – padded out from the trees. The bigger beast, wiser, more experienced, looked for a moment towards our hide. A chill went through me. I had seen predator eyes like that before. Once, in Botswana, Jumanda and I had unexpectedly come upon two huge lions while exploring on foot the land the Bushmen were fighting for. He had stopped me with a casual hand gesture. 'Don't worry, man,' he had said. 'The lions are our cousins, we know them. We just wait here till they move off.'

The lions had looked us over, no trace of fear, not even much curiosity in their amber eyes. I had been ready to soil myself, but Jumanda just quietly stood his ground. The lions' look communicated one thing only – could they be bothered to eat us or not? Having eventually decided not, they unhurriedly rose and sauntered off down the track, roaring from time to time to warn any other lions in the area that this was their territory and they were hunting now. Without Jumanda there and whatever Bushman *nxum* he was throwing at them, I'm sure I would have been the dinner they were now wandering off to find.

Another time, in Yellowstone National Park, I had seen – this time from the safety of my vehicle – a huge grizzly shamble down the snowy hillside and casually take a freshly killed elk away from a small wolf pack. They had given ground immediately, rather than face the dispassionate killing machine that had wandered in among them. Easier to kill anew than to risk those great paws, those enormous teeth. For a moment, noticing me, the great beast had raised its head – its face, incredibly wide across the jaws, giving off a sheer maleness that made one shiver. But it was the eyes – again with that assessing 'Can I be bothered to eat you or is it too much hassle?' look – that made one's DNA recoil in instinctive horror. Our European ancestors had felt it, fearing the dark beyond the cave's mouth, where the bears dwelt.

Now, as we sat in the hide looking out through the window, this was how this big Romanian bear regarded us through the glass. No concern, just a vague assessment, dismissal, before he went to work on the ant heap, pulling it to pieces casually, easily. It was hard not to imagine him doing that to a human ribcage. It was almost fully dark now. Too dark to photograph: night time – the time of predators, the bear's time, his forest. We were merely guests.

'We'll have to wait till he has moved away before we can leave,' said Marius in a low voice. 'It won't be safe to walk out of here for a little while.'

So, for perhaps thirty minutes after the departure of the older bear, who had stayed only long enough to snack before moving unhurriedly on, we held on inside the little cottage hide, Rowan relieved at last to be able to giggle and laugh and sing Scubby songs at will, letting go the tension of being so good, so in control, for so long. As we walked back out through the pitch-blackness, following the glow of Marius's torch up ahead, fireflies danced around us – magical. And to be sharing this with my son, for it to be his idea, a journey he was taking us on, this – indeed – was magic.

The second evening, after a day spent exploring the medieval alleyways of Braşov ('There used to be knights here,' said Rowan, looking up at the city walls that still partly encircled the old town), we climbed even higher into the mountains, driving a good hour until the road became suddenly much, much steeper. We breasted a low pass and paused awhile to take in the view. Ridge after successive ridge rose before us. What did it remind me of? I thought for a moment, looking at the blue lines, each one higher than the last – long, long ridges of wilderness, covered in primeval hardwood and pine. Then it came to me – Appalachia. Years and years before, in another life, when I first came to the States, a raw lad of twenty-one with a degree in history I did not know how to use (but with the story of *The Goth Lords* forming in my head), I had got a job training hunt horses in Virginia, the cradle of America's colonial heritage. They still call it the Old Dominion: farms and woodland, with fox hunting and steeplechasing among the green foothills of the Piedmont, these rising up to the limestone wilderness of the Blue Ridge, covered in old-growth forest, that stretches, ridge after ridge, away towards Kentucky. The barrier to civilization for two hundred years until the trails spilled westwards and the great race for America began.

'These were Ceauşescu's hunting forests,' said Marius, stopping the vehicle for a moment to let us drink in the awe of it. 'Under communism, anyone who came up here unauthorized could be put in jail, maybe tortured.'

'Like in medieval forests,' Rowan chimed in. 'You could have your hand cut off if you hunted in a king's forest.'

Marius raised an eyebrow. 'He knows a lot, your boy. Yes, something like that. Now Ceauşescu has gone and it's all nature reserve. The animals are still here, as they always have been.'

And indeed they were. Over the next ridge, Marius pulled over on to a more level bit of hillside to park – we were to walk the rest of the way to the hide. Almost immediately we caught movement further up the slope – we were being watched by a red hind and her calf. Then I realized the whole hillside was moving. A whole herd of hinds – larger than the red deer I had seen in Scotland where the climate is harsher, the grazing poorer – and their young were grazing across the entire slope, browsing at the young saplings growing there at the forest margins. Again, there was that sense of being in the beasts' domain – such an unfamiliar, even intoxicating feeling in Europe, where so much of our life is based around cities. We forget how much of it is still wild.

The hide commanded an even better view than the ridge where we had stopped. Awestruck by the successions of ever-receding mountains, now touched orange and gold with sunset, I almost didn't notice when – far down in a glade below us – a bear, its fur almost black, emerged from the hushed pines.

'He's too far away for the camera,' said Rowan, not needing to keep his voice down at this distance. As so often these days, he was coming out with things that sounded so adult.

'How do you know that, Scubby?'

'Everybody knows that, Dad. At this distance you need a telephoto.'

This was the non-verbal child that the speech therapists had given up on all those years before. The child that, not three nights ago, had been too weird for the landlady at the guest house. Just how normal did he have to become? The answer, I realized, with a lurch of the heart, was: as normal as people expected him to be. Kristin put it well later that evening, when I brought it up back at the hotel. Rowan was splashing in the bathtub, grumpily washing his own hair and whingeing: 'This is really irritating me! I really hate this!'

'The more "normal" he gets, the less forgiving people are going to be,' said Kristin, sadly, 'and the higher their expectations. It's almost easier in a way if a kid stays more severely autistic. People don't expect them to behave normally and they make allowances for it, even if they write them off. Scub's getting older; he's going to have to learn. It makes me so sad, because I know some people are going to be unkind to him. That's why we have to stick around, and stick together, through thick and thin.'

'Thick and thin,' I agreed. For him – and for us too. For, in the year leading up to this journey, our drifting apart had crystallized into a realization that, as a romantic couple, we had run our course.

We had gone over it together a thousand times, sitting up late, talking into the small hours to try and make sense of it all. There had been tears, sadness. But strangely, once we had admitted that as a couple we were done, it felt oddly liberating. 'I know a lot of people who saved their relationship by splitting,' a friend of mine said, laughing, when I confided Kristin's and my decision to him. There was a lot of wisdom in his words.

Back when Rowan had been at his most severe, and there had been no New Trails, no Horse Boy tribe to rally round, when it had been just the two of us, isolated, desperate, afraid, exhausted, our families thousands of miles away and none of our friends able to cope, we had had a stroke of genius. We would become each other's babysitter, sending each other out one night a week to play, see friends, get drunk, not come back even . . . so that when you *did* come back (the other being only mildly passive-aggressive when you walked through the door the next morning), you came back fresh for the fight. That lightening of pressure, at the very moment when we were starting to pile more and yet more pressure on to each other, saved us, allowed us to be able to see Rowan and each other through the years that followed.

Now, we realized, it was time to do the same. We were not only drifting apart, we were starting to pick at each other more and more, starting to founder on the accumulated years of petty resentment, of the sheer *stuff* that can build up over two decades and then get between a couple. It had been pressing on us both for some time, but until Rowan's final healing was done, perhaps subconsciously neither of us had wanted to risk causing a disruption. But in the 'rest' year between Rowan's third healing with Blue Horse, and this journey into the Eastern European wild, it had become acute.

Then we had a brainwave. We loved each other, right? Twenty years together. Twenty years of mutual support, building, love, friendship, family. What if we were to lighten the load on each other, just as we had all those years before; absolve ourselves from having to carry the weight of each other's emotional needs? What if we lived together as normal, but as friends? What about that? We still loved each other so much, wanted each other's happiness so badly. Our marriage vows (drafted by us), after all, had been to help each other 'thrive and be happy'. Perhaps it was time to live up to them.

Once the decision was finally made, it was as if a filter that had become buried under old dust had been cleaned, unclogged, renewed. As soon as we stopped trying to make something out of something that wasn't there any more, or rather which had changed into something else, as soon as we stopped doing that, took the pressure off each other once more, the living together became easier. We'd always enjoyed each other's company so much, but now it felt lighter, so much lighter. We were less bothered by each other, but we still supported each other, were there for each other, as best friends of twenty-odd years should be.

'I've never understood why people automatically feel they have to divorce when they split,' Kristin said, over wine one evening. 'I mean, if you hate each other, it's one thing. But to break things up – break up the family, break everyone's hearts, including the children's, destroy everything you've built together – just because the relationship has developed into something else, it seems so unnecessary, so violent.'

And as far as Rowan was concerned, nothing at all had changed; we'd had separate bedrooms for some years anyway (I snore and, well, after a while it's just good to have your space). It had been painful to let go of the old dream, our old selves. But the relief, we both admitted, once it was done, was palpable.

So now, sharing a bottle of Romanian red – surprisingly good – we looked at each other across the table, listening to our son splash in the bathtub. 'I still love you, you know, just for the record,' I said.

'Me too,' she winked. We clinked glasses.

So Kristin and I were okay, better actually, but our worries about Rowan were growing. He could still behave with an almost toddler-like unselfconsciousness that was starting to unnerve other people because of his rapidly growing size: suddenly bounding off down the road, or through a crowded airport concourse, bumping into people. He was almost five foot now and weighed over a hundred pounds. People wouldn't tolerate it much longer, I knew. Even though the woman at the guest house, strangely, had seen him at his best, he still did weird things. He'd lift his shirt and stroke his belly, for instance, as he talked to strangers – a way of self-soothing, but one that I could see was beginning to freak people out a little; or pick his nose with great precision and dedication in the middle of a public place; or – as happened the following day – barrel into a playground of younger kids, to their mothers' evident alarm. I still thought of him as small and he thought of himself that way, too, but compared to the little children in the Braşov playground, he was a giant.

We got on a merry-go-round that had separate seats and went round if you made it bounce with your legs: 'Make it go, Dad!' I did, Kristin taking one of the other seats. I kicked my feet off the ground and around we went, all facing each other round the central pole. '*The Simpsons!*' he shouted, Alexandra filming discreetly in the background. 'Do it, Dad!'

I knew the cue, a piece of dialogue taken from a *Simpsons* comic he had bought on a trip two, or was it three years before. Time was starting to blur – I was ageing, and not just in my own eyes. A week or two ago, while in England before coming out to Romania, I'd taken Rowan to a swimming pool near my parents' house and a little boy had asked me, 'Are you his grandad, then?'

'*That remote is mine, boy!*' I shouted, knowing my part as Homer. (The comic strip involved a fight between Homer and Bart Simpson for a TV remote and therefore control of the television itself. Even two or more years on, Rowan still found it hilarious.)

'*Not if I get there first, old man!*'

'*Why, you little . . . !*'

'Choke me, Dad!' Rowan leapt off his seat on the merry-go-round and ran over. Dutifully, I dismounted and – aware that we were out in public – pretended to throttle him as Homer did in the comic strip, while Rowan went, '*ARRRRRRRGH!*'

The Romanian mums watched, bemused. I caught Kristin's eye. He was so innocent, but he was going to have to learn, as Cisco had, to 'fake it'. Would he be able to, though?

It came into focus once more at the bear sanctuary we visited later that day, before our final rendezvous with Marius. The sanctuary was set among unfenced hills covered in sweeping grassland, crossed here and there with belts of oak and elm, that provided common grazing for the cows and sheep of the villages down on the plain. The approach to the sanctuary had been easy to miss – a dirt track off the main road with its growing strip development, big roadside signs for electronic products, little industrial parks. Designed more for carts than cars, the track, by contrast, led us straight back into the pre-industrial age until, almost as an after-thought, it brought us out at the bear sanctuary. Surprisingly for a place that seemed so tucked away, it was clearly well funded, with expansive, attractive enclosures, winding gravel pathways, signs in German and English as well as Romanian, and a young female guide to take us on a tour of the facility.

Rowan was full of restless energy that afternoon and kept bounding off away from the group to go check out the poor bears. They'd been rescued from Gypsies who had crushed their ribs, pulled out their teeth and claws, so as to produce dancing bears that could no longer easily harm a human being. Rescued from backyards where they had been used to fight dogs, people betting on the outcome. One huge beast – bigger by far than the one we had seen shamble into the clearing on the first night – had been blinded, his eyes pierced with needles as a cub so as to make him more tractable. He sat, depressed, alone, beneath a big pine, despite the fact that they had given him a couple of females for company. All the bears here, explained the young, blonde tour guide – who was clearly growing more and more frustrated with Rowan's way-wardness – had been rescued from these kinds of fates.

'Ignorance of the need for conservation is regrettably still a problem with some sectors of our population,' she went on, in good but scripted English. 'But, little by little, we are beginning to rectify this with outreach and education initiatives. We are hopeful that in the Romania of the future such cruel and outdated attitudes will eventually be a thing of the past. Little boy!' she suddenly shouted. 'Little boy! No! You do not do that! It is obligatory to stay with the group! Little boy!'

Rowan had scampered away towards another set of enclosures, Kristin trotting embarrassed in his wake. Today he didn't want to film, so I was manning the camera. I set it down, sighed.

'Little boy!'

And in front of the whole group – most of whom were American and British – I began the mantra that I'd used so many times before: 'I apologize, he's doing the best he can. Have you heard of something called autism?'

My explanation partly mollified her, and the rest of the group was generally sympathetic. I was tempted to ask her if she hoped that attitudes in her country would soften towards more than just bears: towards children, indeed people, who were different. Did she hope that one day they would no longer lock up their autistic children in orphanages and chain them to cots and walls? But I held my tongue.

Indeed, it was not just nature that harked back to older, more brutal times; it was people's minds too. We were in a Europe that, for all its veneer of post-communist modernity, still had its roots deeply in the intolerance of the Middle Ages. There was a reason the old fairy tales were full of torture, suffering and oppression, a reason why this was the land of the vampires and horror.

But then later, when Marius came to pick us up, and started laughing and joking with Rowan, he made my son seem so 'normal' again that it was disorientating. Rowan might not be able to control his oversized (and, in the city, overstimulated) exuberance in a park full of smaller kids, or at the airport, or on a guided tour, but now he was restraint itself. As Marius led us through a wild marshland on the edge of a muddy winding river in the gathering dark, my son kept his voice low as bid and whispered the questions that any normal, interested boy would ask. We were not going to watch bears this time, but to see if we could spot something even rarer: a breeding pair of European beavers – relics of a population that once stretched from Britain across Europe to Siberia, but which now existed in only tiny pockets of isolated pairs.

'This is a location we in the wildlife service keep secret, because we don't want people hunting them,' Marius had confided during the drive there. 'People used to think the beaver destroyed crops – and old habits are hard to break. But actually the beavers are very good for our rivers. I can't guarantee we'll see one, but I wanted to try, because for us, it is something even more special than a bear or wolf or lynx.'

'Yes,' Rowan agreed gravely. 'Hunting and deforestation is making many species extinct. It's the cutting down of the rainforests that's threatening the planet's wildlife and cutting off our oxygen.'

It wasn't the first time he had said this. A few months before, when we had started felling the trees killed by the years of drought, Rowan, returning to New Trails from an outing with Jenny, had spotted us working with the chainsaws, burning the smaller brush as we went, so that it wouldn't go up in the event of more wildfires. He had come charging out of the car. 'Stop that!' he cried. 'Stop cutting down the forests! It's killing the planet and the animals! Stop it now!'

We had explained, promising him we would only take dead trees and that clearing the forest floor would help the saplings come through, which the deer could then browse. He eyed us suspiciously. 'Promise you won't cut down any living trees!'

'We promise!'

Marius was as impressed as we had been. 'That's right, Rowan. I'm glad to see you know so much about ecology. It's very important.'

'I know. Actually, beavers are not endangerous, but the European beaver is still endangered, so we should protect it.' We had stopped by the riverbank now. Marius, knowing the creatures' haunts, was shining a portable spotlight at the overhanging trees of the opposite bank. The night air was heavy and smelled like rain. Thunder rumbled over the mountains at the edge of the plain through which the river ran.

'There!' Rowan was the first to pick up the pair of eyes moving just above the surface of the water.

'Sharp eyesight!' Marius patted his back. 'You'll make a great ranger one day.'

'Zookeeper!' Rowan corrected him.

Marius laughed. 'Yes, we need zoos too, to protect the genetic breeding pool. Here, why don't you hold the light. Like this – that's right . . .'

We had stayed like that, crouching in the dark, watching the elusive animals drift on the surface of the water for a few seconds now and then, until our limbs became cramped. Whenever the shy creatures felt the light had been on them long enough, they would disappear below the surface with a slap of the tail that sounded like a whip crack. 'I'm getting a little bored, I have to say,' Kristin whispered in my ear. Alexandra and I smiled, acknowledging that we were in the presence of obsession – of a positive kind. Marius and Rowan, two born naturalists, were rapt, intent on spotting the eyes of the beavers as they resurfaced each time, whispering together like conspirators. Only when the rain began first to spit, then to come down in earnest did we beat a retreat back to the car.

'Quick, everyone,' Rowan exhorted us as we trotted back, the rain coming down ever stronger. 'Flash floods are dangerous. Don't be slow, come on!'

We took our leave the next day. 'Come back again, Rowan,' Marius said. 'Come back in the winter and I will take you out to look for wolves. They're easier to find in the snow.'

'Goodbye, Marius – you'll miss me.'

Another great bear-laugh. 'I will. I truly will!'

When the time came to make the three-hour train journey back down on to the plain to Bucharest, en route for home, Rowan kept his good humour up even as the carriage became more and more crowded – until eventually we were all packed together in the hot, sweaty coach like sardines. No freak out. No sensory overload from the crowd, the press, the heat. Where had this even-tempered, articulate, tolerant boy, able to take frustration in his stride, sprung from? But I could see he was overstimulated, even so, the stress starting to show.

And then suddenly, out of the blue, he started making me tell him, very, very loudly, in front of all the people crowded into the carriage, about how when I was three or four I had accidentally pooed in the tub while taking a bath with my cousin Bruno, who was two years older than me and somewhat bigger. I had made the mistake of telling Rowan the story just before coming out to Romania, to help jolly him through a rough morning when we were low on bacon. He'd found it hilarious: how I had hoped that I might be able to sneak out of the tub without my cousin noticing because I had thought – correctly, as it turned out – that the moment Bruno saw what I'd done, he would punch me.

Some minutes later, he made me tell the story again. Caught with a choice between this and a possible tantrum in the enclosed, packed-in space, I went along with it. Again and again and again. Kristin looked at me with sympathetic eyes. It was embarrassing, but it was what got him through the stress of being packed into the hot, crowded space. And more than that, as my mouth went into auto-pilot, telling and retelling the story in its scripted cues while my mind wandered elsewhere, it gave me an idea. An idea for how to start weaning him from these last vestiges of toddlerish behaviour – at least in public – and start transitioning into Cisco's world of faking it for the unforgiving, neurotypical, world.

Humour – it would all come down to humour. It always got him through – was always the right approach. As was proved as the day dragged on, for our plane didn't leave until the evening and there was still a lot of time to kill. By the time we got out of the train and had taken a taxi to the zoo – which he had been building up in his mind, fighting through his growing tiredness, the humid heat and traffic of the Third World shambles that is Bucharest – Rowan was on the edge of total meltdown. Exacerbated by the fact that when we finally made it to the zoo, it was oddly disappointing – a few exotic animals but also some that were decidedly not, including (I kid you not) enclosures labelled 'Cow', which turned out indeed to be a cow, and 'Horse', which, yes, was a horse. The afternoon, under the tall, thin, melancholy-looking oaks, was so hot and draining. He began to whimper, and whine. 'When can we go to a real zoo?'

'You know,' Kristin confided, 'I really don't want to do these big, difficult Scubby trips any more. I have to admit it, I think I'm done. If you and Scub want to do them, that's your thing. I think I've reached my limit.'

'Fair enough,' I said. And indeed, after all she had been through, it was.

But as the hot, frustrating afternoon wore on, with long, long queues at the airport and nothing to eat and crowds and jostling, I managed to keep his mood afloat with the Bruno bathtub poo story, retrieving the situation from all-out tantrum every time it edged to the brink, and all the while formulating my plan.

As we settled into our seats to fly home, his mood at last lifted. 'So that was the European brown bear,' I said. 'Where shall we go for next year's Endangerous trip?'

Rowan looked at me and smiled. 'It's a surprise. Now, tell me the story of you in the bathtub again.'

I took a deep breath, catching Kristin's eye. 'Well, Scub, when I was three or four I was in the bathtub with my cousin Bruno . . .' Already he had begun to giggle once more.

Back at home, we started putting the video together for the first episode of *Endangerous*. 'It has to be silly,' said Rowan. We rose to the challenge: me hiding in the green undergrowth *whisper whispering* in my best David Attenborough voice: 'We've spotted a bear and he's just over there, eating a salmon and . . .' The camera (a hand-held) pans back and reveals the fact that I'm actually in our kitchen, hiding behind a large potted plant, and the bear in question is one of Rowan's toys, but I go on, undaunted: '*Ursus arctos*, the European brown bear is actually the same species at the American brown or grizzly bear. Now endangered in the wild, it still holds on in remote corners of Eastern Europe and Scandinavia, with a few scattered individuals in the Alps and Pyrenees and the mountains of Italy. Similar in size to their close relative the American grizzly bear, they can be very, very dangerous if disturbed, and . . .'

'Um, Ru,' says the person holding the camera. 'It's a toy bear.'

'Don't be silly. Anyway, as you can see, the European brown bear is an omnivore, eating everything it can: fruits, berries, hunting small animals and catching fish like this salmon. Highly territorial, we need to keep a safe distance or . . .'

'Rupert! It's a toy bear! This is your kitchen!'

'Shhh! If you disturb him, he might . . .'

'Rupert! Stop it! It's a toy bear! This is your kitchen! This is silly.'

I flapped my hands, looked down. 'Okay, I guess it is a bit silly. Sorry.'

Peals of laughter from Rowan. He had written the sketch himself.

He and Jenny downloaded an easy animation programme from the web and added a sequence on language, because Rowan had finally started to become interested – after years of resistance – in the plethora of languages he'd heard on his trips abroad, including Romanian. He created two girl characters, Jennifer and Allison, for whom 'School is *soooo* boring', and so they head off into outer space to meet Grumpus Pumpus the Space Monkey who takes them on a journey to the source of our European language, Proto-Indo-European, which resides in space because no one really knows what it sounded like. Grumpus Pumpus then takes them to the Italy: 'Here we are at the Colosseum, in Rome, whose language used to be Latin, the root of modern Italian and Romanian. We still use Latin to classify animals like the endangerous

brown bear, *Ursos arctos*, which means "bear from the north".'
Then characters find themselves superimposed on a real Roman
ruin – long stone benches with holes at regular intervals.

'What is this?' asks Allison. 'A communal toilet,' replies Grumpus Pumpus. 'The Romans liked to have a little chat when they
went to the toilet, you know. But they didn't call it a toilet, they
called it a *latrina* – which is where the English word "latrine"
comes from.' Then there's a terrible fart sound, making the girls'
hair stand on end. 'What was that?' 'I'm sorry,' says Grumpus
Pumpus. 'I just really had to go to the lavatory.'

Finally they find themselves in Berlin, Grumpus Pumpus standing atop the Brandenburg Gate. 'This is Germany, where they
speak German, which, like English, is a Germanic language,
though English is mixed with Latin too. Some German words we
use in English: "Lager"' – a pint appears in front of Jennifer – 'and
"Hamburger"' – and a burger appears in front of Allison: 'Oh
yum, can I eat it?' Grumpus Pumpus flies into a rage – it's *his* hamburger. Allison throws a tantrum as she wants to eat it herself. 'Oh
well,' says Jenny. 'It's time to go back to school anyway.'

Then we cut back to the bears – the amazing footage Rowan had
taken in the hide – with bear facts to follow; then a sideways foray
into vampires, Dracula and Castle Bran – the House of Blood – with
a cameo appearance from Evil Mummy; a look at the civet family in
general, of which bears are the largest genus; the New Trails girls
going to the refrigerator to get 'bear snacks' and the 'bear refrigerator' eating them. And finally a 'Gangnam Style' dance sequence
with all of us in animal masks. 'It's the Endangerous Project and I'm
the director!' Rowan shouted during filming. 'Dance sillier!'

So we did. And the first episode was born.

And with that, something in Rowan clicked – an inner writer
and director blossomed with startling results. During one history
period at New Trails – we were studying the Renaissance –
Rowan made us enact Henry the Eighth cutting off his wives'
heads, each head consisting of an onion with a sad face drawn on
it that was held up in front of the real heads of some of the female

staff as they each knelt in turn to receive a blow from the sword. 'King Scub the Eighth' pronounced a sentence of death for 'not being silly enough' and countered our protestations that the real King Henry actually beheaded only two of his wives with a regal 'I'm rewriting history!' as, one by one, the onions went bouncing off the mounting block, rolling on to the flagstones of the front yard while the dogs looked on, bemused.

Then Rowan discovered William Shakespeare. 'I'm going to write a play!' he announced, and – good as his word – promptly sat down to do so. This, the boy who had been unable to speak! One Sunday afternoon after he'd finished the play, he and I and one of the working students at New Trails – a British girl called Vicky – drove out to Winedale, between Austin and Houston, where some decades before a wealthy Texan Shakespeare aficionado had built a facsimile Globe Theatre out among the oak trees, cactus and mesquite. The university did a summer Shakespeare season there, but I suspected that now, three months before that started, the place would be empty. We drove out that afternoon and found it – as I had suspected we would – unmanned, hopped over the fence and crept on to the deserted stage.

The play was called *William Shakespeare Comes Back from London and Anne Hathaway Gets Cross* and Vicky and I had rehearsed the title roles. Looking about him on the stage, Rowan was enchanted. 'We need music!' he cried.

'Er,' I mumbled, 'I can sing something medieval-ish before we come on to the stage, if you like.'

'Yes! Music, maestro!'

Music, maestro? Where had he got that from – some cartoon, perhaps? 'Um . . .' I fished for something in my head and came up with a sort of truncated 'Greensleeves'.

'Now we need lights!'

'I'll tell the lighting man to get the spotlights working, Scub. In the meantime, if you go up those little steps behind you, you'll find a director's box where you can look out over the stage and tell us what to do.'

Rowan was up the short flight in a heartbeat, then reappeared at the gallery balustrade. 'Okay – music!'

I did my tortured version of 'Greensleeves'.

'Lights!'

'Spotlights, please!' I shouted to the imaginary man up in the lighting booth.

'Action!'

From opposite ends, Vicky and I walked on to the stage.

'My Lady Anne,' I bowed.

'Fie upon thee, sir!' Vicky stamped her foot and turned her back to me. 'You gallivant off to London, leaving me and the children here to starve, while you wine and wench and gamble! And now you come back and expect me to . . .'

'But I have missed you, my lady! Thought about you night and day! I have written you a sonnet . . .'

'A pox on your sonnets – I need money!'

'But I have been selling my sonnets! I have brought money! But the best sonnet . . .' I moved up, taking her shoulders tenderly, 'I saved it for you. Would you like to hear it?'

She softened. 'Very well. Tell it to me.'

I took a breath. 'Shall I compare thee . . .'

She looked around, eyes fluttering.

'. . . to a warthog. Thou art more hairy, and yet more smelly.'

Surprise, indignation, anger – Vicky was a good actress.

'Fart winds come out from your bottom.'

'I can't believe this! No one has ever been so insulting!'

'And make everyone pass out from the smell.'

Vicky/Anne picked up an imaginary frying pan and – 'PWANG!' – knocked me over the head with it.

Giggles from the director's box. Rowan came down the stairs, stopped at the bottom and bowed. 'All original work.'

Then he clapped his hands: 'Now again, with more feeling! Music!'

Vicky and I had to repeat the performance some forty or so times before Rowan was satisfied. 'That was amazing, Scub,' I told

him, as we drove home. 'I mean, really. The play's really good –
timing, physical comedy, everything. I'm really impressed. Truly.'

We drove in silence for a while. 'Should we film this as part of
the Endangerous Project?' I asked.

'Or . . .'

'Or, um, we just leave it as its own play.'

'Correct, Dad.'

'What about Endangerous, though? Where do you want to go
next? We could go anywhere – Africa, Asia, South America, Yellowstone here in the USA . . .'

'Or . . .'

'Um . . .' We were back in autism enigma-speak. I fished for
what he might be wanting me to say. 'Or . . . we could . . .'

'We could . . .' he encouraged me.

'Go to zoos? Zoos rather than the wild: is that it?'

'Zoos!' he confirmed. 'Or . . .'

I racked my brains. Then it came to me; this was where this
whole homeschooling adventure had begun: Gerald Durrell's *My
Family and Other Animals*, the inspiration behind our entire Horse
Boy Learning approach – exploration, play, all involving animals,
nature. Durrell had grown up to be a zoologist. Was this where my
son was headed?

'Or,' I ventured, 'we could have our own zoo?'

'Our own zoo!' Sudden, absolute joy. 'We're going to need
some elephants, giraffes, exotic antelope and deer species, penguins, alligators . . . and breed endangered species to go back into
the wild, because the animals are in danger of going extinct – *in
danger of going extinct*,' he repeated to himself at the end, as he did
when he wanted to affirm something.

'Right.'

And so arrived, at New Trails, two European fallow deer, a
male and a female, both snow white (the 'white hart' of medieval
lore), whom Rowan christened 'Elliot' and 'Gazelle'. They were
completely wild upon arrival, but within weeks Rowan and his
'ladies' had the pair eating from their hands. Then came Dexter,

a young Nubian ibex (an endangered wild goat species from northeast Africa) of extraordinary sociability and charm, who promptly moved into the house with the dogs and came for cuddles on the sofa. Then a pair of Japanese Sika deer – Steven ('with a *v* not a *ph*,' insisted Rowan) and Amethyst – both so chilled out that almost upon arrival you could stroke their soft, luxuriant brown coats with barely visible spots. Our 'reptile house' (the upstairs landing) held the leopard geckos, a Jackson's chameleon from Madagascar with a striking horn on its viridian head, tree frogs, various snakes and, in Rowan's bedroom – right above where his head was when he slept – a tarantula and an emperor scorpion, which had babies. For a boy with anxiety issues, he seemed completely unconcerned that these two creepy monsters might escape in the night – as I would have been. Back over at New Trails, I was instructed to raise the height of the fence around one of the lower pastures to seven feet in anticipation of what Rowan promised would be 'several antelope species from Africa and India', yet to come.

'I should have known,' Kristin said ruefully, 'that when he said he wanted to be a zookeeper it'd mean we'd have to have our own zoo!'

And gradually Rowan – who had hitherto delegated the looking after of all the various New Trails animals to us – began feeding, watering and seeing to his animals himself. Taking responsibility – even going out into the dark to make sure the animals had water or were securely locked in their houses for the night. First thing in the morning, he'd be up to feed them, let them out – all unbidden.

The Endangerous Project had ignited Rowan's creative spark and filled New Trails up with animals, but the sense of storytelling, of role play, that it engendered meant I could at last follow up on the idea I had had in Romania when Rowan had made me repeat my infant bathtime poo accident story ad nauseam on the train.

The power of a story, especially if it was funny, was the one thing that could take Rowan out of himself, allow him to view situations and himself from the outside – advanced perspective taking, in other words. Finally we could tackle the social issues that had been worrying us, now that he was getting so big, without shaming him, without distressing him. All through story, through humour. Jenny and I began to make up funny sketches about what would happen if Grumpus Pumpus arrived from outer space and found Rowan running around naked where strangers could see him. 'He'd go: "Nooooooooooooo – what if a bad adult sees that!"' Rowan found it hilarious and ran around for a week going '*Noooooooooo – what if a bad adult were to see me!*' And soon afterwards began wearing pants when he went outside, and when people came to the door.

'And what would happen,' Jenny said, 'if the police saw a huge monkey like Grumpus Pumpus running headlong into a crowd? They'd say, "Noooooooooooooo!" because people would be knocked flying left and right, and then they'd say, "Grumpus Pumpus, you're under arrest for being too Chargey-Aroundy and we hereby sentence you to four million years of having a cold bath with someone you dislike." And Grumpus Pumpus would say: "Nooooooooooooo!"'

Rowan would jump in, make the story his own, and pretty soon stopped running headlong into crowds of strangers. We had found the key.

Was this what Ghoste had meant when he said the guardianship would pass from Betsy to me: that I would use what I knew – story and its craft – to help Rowan's transition out of childhood and into the rest of his life?

One crisp December afternoon at New Trails, as Rowan approached his twelfth birthday, I watched a young autistic boy and his siblings playing in the petting zoo enclosure with the deer, the bunnies, the tame pigs, the ducks that Rowan had rendered so tame you could pick them up and press a special point on their chests, upon which they would automatically quack – much to the delight of the little autistic boy. He was all the more delighted because it was Rowan himself – the little boy was in awe of older boys – who was showing him how to do it.

'Now,' said Scub, 'you pick him up like this – that's right – and press your finger here.'

'*Quack!*' went the duck.

'*Quack!*' said the little boy delightedly. '*Quack!*' he repeated, while his sister stroked the velvet backs of the sika deer and his brother fed carrots to the three little pot-bellied pigs, Ronnie, Henrietta and Frannie (pronounced, for some strange reason known only to Rowan, 'Fray-nie'), who had come nosing in to ask for treats.

'Ducks go quack!' the little autistic boy declared suddenly. His mother, watching, promptly burst into tears. It was the most words he had ever spoken.

The healers in Mongolia had said that Rowan would become a shaman. At the time I had resisted the idea, not wanting to write a script for him. I knew how rigorous that road was, did not want to push Rowan into anything like that. If at some point in his life it was his own decision, then well and good, but it would have to come from him. Now I wondered if it wasn't happening right in front of my eyes.

'Want to try again?' Rowan showed the little boy once more how to pick up the duck – a Muscovy called George – and find just the right spot to press for the *quack*. 'Right here, you see – press here, like this . . . There you go . . .'

'*Quack!*' said the duck.

'Ducks go quack,' the little boy said again. Rowan had got the child talking. Tears sprang to the corners of my eyes, too. Next to me I saw Jenny looking away, hiding her own.

Epilogue

The Dream Whisperers

It's ten in the morning: time for Rowan to start his school day. The subject this week is electricity, and Rowan is building a small robot from a kit. Its name, when finished, is to be 'Tin', as the body is made from an old tin can. Betsy is waiting – saddled – at the front door, held by two of the working students from New Trails, patiently waiting for Rowan to finish his computer game. 'I just have to finish this round! I'll be right there!'

Betsy is still with us, and as good as new again. Two years after her sudden, alarming weight loss, and after much care and attention, she is back in light work again. At almost thirty, she looks great, is back to being Rowan's morning ride to our school that is not a school. They love each other, start the day together. But we aren't allowed to call her the 'School Bus' any more. A few weeks ago, he'd said to me: 'That's a crazy idea, Dad. Betsy's a horse! She can't be a machine!'

I'd admitted, somewhat sheepishly, that he was right.

'We have to call it the San Antonio Zoo Train when Betsy comes to pick me up.'

'But . . . that's a machine too.'

'I know! I'm being inconsistent!'

That same week, we had received an unexpected visitor: the superintendent of schools from our home town of Elgin. I invited her in, gave her a cup of tea and asked what I could do for her.

'I want to know why you took your son out of school,' she said.

My blood ran cold for a moment. Then, recovering myself, I thought, *Well, fair enough*, and told her. 'Because it was hopeless,' I said honestly. I described the holding pen with no windows that had served as a classroom; the shadeless concrete playground that the kids never went into anyway; the teacher who had no idea how to get communication from the kids in her class; the teaching assistants who would simply turn on the TV to drown out the kids' stimming and sit there drinking sodas and eating junk food, batting the kids' hands away as they tried to grab it from them, yelling at them . . .

She heard me out, sipping tea while I outlined the Horse Boy Learning homeschool programme that Jenny, Iliane and I had evolved over the past few years, and how we mixed it with Kristin's self-compassion work. Then I asked her why she had come.

'I was wondering if you'd come in and train our staff,' she said.

For once, I was speechless

So here is what I believe: autism is not a problem to be fixed. Autism is a collection of gifts, a skill set, a wonderful way of being. Its gifts include an intellect that operates without the distraction of social conditioning – an ability, therefore, to focus intently on the task at hand without being distracted by that pretty girl, by thoughts about whether this is going to please anyone, or about whether achieving this task will put them higher or lower in the group's pecking order. This egolessness would take me – and most neurotypical human beings – decades of rigorous spiritual practice to attain, if indeed it were possible at all. Most autists seem to be born with it. Sure, they suffer from anxiety, but on the whole they don't suffer from the psychological anguish that we neurotypical – or perhaps it would be better to say 'ego-typical' – humans do. Am I tall enough? Thin, handsome or pretty enough? Rich or successful enough? This enough or that enough? My own ego – and probably yours too, if we're both honest – is an 800-pound gorilla that I am constantly doing battle with, and usually losing. Occasionally, very occasionally, I manage to use my ego the way it is supposed to be used: as a tool to help get things done, a motivator, the horse that pulls the cart. But normally the bloody thing controls me, not the other way around.

And I'm not the only one. Neurotypical people chuck themselves off bridges every day because of this endless feeling of not being good enough, this endlessly niggling inner critic. Being mainstream, being 'normal', seems to be no Holy Grail.

Sure, there are huge challenges that go with autism, especially in the early years. When a child cannot speak to you, is locked completely into their world, is shut down by sensory overstimulation, cannot make friends, cannot toilet train properly, then, yes, one must address these challenges. But the longer I am in on this autism adventure, the more adult autists I come across who do participate economically, who have love lives, careers, who contribute their gifts to the general good: Dr Temple Grandin, Cisco Buitron (who now works for Horse Boy Foundation as a consultant), Daniel Tammet, Tito Mukhopadhyay, Donna Williams, Naoki Higshida . . . If you don't know who these people are, you should. They are helping to shape a new generation.

Sure, not all these autists, successful as they are, live independently, start a family, buy their own apartment, drive their own car – though some do. But even the Western notion of the path to success – of leaving home, forsaking your clan, renting an apartment in the big city, setting up your own nuclear family in the suburbs – is something very, very few people on planet earth actually do. Most people still live as our forefathers did – in village settings, rural extended family networks, where mutual and group support is a given. Where people live surrounded by nature, animals, each other – tribe. And these people seem to be the happiest, the most fulfilled.

Our own culture's experiment with privacy at all costs, with the nuclear family that lives unconnected from its neighbours, with so-called independence – the idea of breaking away from your own family and those around you, the cult of the rugged (or by now rather soft around the middle) individualist – seems to lead mostly to unhappiness, depression. It's all very well living that way, but when a crisis hits, whether the crisis is banal, like not being able to start your car, or real, as in a medical emergency, you need to have people around you.

The shamans to whom we had travelled – whether in Mongolia, southern Africa, Australia, the States – none of them adhered to this individualist myth; and it could be argued that their cultures are more successful than ours. For despite all attempts to wipe them from the planet, they have held doggedly on, living a life whose quality cannot be measured in money but in what the Dalai Llama and others like him call 'gross national happiness'.

And when you spend time among these cultures, you cannot help but notice that their healers and shamans almost always display neuropsychiatric disorders of one sort or another. Ghoste had been, in his own words, 'a child in his mind' until late childhood, suffered seizures until his late twenties, and still had fainting fits and bouts of neurological illness even when we went to see him. Think of Besa, flapping and jumping, toe walking and speaking in riddles and not looking one in the eye, while, at the same time, having a wife and family and hunting and gathering for himself, while also healing countless people who came hundreds, sometimes thousands of miles to see him. Harold likewise had stories of seizures and other troubles from his youth. Blue Horse confided that he too had had episodes of weakness and mental instability. In their cultures such symptoms were regarded, not as a disqualification from society, but as a prerequisite for the job. They were fully integrated into their society, not marginalized from it.

We Westerners often kid ourselves that we are practical people, but we aren't really. Imagine what it's like when winter comes to the mountains of southern Siberia, the Mongolian steppe; when the dry season hits the Kalahari and only certain cracks in the ground can let you know if there is a water-bearing tuber hidden there – a life-saving drink that you might have to dig down through three feet of rock-hard clay to reach. These are not whimsical people: they are completely concerned with survival. If it doesn't work, they don't do it. They have no institutions to put people in. If a person *can* do something, they *do* do that thing.

Everyone contributes. And whatever one thinks of the merits or otherwise of shamanism, people in these cultures fall sick and get better without much access to Western medicine. The point is, if almost every group of people that predates industrialized society has a way of integrating neurologically different individuals into the core of their culture, then why haven't we? Why are our avenues of economic and societal participation so narrow?

We had better answer these questions, if only for economic reasons. If the current figures for autism at the time of writing are true – one child in eighty-eight over the age of eight, and one boy in fifty-six – then if you tried to institutionalize all these people, tried to keep them outside of the economic mainstream, the economy would simply implode. Things are about to change radically in our society – and probably for the better. With all these egoless people entering the workforce, imagine how, in twenty years, business will have changed.

And this is where it gets interesting. Is this massive rise in autism even autism at all, in its classic sense, or is it in fact due to the impact of a much higher level of toxicity in the environment on the foetus in the womb or the child once it is born, producing autism-like symptoms? The science seems to be pointing that way. There is a huge controversy over whether or not vaccination is part of the picture. But it goes way beyond just vaccines: recent studies have shown how plastics breaking down in the environment can act like hormones on the body, causing metabolic changes. Industrial heavy metals like lead, aluminium, mercury and cadmium can result in autism-like symptoms if present in the body in too high a degree. Pesticides, fertilizers, pharmaceuticals that leach into the water supply . . . What we know is that the world is much, much more toxic now than it has ever been. When I first went to Africa or India, no one had a mobile phone – now everyone in the world does and they chuck them away every three months. When I was younger, you didn't get a plastic bag in your average grocery store. When I was a boy, no one in China had a car.

Even if the food you eat is organically grown or foraged in the wild, that isn't enough. Toxins are in the soil and the water now, in the oceans and the rain, and they are affecting our children – and us.

It seems very clear that our species is on the brink of an environmental crisis. An environmental crisis that has been largely caused by the human ego: greed gone wild. But – and this is where it gets even more interesting – is it possible that this very crisis is bringing our species its own antidote? Are we starting to breed a new generation of egoless, or let's say much *less* egotistical, humans? Do we, as autism parents, have a front-row seat at the accelerated evolution of our species? Individuals with the same intellect as our own, or possibly greater because it is unhampered by the negative effects of the ego; individuals who can create technologies without greed, who will bring us back to a post-industrial version of the more authentic human way to live? Is autism going to save our planet? Or rather, is autism going to be part of what saves *us*?

Rowan is cooking his own noodles. Just before his twelfth birthday, he started taking over his own cooking. He's annoyed with me. 'Dad! There's MSG and high-fructose corn syrup in this ramen sauce you bought. You should buy the organic stuff!'

'You're totally right, Scub, I will. Sorry.'

It still seems incredible how far he, we, have come.

He recently told me that he wants the *Endangerous* programme to be a TV project, but that he wants to make a season or so of episodes for fun himself, and then have someone else to make it for real television. So, leveraging the recent success of *The Quest*, we're pitching it to TV companies, and it looks like it may fly. If it does, the intellectual property is his – if there is a royalty, the money is his. Rowan, an autistic boy not yet into his adolescence, earning from his own ideas. It shows what is possible.

It seems that these children are dream whisperers. That if you are ready to give up your dreams for them, put yourself into service to fulfil their dreams, then by some strange, shamanic alchemy your own dreams begin to come true. All the writing and film projects, all the horse training I had really wanted to do since childhood came about only when I first gave up my dreams for Rowan, then put them into service for him and the other families. And through the fulfilment of those dreams, I can stay in the game, serving Rowan and the other families that come into our orbit until the day I die – or even, if I can set the financial structures up properly, beyond. Because like it or not, I'm in for good, for life, for always.

You are familiar perhaps with the Native American concept of the 'dream catcher', a hoop with a web in it that supposedly catches dreams as you sleep. My question is – what do you do with the dream once you've caught it? You have to tame it, gentle it – *whisper* to it, if you like – so that you can ride it to its fruition. Just by reading, just by engaging with this story, by caring enough to give your time and attention to it, by spending the money you spent to buy the book, which supports the work at New Trails and beyond, you have put yourself in service to the dreams of those we serve.

So there is a question you must ask yourself when you go to bed tonight. The most important question of all: *What are my dreams? What are the dreams I've had since I was young, the ones I never pursued fully because at some point life intervened?* You may have forgotten them. Dreams tend to get broken, shat on, buried by the trials, disappointments and vicissitudes of life. But that is actually a fertilization process. The dreams don't go away. They put down roots and, with a little watering, can be revived, called back into being – bigger, stronger, better than before.

If you have forgotten, ask yourself anyway, and about thirty-six hours after you ask yourself that question, you'll be sitting in traffic, or on the toilet, or in some other random moment, and it'll go like this: *bubble bubble bubble – PING! Ah yes! That was it! That was the dream!* And then almost immediately there's a pain reaction and you push it away. *Arrrgh, I can't have it!*

This time, though, the rules are different. Because of the service you are rendering simply by engaging with this story, your willingness to engage and help the dreams of those more vulnerable than yourself, this time you *can* have it. This time you will. In fact, it's already happening. And I look forward, as the years go by, to meeting some of you if the winds of fortune so allow, and finding out how some of those dreams are starting to come true.

And now the story is shifting, as stories are wont to do. The old guard is starting to fall. We received word through Tulga – we have remained in touch since Mongolia – that Ghoste has been gravely ill. The first time he suffered a stroke he was cared for at home, in his teepee. But the second one was shattering – it cost him the use of his left side and meant he had to be taken into hospital in the distant capital, Ulaanbaatar. The costs of the treatment were prohibitive, but when Tulga told us, we didn't hesitate. We owed Ghoste so much. It felt good to give something back – a debt at least partially repaid. But how long Ghoste will be able to go on healing, giving of himself as shamans have to, we don't know.

Then Jumanda contacted me to tell me that Besa had passed away. I still don't quite know how to process that. In many ways, it felt as though my life – my spiritual life at least – began when I met Besa all those years ago under that acacia tree in western Botswana and he told me, for the first time, about healing – the only coherent conversation I had ever had with him.

And now he was gone. What did that mean? Am I now old Besa and Rowan Little Besa, as I had been?

'Besa's an ancestor now,' said Rowan, when I told him, just as he had when Uncle Terry died. And as an ancestor, Besa is going to be needed, and soon. More or less at the time of his death we got word that the Botswana government was getting ready to try and re-evict the Bushmen once more and reverse all the gains they had won. The government started by banning the Bushmen's lawyer, whose fees we had been fund raising for these past ten years, from re-entering the country. Jumanda warned me that a new assault on the First People was coming. As I write, we are putting together a new strategy. But I have faith. The Bushmen have always prevailed – the Light always does, in the end.

Kristin and I still live in the same house – or rather, I've built myself a little man-shed in the front pasture right outside the house. I use it for writing and sleeping, although I still frequently bed down on a mattress outside Rowan's door if he's having an insecure night. 'You're my guardian,' he told me, echoing, or perhaps confirming Ghoste's words of seven years ago. 'Because sometimes I get scared there are monsters in the woods.'

'Don't worry, Scub,' I told him. 'I used to as well; even though they're not real, it doesn't stop us thinking they might be.' I thought a moment. 'But if it scares you, we don't have to live out here. I mean, if you wanted to move into the city, if you felt safer there, we could do that.'

Rowan looked at me as if I was mad. 'No, Dad! I'm a countryside person! I love it out here where it's peaceful and quiet and beautiful. I never want to live in a city. I want to live right here. This is my place.'

'Okay, then. But whenever you feel a little scared at night, I will sleep outside your door and make sure you are safe. We can have little chats through the door till you go off to sleep. And in the morning when you wake, you'll find me there.'

So these 'guardian nights', as he calls them – where I sleep like a bodyguard outside his door – have become another of our rituals. He doesn't always ask for them, but I cherish it when he does, because these are the last months of his childhood, and every second is precious to me.

Kristin and I still take him out together as normal, frequently hang out over a glass of wine or dinner in the evening, just as we always did. We support each other. She has someone; I have someone too. But the family has not contracted, split, as so many do. It has grown stronger, into more of a tribe. We all have our eye on the same ball – Rowan – and because of that, our *stuff* can take a merciful second place. As far as Rowan is concerned, there is no change, no failure of support. He knows he's number one and that we intend to keep it that way.

At first we thought we were the only ones to do this, were almost embarrassed to tell friends and family that we had split but remained together as friends. Weirdly, it's so much more socially acceptable to divorce, break the family apart, destroy what was built, than it is to go on as before, with the sole exception of romantic involvement and all the responsibilities and pressure that go with that. Why – to feed the pockets of divorce lawyers? But we are not the only ones. In fact there is something of a movement afoot, it seems; separated but not separate, something along those lines. People are starting to publish memoirs, websites about it. Perhaps that will be the next story.

So yes, at twelve, Rowan is approaching the end of childhood, the beginning of manhood. When he woke up last year on his eleventh birthday, he wouldn't speak for two hours, for fear his voice might have changed. It still hasn't, in fact – but one day soon it will. His pleas of 'I don't want to grow up' have gradually changed to 'Well, it might be okay to grow up sometimes, as long as I can go back to being a kid again in between.'

It's what we all want, no?

Last Christmas I was reading him to sleep with *The Hobbit*. He was taking ages to get sleepy: restive, laughing at half-remembered jokes in his head, finding it hard to settle down. A part of me was impatient for him to go to sleep, so I could go back down and join the good cheer of the quiet Christmas party we were having with friends. Then another, saner, voice said: *This is the last Christmas you will have with him as a full-on child. Look at him. Commit his child's profile to your mind's eye. Do not wish yourself anywhere else. Be here now, for soon it will be another time, another place, and this will be no more than a memory.*

Since then another year had come and gone. It's a beautiful Texas midwinter day – mid-January but one of those days when, for a brief spell, the weather thinks that spring has arrived early. A good day for digging fence posts. We are putting in the new pens for Rowan's deer and the antelope that will soon be coming.

'New Trails is going to be an animal rescue for exotic species,' Rowan announced recently. 'A zoo sanctuary where animals that have been abandoned or need rescuing can come.'

So we're doing it: our licence for wildlife rehabilitation is in the works. We will be able to take in injured or orphaned indigenous animals – deer, bobcats, raccoons, coyotes – as well as the African and Asian species that many people in Texas have, and which sometimes get abandoned. An eland is waiting for adoption, apparently, and some addax – perhaps the world's rarest ungulates, barely holding on in their natural habitat in the Sahara. Bubbles, the super-affectionate African crested porcupine who likes her belly scratched and to lick your hand, arrived recently. And Mr Squeaky, an Asian small-clawed otter, is also waiting for adoption.

My arms ache from the digging, but it's a good ache. Rowan presented me with his calculations of the surface area of the newest pen – 8,000 square feet – which he, Jenny and Iliane all measured out together. 'Its rough animal-carrying capacity, Dad, is four large antelope and up to ten smaller ones.' The deer and antelope will share with the foals, who are now almost two years old, the next generation of Horse Boy horses, because Betsy will be thirty next year, and some of our other stalwarts are getting on, too. We must look to the future. Rowan certainly is.

Just yesterday morning – it been one of my 'guardian nights', so I was sleeping on a mattress outside his room – Rowan said, through his door, 'Hey, Dad!'

'Hmm?' I was just coming awake.

'I think eventually we'll probably maybe have to rescue elephants. Ones that are getting too old for circuses, who need to retire.'

Immediately an image sprang into my still half-dreaming mind, of children learning in a school that consisted of a wide platform attached to the back of an elephant, learning their curriculum as the great beast rocked them slowly and steadily through the Texas countryside.

'Sounds good, Scub.' And I have no doubt it'll happen: knowing Rowan, it's just a question of time.

Time. It's flying by faster than I would wish it to. What will the future hold? Will Rowan grow up to eventually run his own endangered wildlife sanctuary? Zookeeper and naturalist: it seems pretty likely. Not a bad life for his old mum and dad, not to mention his tribe, to share.

'Oh, and Dad!'

'Ye-es . . .'

'We can start Endangerous again. It's going to be Patagonia.'

'Why Patagonia, Scub?'

'Penguins!'

'But penguins aren't endangered and dangerous.'

'They're endangered by dangerous animals, though. Like mankind. *Mankind*,' I heard him whisper it to himself as he often did when confirming things in his mind.

'I guess you're right about that.'

'And we're going to have to build a penguin habitat at New Trails.'

'Ah. Well, I guess when we're ready.'

'Fine!' he said grumpily. 'When can I not be patient?'

'Well, Scub, if you're like me, you'll actually be impatient all your life, but eventually, even if you don't want to, you'll learn to be patient anyway. Because in my experience, no matter how impatient I am, life always seems to make me wait. But I get there in the end.'

Big sigh. 'I *guess*.'

I know how he feels.

Over breakfast I reported the intended trip to Kristin. She chuckled. 'Patagonia? You guys are on your own with that one. My wilderness-bashing days are done! But I'll help buy fish for the penguins when they arrive.'

So now, as I sit writing these last words, the warm false spring outside the window calling me, I have just seen something amazing. Rowan knows I have to write, so last night he said: 'Tomorrow I'm going to call Jenny at eight o'clock and go over to help the girls feed the animals. You can come over when you're done.'

'You're going to call Jenny?'

'Yes, Dad.' Only a week ago, Rowan finally started – after years of resistance – to use the phone. Next it'll probably be driving lessons.

'Okay, I can walk you over there in the morning, no worries.'

'I'm not vulnerable!' he said crossly, and a little cryptically.

'Er . . . okay – does that mean you really want to take yourself through the woods to New Trails by yourself?' He had never done this before.

'Yes, I'll be fine. I want to.'

'Okay.' I looked at Kristin, who raised her eyebrows and put on a silent *wow!* face.

'Okay.'

And so this morning, after climbing over my mattress outside his door – for last night was a 'guardian night' – he fixed himself breakfast, got dressed, dialled the number for Jenny and said: 'Hey, Jen, I'll be over there in, like, ten minutes, okay?' as if he'd been using the phone all his life. Then, as Kristin and I watched from the living room, he went out through the back porch, giving us both a casual wave and – with a 'Bye, Mum. Bye, Dad. Love you!' – skipped off down the slope and into the woods towards school, the little dreadlock that always seems to form at the back of his head bob-bobbing as he went. His own man, at last, free in a world of his own creation.

Kristin and I looked at each other, taking the moment in, letting it settle into our hearts.

Later, when Jenny popped in to fetch some supplies – Rowan still busy with the working students and the animal pens – she put her head round the door. 'I just have to tell you what he said when he got to New Trails. I was waiting for him near the edge of the woods just to make sure he got there safely.'

'What did he say?'

'He looked up at me as he went by and said: "Things are changing, Jen." And then he just smiled.'

Acknowledgements

It goes without saying that every story is a result of a team effort, but in this particular case, before the usual acknowledgements of editors, publishers and so on (without whom there is no book and whose names should be on the spine alongside the author's), a story within a story needs to be told.

If I have learned one thing over the past few years it is that no family can do it alone – whether there are special needs or not. It all comes down to tribe. The Horse Boy tribe has grown into something international and wonderful – an incredible network of mutual support that goes way beyond just horses and autism and has much more to do with shared love and a passion for life, for love, for healing and for just plain finding out about stuff.

There would be no Horse Boy tribe without Jennifer Ann Lockwood and Iliane Christine Lorenz. You two exceptionally talented people know that true strength lies in only one place – loving kindness. Jenny, you have been a mentor and adviser not just to Scub but to me too. Your development of Horse Boy Learning has been pure genius. Iliane, as Scub's 'evil adviser' you have indulged his humour and supported his interests way beyond the abilities of most people – building with your bare hands yet more animal cages for the ever-growing New Trails Scubby Zoo, coordinating the universe of everything Horse Boy with tireless energy and love.

Also, Ginny Jordan – without whom there would be no Horse Boy, period: for the full story, see the Acknowledgements in *The Horse Boy*. And Lisa Selz, without whom the work of the Horse Boy Foundation could never have had such wide reach. These two women represent forces for good in the world that go far, far beyond Horse Boy and its endeavours. It is good to know that there truly are people like them working behind the scenes of society for the general good in ways we can only guess at. Next time you are feeling depressed about corporate greed and government chicanery, just remember that there are individuals like Ginny and Lisa – many like them, in fact – striving to make the world a better, not a worse, place, and that the benefits of their philanthropy trickle down in the way that they are often supposed to but seldom seem to in reality. So, Ginny and Lisa, and those like you, we salute you.

Josh and Laurence, our other New Trails stalwarts – two geniuses whom we are lucky to have working with us. Erin Brownrigg, too. Isabella Marini for taking us into the next generation.

Martha Lamarche for being the most extraordinary autism mum. Thalia Michelle the same. And of course the much, much wider Horse Boy tribe. Thank you for the work you do.

Okay, now the book stuff. If anyone bothers to read acknowledgements, then here is a tip. If you ever decide to write a book, hire Eleo Gordon as your editor. She is old school, which means she is a servant to the story. She will make your book what it ought to be. Kate Parker the same.

If you're looking for an agent, you budding writers, all I can say is that you should try and break down Elizabeth Sheinkman's door at William Morris Endeavor.

And then, perhaps most importantly, thank you to Ghoste, to /Kunta, to Harold, to Blue Horse.

And to Betsy. Always Betsy.

Rupert Isaacson
Elgin, Texas
www.horseboyfoundation.org
www.horseboyworld.com

2016 Update

On a cool, rainy morning in May 2015, Betsy passed away of old age, at the age of 30, dying peacefully in her home pasture on her own terms, with dignity, surrounded by those who loved her. Over the previous year she had had difficulty digesting food until finally, no longer able to get up, she lay where she had slept, allowing us some final hours to be with her, to love her, until the lights at last went out. We buried her on the exact spot where she and Rowan had first met, 11 years and one month before. We planted a weeping willow on her grave. A candle burns there each night.

Her legacy continues. Horse Boy Method, the therapeutic riding approach she and Rowan helped to create, is now in 11 countries and rising. The two programs that do not include horses but involve the kinetic learning techniques learned from working with the horse: the homeschooling module – Horse Boy Learning – and Movement Method, the brain training technique that works in homes, gardens, classrooms, parks, anywhere, also live on – inspired by the oxytocin/brain/nervous system connection that Betsy and Rowan helped us discover. The three programs have now been studied at the University of Texas, the University of Belmont, the University of Osnabrueck in Germany, the University of Gothenburg in Sweden and the University of Nottingham Trent in the UK. Doctors in Germany are recommending the programs for autism parents and practitioners alike. The German Kuratorium for Therapeutic Riding is looking at Horse Boy as an official approach.

Because of this one, incredible horse, and the amazing connection between her and Rowan, there are more options for autism families than ever before – options that are more effective, more joyful, more adventurous, more fun; options that help prepare people with neuro-sensory conditions of any kind to truly swim in the 'normal' world while still being themselves, rather than trying to mold them into people they are not. You don't need a horse, you don't need land, you just need to let your child lead you, following their passionate interests, outside, in nature, in movement. Put these things together and the over-active nervous system calms, the happiness/communication hormone oxytocin is produced, the vestibular system, which is responsible for attention, is activated, the cerebellum begins to produce the brain communication system known as purkinje cells, which gets the pre frontal cortex - responsible for reasoning and emotional regulation going. The over-active fight/flight reflex (the amygdala) is finally switched off, freeing the child or adult from being endlessly trapped in a state of anxiety and opens them, at last, to learning.

We now know the science behind it all, but ultimately it's about happiness, about love. Science that leaves out the happiness component never works in human terms. Science that prioritizes it does.

Anyone can learn Horse Boy Method, Horse Boy Learning or Movement Method – to get trained whether as a parent or a practitioner go to horseboyworld.com. To help us continue to offer these programs free of charge to local families, and to train low income parents and practitioners on scholarships, donate at horseboyfoundation.org.

Betsy's legacy, the Horse Boy tribe is now worldwide: join us and help us build a better world for autists, for those with neuro-sensory conditions, for us all.